PLAZA of
Sacrifices

DIÁLOGOS

A series of course-adoption books on Latin America:

Independence in Spanish America: Civil Wars, Revolutions, and Underdevelopment (revised edition)—Jay Kinsbruner, Queens College

Heroes on Horseback: A Life and Times of the Last Gaucho Caudillos— John Charles Chasteen, University of North Carolina at Chapel Hill

The Life and Death of Carolina Maria de Jesus—Robert M. Levine, University of Miami, and José Carlos Sebe Bom Meihy, University of São Paulo

The Countryside in Colonial Latin America—Edited by Louisa Schell Hoberman, University of Texas at Austin, and Susan Migden Socolow, Emory University

¡Que vivan los tamales! Food and the Making of Mexican Identity— Jeffrey M. Pilcher, The Citadel

The Faces of Honor: Sex, Shame, and Violence in Colonial Latin America—Edited by Lyman L. Johnson, University of North Carolina at Charlotte, and Sonya Lipsett-Rivera, Carleton University

The Century of U.S. Capitalism in Latin America—Thomas F. O'Brien, University of Houston

Tangled Destinies: Latin America and the United States—Don Coerver, Texas Christian University, and Linda Hall, University of New Mexico

Everyday Life and Politics in Nineteenth Century Mexico: Men, Women, and War—Mark Wasserman, Rutgers, The State University of New Jersey

Lives of the Bigamists: Marriage, Family, and Community in Colonial Mexico—Richard Boyer, Simon Fraser University

Andean Worlds: Indigenous History, Culture, and Consciousness Under Spanish Rule, 1532–1825—Kenneth J. Andrien, Ohio State University

The Mexican Revolution, 1910–1940—Michael J. Gonzales, Northern Illinois University

**Series advisory editor: Lyman L. Johnson,
University of North Carolina at Charlotte**

PLAZA of Sacrifices

Gender, Power, and Terror in 1968 Mexico

ELAINE CAREY

UNIVERSITY OF NEW MEXICO PRESS
ALBUQUERQUE

11 10 09 08 07 06 05   1 2 3 4 5 6 7

Library of Congress Cataloging-in-Publication Data

Carey, Elaine, 1967–
  Plaza of sacrifices : gender, power, and terror in 1968 Mexico /
Elaine Carey.— 1st ed.
      p. cm. — (Diálagos series)
  Includes bibliographical references and index.
  ISBN 0-8263-3544-6 (cloth : alk. paper) — ISBN 0-8263-3545-4
(pbk. : alk. paper)
  1. Student movements—Mexico—History—20th century. 2. College
students—Mexico—Political activity—History—20th century.
3. Massacres—Mexico—History—20th century. I. Title. II. Diálogos
(Albuquerque, N.M.)
  LA428.7.C36 2005
  378.1'981'097253—dc22

                              2005000960

Book design and composition by Damien Shay
Body type is Utopia 9.5/13.
Display is Stencil and American Typewriter.

For
Javier
and
Lucas

Contents

Acknowledgments

Many people in Mexico and the United States have contributed to this project since it was a doctoral dissertation. I am grateful to my dissertation director Enrique Semo who discussed this project with me for over ten years. He has been an encouraging, and at times demanding, mentor through the years. His, as well as his family's, friendship and advice have been invaluable. Lourdes Estevan, Aída González, and Lilian Liebermann opened their homes to me and provided tremendous insight into contemporary Mexico and the role of women. Carmen Landa not only consented to an interview, but helped me to contact other women in the movement and kept me aware of feminist events while I was living in the Federal District. Marcelino Perelló and Mercedes Perelló gave me their companionship as well as their personal histories of the movement. My lunches with them and other 1968 activists are memorable. Raúl Jardón's exceptional research was invaluable. He consented to an interview, and he kindly shared his unpublished manuscript. His and Marcelino's own histories led me to reconceptualize my gender focus. Alejandro Pelayo introduced me to the many films of 1968, and graciously shared his own research on film and 1968 with me. Because of his influence, I have continued to follow the release of films and documentaries on the movement. Other people took the time to discuss their experiences in and/or analysis of student movement and its aftermath: Susie Glusker, Lilia Granillo, Miriam Hamdan, Alejandra Herrera, Marta Lamas, María Llamas, Roger Magazine, Carlos Monsiváis, Veronica Ortíz, Caroline Pacheco, Elena Poniatowska, Carmen Ramos Escandon, and Vida Valero Barrós. In 2000, Margarita González de León also graciously opened her home to me where over breakfast before I went to the archive, she and her son Antonio González de León discussed this project with me. Being from the two generations on either side of those that came of age in 1968, their perspectives of the impact of the student movement were compelling. During my research breaks, Fumiko Nobuoka and Raúl Martínez idled away their days with me in bookstores, galleries, and museums. In Detroit, Miriam Bannon, Thomas Florek, SJ, Javier Saravía, SJ, and Alberto Vargas, SJ, provided me insight into the role of the Mexican Catholic Church in 1968 and the following social movements.

For their analysis and institutional support, I would like to thank Mercedes Barquet, Dalia Barrera, Luz Elena Gutiérrez, Julia Tuñón, and Elena Urrutia of the Programa Interdisciplinario de Estudios de la Mujer (PIEM) at El Colegio de México. Their advice, encouragement, and challenges continue to influence my study of women and 1968. Thanks and gratitude are also due to the archivists, librarians, and employees at the Archivo General de la Nación, Biblioteca Nación, Centro de Estudios del Movimiento Obrero y Socialista, Archivo Histórico de Universidad Nacional Autónoma de México-Centro de Estudios Sobre la Universidad, El Colegio de México, the Hermeteca Naciónal, and the Fototeca Nacional. In particular, I would like to thank L.C. Cecilia Ramírez and L.C. Leticia Medina for allowing me to photograph and reproduce the student propaganda. In the United States, I have benefited from the archivists and staff of the Hispanic Reading Room at the Library of Congress, Latin America Video Archive, the New York Public Library, and the libraries at the University of New Mexico, the University of Detroit Mercy, Arizona State University, and St. John's University.

In preparation for this manuscript, Lyman Johnson and David Holtby at the University of New Mexico Press have continually given their advice and encouragement. Evelyn Schlatter has been an advocate, editor, and critic of this project since it was a thought in graduate school. I constantly tested the boundaries of our long friendship by asking her to read "just one more draft." My colleagues at the University of Detroit Mercy also helped in invaluable ways, but I would like to particularly thank Hugh Culick, Roy Finkenbine, Brian Nedwek, and Sarah Stever who were my academic mentors in my first years in the academy. Many people have read parts of this manuscript as a dissertation or revised drafts through the years, and they have offered invaluable advice and suggestions: Rodney Anderson, Michael Barry, Mauricio Borrero, David Farber, Linda Hall, Fred Harris, Robert Himmerich y Valencia, and Rosemary Weatherston. Other people have read or heard sections of the manuscript and have contributed their comments and criticism on the theme: Kristina Boylan, Barry Carr, James Cockcroft, Mary Coffey, Deborah Cohen, Rafael Franco, Lessie Jo Frazier, David Maciel, and Ken Mitchell.

My research for this project was originally funded by a Fulbright-Robles García grant from the United States Information Agency and the Mexican government and several awards from the University of New Mexico: a Graduate Achievement Award from the Office of Graduate Studies and two grants from the Student Research Allocations Committee. I also received two summer research grants from the University of Detroit Mercy and course reductions from St. John's University. While developing this manuscript, I attended the conference "Los Olvidadas: Gender and Women's History in Postrevolutionary Mexico" coordinated by Gilbert M. Joseph, Jocelyn Olcott, and Mary Kay Vaughn in 2001 and the National Endowment for the Humanities summer institute "Hispanic Gendering of the Americas: Beyond Cultural and Geographical Boundaries" in 2002 led by Asunción Lavrin and K. Lynn Stoner. The conference and the institute and all the participants further instructed my perspectives on gender history.

During the entire process of researching and writing, I have received enthusiastic support from my parents, Andrea and Dan Carey, my maternal grandparents Marie and Jim Stofer, and my siblings Brian and Erin. "*Mi familia de otro lado,*" the Alvarez Isasi family, Javier, Amada, Bertha, Carmen, Liliana, Ileana, Jorge, and Raúl have given me a second home and continue to furnish an on-going, and at times irreverent, commentary on contemporary Mexican politics, society, and culture.

Lastly, this work is dedicated to an ex-student activist and to a future student activist. Javier Alvarez Isasi enthusiastically followed my research through the years. He tirelessly discussed the theme, introduced me to student activists of my own generation, and constantly updated our 1968 archive. Lucas Alvarez-Carey entered the world as the project was being finished bringing both Javier and me great joy.

List of Acronyms and Organizations

Asociación de Padres de Familia de Estudiantes de IPN
  (Association of IPN Students' Parents)
Banco Nacional de Crédito Rural
  (National Bank of Rural Credit, BANRURAL)
Central Nacional de Estudiantes Democráticos
  (National Center of Democratic Students, CNED)
Ciudad Universitario
  (University City, CU)
Coalición de Organizaciones de Defensa de los Valores Nacionales
  (Coalition of Organizations for the Defense of National Values)
Coalición de Profesores de Enseñanza Media y Superior Pro-libertades Democráticas
  (Coalition of Teachers of Secondary and Universities for Democratic Liberties
  The Coalition)
Coordinador de Comités de Lucha
  (Coordinator of the Committees of Struggle, Coco)
Comité Coordinador del Movimiento de la Huelga del IPN
  (the Central Coordinating Committee of the IPN Strike)
Comité de Padres de Familia en Apoyo al Movimiento
  (Committee of Parents in Support of the Movement)
Compañía Nacional de Cámaras Industriales
  (National Staple Products Corporation, CONASUPO)
Confederación Nacional Campesina
  (National Peasant Confederation, CNC)
Confederación Nacional de Organizaciones Populares
  (National Confederation of Popular Organizations, CNOP)

List of Acronyms and Organizations

Confederación de Trabajadores Mexicanos
    (Confederation of Mexican Workers, CTM)

Consejo Nacional de Ciencias y Tecnología
    (National Council of Science and Technology, CONACYT)

Consejo Nacional de Huelga
    (National Strike Committee, CNH)

Federación Nacional de Estudiantes Técnicos
    (National Federation of Technical Students, FNET)

Frente Revolucionario de Acción Popular
    (Popular Action Revolutionary Front, FRAP)

Frente Revolucionario Estudiantil
    (Revolutionary Student Front, FER)

Instituto Mexicano de Protección a la Infancia
    (Mexican Institute for Infant Protection, IMPI)

Instituto Nancional de Fondo para la Vivienda de los Trabajadores
    (National Institute of Workers' Housing Fund, INFONAVIT)

Instituto de Seguridad y Servicios Sociales de los Trabajadores del Estado
    (Institute of Insurance and Social Service of State Workers, ISSSTE)

Instituto Politécnico Nacional
    (National Polytechnic Institute, IPN or Poli)

Juventud Comunista Mexicana
    (Mexican Communist Youth, JCM)

Liga Comunista Espartaco
    (Communist Spartacus League, LCE)

Liga Comunista de 23 de septiembre
    (Communist League of the 23 of September, LC-23)

Movimiento Universitario de Renovadora Orientación
    (University Movement for Renovated Morals, MURO)

Movimiento Revolucionario de Maestros
    (Revolutionary Teachers' Movement, MRM)

Mujeres de Acción Católica Mexicana
    (Women of Mexican Catholic Action)

Partido Communista Mexicana
    (Mexican Communist Party, PCM)

Partido Acción Nacional
    (National Action Party, PAN)

Partido Agrario Obrero Morelense
    (Morelos Agrarian Worker Party, PAOM)
Partido Revolucionario Institucional
    Party of the Institutional Revolution, PRI)
Partido Revolución Mexicana
    (Party of the Mexican Revolution, PRM)
Secretaría de Educación Pública
    (Secretariat of Education, SEP)
Sindicato Mexicano de Electricistas
    (Mexican Electricians Union, SME)
Sindicato Nacional de Trabajadores de la Educación
    (National Union of Workers in Education, SNTE)
Sindicato de Trabajadores Ferrocarrileros de México
    (The Mexican Republic Railroad Workers' Union, STFRM)
Unión Cívica de Padres de la Familia de UNAM
    (Civic Union of UNAM Parents)
Unión de las Mujeres Mexicanas
    (Union of Mexican Women)
Universidad Autónoma Metropolitana
    (Metropolitan Autonomous University, UAM)
Universidad Nacional Autónoma de México
    (National Autonomous University of Mexico, UNAM)
Uniones y Sociedades de Padres de Familias de la UNAM and IPN
    (Parent Unions and Societies of UNAM and IPN)

Introduction

On October 2, 1968, the Mexican government sanctioned a massacre of student protesters in the Plaza de las Tres Culturas in the Nonoalco-Tlatelolco housing development in Mexico City. Officially, the government-supported newspapers estimated the number of dead to be forty-nine, but other estimates exceeded seven hundred. The brutal response of the Mexican leaders toward their youth haunted the capital and the country in the years to come. In the wake of the October 2, 1968, government massacre, weary, divided, but enraged students gathered to discuss the continuation of the student strike that had rocked the city since late July. In a public forum sponsored by the *Consejo Nacional de Huelga* (the National Strike Committee, CNH), a brother and a sister squared off. In that public meeting, student activists had gathered to debate whether they should call an end to the strike that had paralyzed Mexico City or to continue and escalate it. Marcelino and Mercedes Perelló were not newcomers to social activism or to terror. Due to the death, detainments, and continued violence, some activists wished to end the strike and return to classes. Marcelino was one of the CNH members responsible for making such a decision.[1] His sister Mercedes arrived at the meeting as a representative of political prisoners who had been detained before and during the movement. As the wife of a political prisoner and a leftist activist, Mercedes adopted a hard line when she demanded the continuation of the strike.[2] Marcelino was furious. First, Mercedes was intervening in a CNH meeting; and secondly, he felt that she was emotionally blackmailing him and other members of the CNH because she was the wife of a political prisoner. She was not alone in her demand for a continuation of the strike. Hard-liners in the movement argued that the government left them no choice but to continue to take to the street. If need be, some argued they should escalate the movement to armed urban guerrilla warfare.

1

Introduction

The Perelló siblings' history and experiences in the movement exemplify the changes that took place in Mexico in the years following the presidency of Lázaro Cárdenas (1934–1940). Marcelino, a CNH member, had emerged as a prominent voice in the movement when he was chosen to engage in a public dialogue with the administration of President Gustavo Díaz Ordaz. Mercedes made up the rank and file, more ideologically left and more radical than many CNH members. Activism was in their blood. Their father was a Catalan journalist and nationalist who was implicated in a bombing plot to kill the king, Alphonso XIII. He met their mother through the letters she wrote him while he was in prison.[3] The senior Perellós immigrated to Mexico, fleeing the Spanish civil war. In Mexico, the family opened a small bookstore in the Zona Rosa, a favorite spot for Mexican intellectuals to gather to argue and debate the issues of the day. By 1968, Mercedes, who had studied psychology, became immersed in student and radical politics. Marcelino, a student at the *Universidad Nacional Autónoma de México* (National Autonomous University of Mexico, UNAM), also became involved in student and radical politics.

The 1968 Mexican student movement changed their lives as it did the lives of their entire generation. With the repression of the movement, Marcelino was forced to flee Mexico to avoid incarceration and perhaps even death. He was smuggled to the United States from where he fled to France, Romania, and ultimately to Spain—the country his parents were forced to abandon—where he remained in exile until 1985. His sister Mercedes did not flee Mexico, since her husband was imprisoned serving a two year prison sentence for his activities in the movement. Keeping to her Maoist ideology, she "went to the people," and worked in labor and social justice struggles.

The Perellós' tale parallels the stories of countless other student activists. Their experiences and those of their fellow activists embody the tensions between youth and government, between children and parents, and between men and women. In their youth, University City, the barrio that housed national university, opened in southern Mexico City. The Perellós took their places at UNAM as did many young people whose parents had benefited from the Mexican Economic Miracle during the 1940s to the 1960s when the economy grew at a staggering rate. Like their peers, the Perellós had great hopes for the future, but they were keenly aware of the socioeconomic discrepancies that continued to exist in Mexico despite its economic prosperity. The Perellós, like countless other young people gained access to higher education due to the economic boom, but they also observed the socio-economic disparities around them. Furthermore, the international youth culture, whether rock-n-roll, clothing, language, or political and social movements, influenced Mexican youth. Many young urbanites of Mexico City embraced these cultural changes that seemed to defy Mexican nationalism, but the ever adaptable government assimilated certain cultural preferences of Mexican youth. However, by 1968 the international youth culture was highly politicized, and Mexican adolescents and young adults challenged their government, and in so doing, according to the government, they endangered the progress of the revolution. Of course, by the 1960s the *Partido Revolucionario Institucional's* (Party of the Institutional Revolution, PRI) saw itself as the embodiment of the revolution.

The 1968 Mexican student movement was a response to political, social, cultural, and economic shifts that occurred in Mexico in the wake of the Mexican Revolution. Contemporary scholars of Mexican history have explored post-Mexican Revolution society. Certain historians have questioned the concept of the monolithic state, and they have exposed the agency and response of the Mexican people to negotiate, construct, or craft daily life, nationalism, culture, and gender.[4] In the post-revolution economy, there existed contextual and shifting cultural implications of modernity. Recent historical studies have demonstrated the conflicts of modernity as it played out in comics, films, popular music, and the counterculture.[5] These works also examine how modernity clashed with gendered constructions of power within the Mexican Revolutionary family. Moreover, how the ruling PRI manipulated popular culture, revolutionary idealism, nationalism, and modernization for its own purposes.

In order to understand the Perellós and their comrades of the 1968 Mexican student movement, they must be situated in the context of the rise of youth culture and the concurrent international student movements. However, it must be noted that they and their generation had a more intimate knowledge of and were consumed by the events that took place directly around them in Mexico. Thus, in the context of the 1968 Mexican student movement, there is an intersection of the internal shifts combined with the rise of the international student movements that have their legacies in the global post-World War II world. These influences collided on the streets of Mexico City in the summer of 1968 when young people attempted to establish a dialogue of reform with their government. Students employed the revolutionary language that historically was theirs as heirs of the Mexican Revolution, but they also embraced international revolutionary rhetoric. They incorporated models of resistance that were international as well as national. Moreover, they defied certain gender constructs through the activism of young women. Yet, the students also employed aspects of traditional Mexican gender perceptions in their organizing, propaganda, and overall movement. The challenge for the students was not solely their issues with the Díaz Ordaz administration and the Mexican government generally, but also a confrontation with modernity, nationalism, and relations between individuals and the state.

The student movement was a social uprising against an oppressive, monolithic, and paternalistic construct of the state, and it emerged as an abomination to sanitized hopes of modernity and control propagated by Mexico's political elite in the 1960s.[6] The image of the president as the father of the revolutionary family came under attack in Mexico for internal and external reasons. Young people experienced a very different Mexico from that of the 1940s and 1950s. By the late 1960s, it was more evident that the economic boom had never proven to be the salvation of the masses that it had been purported to be. The inability of the economy to benefit the masses contributed to labor and social protests. Mexican intellectuals of the 1950s and 1960s captured the malaise of the nation and engaged in public criticism of the concepts of nation, culture, the state, and power. Moreover, intellectuals, writers, and artists directly criticized the centralized authority of the PRI that had been in power since the 1920s. With the international youth discussions of democracy and freedom in the 1960s, Mexican youth believed that they too could harness these shifts to bring profound social and political change. What most youth did not consider was the response of the individuals and entities that they were confronting and the illusion that their opposition jeopardized. In addressing the creation of modernity, power, and national culture, Mexican cultural theorist Roger Bartra wrote:

> [E]very once in a while the great show is interrupted by out-
> bursts that invade the scene and disrupt national harmony.
> That is what happened in 1968 when unforeseen characters
> shattered the cultural continuity of the comedy in which
> national destinies amorously intertwined with universal,
> Olympic history. The idyllic romance was thwarted, and the
> responsible paid very dearly—right there in the Plaza of
> Three Cultures—for the crime of having raised the curtain
> ahead of time.[7]

This study considers how Mexican youth in 1968 provided the world a peek at the social, cultural, and political crisis brewing in Mexico.[8] The Mexican student movement was part of the international student protests, but more importantly, it must be understood as part of a continuum of social protests in Mexico. Furthermore, the student uprising demonstrated the crisis within the ideals of the Mexican revolutionary family and nation. This work pays close attention to how gender played out in the movement and how the movement was a significant chapter in the continued renegotiations of power, culture, gender, and modernity. In this analysis, it must be noted that the Mexican student movement was never specifically about achieving equality between men and women. Instead, the movement, while not attaining political success in 1968, reached far beyond its historical time and space by contemplating and questioning Mexican power structures overall, whether between the state and the individual, between parents and children, or between men and women.

The study of gender must consider the agency of the oppressed and marginalized to be historical and significant actors, but also the subtleties of power and those who yield it.[9] Recent Latin American gender studies have expanded to consider both masculinity and femininity; moreover, scholars also have begun to contemplate how gender reveals the differences between powerful and powerless, dominant and submissive, and significant and insignificant.[10] As gender scholars studied manhood they found that masculinity is less about the attempt to dominate women and more about the struggle against domination by another individual or group. Historically, not all men have benefited from the same form of masculine privilege, and that discrepancy was painfully evident in Mexico.[11] Young Mexican middle class, educated, urban males encountered a regime that was unwilling to share its power and authority with young men regardless of the fact that these men came from the same socioeconomic, educational, and privileged backgrounds as that of the politicians.

I examine here both men and women as significant actors whose experiences in the movement differed according to age, gender, class, and the potential for power. Both young Mexican men and women were influenced by the events in Mexico, the Cuban Revolution, the Vietnam War, the international student protests, and youth culture. All of these political, social, and cultural events undermined certain established Mexican gender constructs. On the one hand, the Mexican government deemed politicized young men as deviant, suspicious, seditious, and dangerous because they embraced foreign influences as represented in youth culture while at the same time they resisted co-option into the ruling party. Women, on the other hand, were not seen in such a politicized way because they were not seen to have the same potential for power as their male counterparts. Thus, women's gender struggles were more subversive and transgressive *within* the movement. Through their actions, young and politicized women ruptured the natural routine of feminine activities that were replicated in private and public spaces bound by history and tradition. Subverting traditional constructions of femininity, young, urban middle-class, educated women activists constructed new identities and possibilities in the movement, in the streets, and in their homes.[12] During the entire movement, female activists pushed their substantive roles to challenge gender expectations. The mobilization and activism of young women in the movement led to further questioning of gender expectations and roles in the years immediately following 1968 contributing to a second wave of Mexican feminism in the 1970s.

The mobilization of middle class, educated, young men and women was unprecedented in 1968.[13] Not because students protested, but because their demands for democracy and civil liberties in 1968 went far beyond simple student concerns about tuition increases and exams. Those demands spilled over to all sectors of the population and out into the provinces. Thus, those young people—benefactors and heirs to the Mexican Economic Miracle but products of the 1960s—questioned their government, their society, and themselves.[14]

To capture the influences on Mexican youth in 1968, Chapter One, "La cruda de guerra mundial: Converging Forces" considers the historical events and atmosphere that led to the student movement of 1968. It examines global and local events and people who inspired *la generación del '68*. In 1959, the victory of the July 26 Movement in Cuba captivated the world. Mexican youth found a new model of modern, educated, upper middle class revolutionary leaders in Fidel Castro and Ernesto Guevara. The Cuban revolutionaries served as models, particularly for young men, but also for the entire generation of the 1960s in Mexico and beyond. Combined with the new image of a middle class and educated vanguard, Mexican youth borrowed sophisticated language, rhetoric, and criticism from Mexican intellectuals who bemoaned the revolutionary transformation and criticized the one-party system and corruption that embodied the power-hungry PRI. Mexican students did not have to look beyond the borders of Mexico for inspiration to organize a mass social protest. The crisis of the Mexican Revolution already had emerged in the late 1950s and early 1960s. In the streets of Mexico City, students found new models of ideology, organization, and politics among workers and peasant movements.

How these influences converged on the streets of Mexico City in the summer of 1968 and contributed to the movement is the subject of Chapter Two, "Los chavos en la calle: The Beginning." In this chapter, an unlikely event—a street skirmish between students and police—triggers mass student mobilization. Concentrating on the early stages of the movement, this chapter analyzes how male student activists became a threat to the government. Using editorial cartoons and speeches, government officials and the press immediately embraced gendered language and painted the students and the left as foreign, deviant, and dangerous. The male student activist was embodied as the enemy of the revolution. While engaging in a rhetorical battle with the press, students also organized the first mass marches and developed the infrastructure of the movement that defied gender constraints, particularly in the *guardias*.[15] The guardias and early organizational methods contributed to clashes between male and female activists due to their own perceived notions of proper gender roles.

Chapter Three, "Los dueños del mundo: The Mobilization of the People," contemplates how the students were able to mobilize the people of the Federal District through their organizational methods, their use of the brigades, and how they rallied parents. In August, the students issued their Six Point Petition in which they specifically outlined their demands, reflecting the demands of workers' movements in the 1950s. With their marches, brigades, and petitions, young men and women circulated throughout the city to propagandize the movement. By transgressing physical space and gender boundaries, men and women engaged in heated negotiations over who performed what duties and what was suitable for men versus women. Students also organized parents because they saw them as natural allies. Although this may have been true for many male activists, parents undermined young women's ability to join the movement. Moreover, this chapter returns to Marcelino Perelló when the CNH chose him to be one of the spokespersons for the students in public dialogues with the Díaz Ordaz administration. Once recognized, Perelló became a target of suspicion because he represented the vanguard male activist.

Chapter Four, "Es una provocación: The Destruction," describes the government's ultimate response to students' actions. By late September and with the opening of the Olympic games approaching, the Mexican government had grown tired of what it saw as the students' shenanigans. Invoking patriarchal and paternal authority, the Mexican authorities sought to remove the bases of student operations on various campuses. They also targeted individual student leaders through the use of detention, threats, and co-option. The government's use of rhetoric exemplified their reassertion of control and power yielded by the patriarchs within the revolutionary family. The chapter concludes with a discussion of the massacre in the Plaza de las Tres Culturas on October 2, 1968. Although successful in destroying the movement, the brutality of the attacks undermined the power of the president and his party and drew greater criticism to the patriarchs of the revolution.

Chapter Five, "Apertura Democrática: Masculinity, Power, and Terror," examines how the movement continued and how the government responded to its tarnished image of power and authority. In 1970, Luis Echeverría became president. His responses to the students and the outcomes of the movement expressed the limitations of the sociopolitical and gendered constructions of state power. Echeverría responded to student pressures by introducing the "Democratic Opening" which involved releasing political prisoners and offering governmental and bureaucratic programs and positions to ex-activists. However, when defied, the president turned to violence. He initiated a Dirty War against ex-activists who deflected his overtures. Ex-activists also never agreed on a united stance or front, and they responded to Echeverría's quixotic administration in a similar fashion. In the Federal District, young people continued to organize and protest, while ex-leaders, particularly young men, were co-opted into the regime.

Many of Echeverría's policies to bring activists into the government and back into the revolutionary family focused on male activists, but he also attempted to appease women with the hosting of the 1975 Year of the Woman. The last chapter, "La nueva ola: Gender Rebels" examines how young women transformed their mobilization in the 1968 movement to develop a feminist movement that contradicted the vision of the Mexican government. As young women began to question the rhetoric of independence, freedom, and democracy during the 1968 student movement, they furthered that line of questioning to contemplate how these concepts were gendered constructions that never fully extended to them.

Chapter One

LA CRUDA DE GUERRA MUNDIAL:
Converging Forces

In the spring of 1968, Mexican President Gustavo Díaz Ordaz may have gazed from the windows of the presidential palace to observe the finishing touches being added to the Federal District in preparation for the XIX Olympiad, the international showcase of Mexico. His administration had sponsored the construction of a modern metro system, hotels, and sports facilities that included a stadium decorated by muralist Diego Rivera.[1] Other construction projects included high-rise apartment buildings and wide boulevards that passed by sculptures erected by participating countries in the celebration. The "modern" Mexico was the first nation to host the Olympic Games in Latin America and in a "developing" country. To the outside world, Mexico appeared stable, democratic, and at a critical juncture to enter the developed world.

In 1968, Mexico did appear to be on the brink of entering the modern world with the games, the economy, and a vibrant cultural life, but in July young men and women were in the streets rioting and demanding political change. What led to the outbursts on the streets? There were external and internal influences that merged in the 1950s that created new concepts of gender and political activism for Mexican youth. One of the influences was the Cuban Revolution, but the internal factors for the student movement were linked to the growing criticism of the Mexican Revolution that was particularly evident in the labor struggles of the 1950s and 1960s. These struggles foreshadowed the violence that took place in 1968.

Mexican youth were influenced by revolutionary movements in the developing world, as well as the youth uprisings in Europe and the United States. Along with revolutionary and social movements, students of the 1960s lived in a completely different world than those who came of age in the 1940s and 1950s. One of the most profound events in contemporary Latin American history was the Cuban Revolution that contributed to new intellectual trends and revolutionary fervor among middle class youth who were mesmerized by the success of young men and women much like themselves. College and high school activists drew inspiration from Ernesto "Che" Guevara and Fidel Castro who exemplified a new image for Latin American youth. Although the Cuban revolutionaries were imprisoned and threatened with deportation in 1956 while organizing the revolution in Mexico, in February 1959, the *barbudos* (the bearded ones) returned to Mexico as heroes.[2]

For Mexican youth that came of age in the late 1950s and 1960s, the Cuban revolutionaries images combined with growing criticism of the Mexican Revolution as a revolution betrayed. That criticism was found in the pages of books and on the streets of Mexico City. In essays and novels, intellectuals considered the role of masculinity in Mexico's cult of power. The members of the *Partido Revolucionario Institucional* (Party of the Institutional Revolution, PRI), Mexico's so-called revolutionary leaders were not like Che and Fidel, young, exuberant, straight-forward, and successful. Instead, the Mexican status quo appeared bourgeois, staid, manipulative, and violent.

With the intellectual criticism also came other internal forces that contributed to the student movement of 1968. The labor movements of the 1950s and 1960s challenged the so-called Mexican economic miracle and questioned the survival of the Mexican Revolution. These labor movements emerged in the wake of the dismantling of the state apparatus constructed by Presidents Alvaro Obregón (1920–24), Plutarco Elías Calles (1924–28), and Lázaro Cárdenas (1934–1940). The 1950s and 1960s ushered in the collapse of the clientelist state constructed in the 1920s and 1930s that brought labor and peasant organizations into the state. Cárdenas' successors moved away from traditional bases of power, labor and peasant organizations, to court foreign powers and domestic industrialists and bankers to invest capital. A class struggle emerged because many people were left on the periphery of the political process and economic growth.

Consequently, workers, students, and teachers challenged the emerging status quo, and found themselves the targets of violence. The events and people that influenced the *generación del '68* challenged the official appearance of Mexico as a modern and democratic nation. With youth in the streets rioting in 1968, the conflict between the students and their elders represented a continuum of struggle between the powerful and the powerless that had its legacy in the Mexican past.

We are with Che Wherever He Goes: El Che and the Cult of Masculinity

In the 1960s, Mexican students combined their national icons and shifting cultural ideals with an international revolutionary movement. Ideologically, the movements were influenced by a range of individuals from Karl Marx to Ho Chi Minh to Herbert Marcuse. The most important and widely followed and recognized was Cuban revolutionary and Argentine *Comandante* Ernesto Guevara—El Che. As Mexican writer and 1968 student activist Paco Igancio Taibo II described at the Socialist Scholars Conference in 1998, "I am one of the children of Comandante Guevara...I was raised with the idea that Che was the man to follow."[3] Student activists who came of age in the 1960s, like Taibo, identified with Che, Fidel Castro, and the Cuban Revolution.[4] To them, the Cuban Revolution represented the possibilities and hopes of Latin American youth and the oppressed.

The Cuban Revolution began on July 26, 1953, when Fidel Castro led other revolutionaries in an attack on the Moncada barracks. It was a suicide mission and almost one-third of the combatants were killed. Following the attack, Castro and his brother Raúl were captured, tried, convicted, and sentenced to fifteen years hard labor. In 1955, the Cuban dictator Fulgencio Batista issued a general amnesty, and the Castro brothers fled Cuba. They spent part of their exile raising funds for the revolution in New York and organizing their return in Mexico. It was in Mexico, that they met Argentine Ernesto "Che" Guevara.

The meeting between Ernesto Guevara de la Serna and Fidel Castro took a circuitous route. Guevara was born in 1928 in Rosario, Argentina. Although frequently bed-ridden due to asthma, he did complete primary and secondary school.[5] After which, he studied medicine receiving his MD in 1953. It was during his university studies that Guevara began to travel. He took his first trip on a motorcycle he built in 1949. During his summer breaks, he traveled through South American countries keeping a journal of his experiences.[6] Once he graduated from medical school, he went to Bolivia and then to Guatemala.

Guevara's time in Guatemala changed his life. He witnessed the United States backed overthrow of Jacobo Arbenz in 1954 that contributed to his anti-imperialist views.[7] He also met Cuban exiles who were with the Castro brothers on their infamous attack on the Moncada barracks. These Cuban exiles gave him his nickname "Che," and they also became his link to Fidel Castro. After Arbenz's overthrow, Guevara went to Mexico. Outside of a hospital where he worked, Guevara ran into Ñico López, a Cuban exile and rebel who he had known in Guatemala. López introduced him to Raúl Castro, who in turn, introduced Guevara to his brother Fidel in the summer of 1955.

In Mexico City, the two revolutionaries met and changed the course of history. Guevara joined Castro's July 26 Movement's return expedition to Cuba as a medical officer. Guevara, Castro, and eighty other men landed together in Cuba in 1956, and fought Batista's forces until 1959. Guevara led his own column that was responsible for the decisive victory at Santa Clara with assistance from the local population in December of 1958. The following month, the July 26 Movement took Havana and control of the government. Young, educated, upper middle class radicals had toppled a United States backed dictatorship.

The images of the Cuban rebels arriving in Havana marked the following Latin American generations. To student activist Marcelino Perelló, the 1960s with all its hopes and aspirations for Latin American youth began in January of 1959. Another 1968 activist Sócrates Campos Lemus saw the Cuban Revolution as the most important influence on the students. He stated in an interview. "Of course, there were people influenced by different movements and political currents of the time. You can not know what an enormous influence, cultural impact, and political mobilization the Cuban Revolution had. We saw it as a liberating movement in many aspects."[8]

During the Mexican student movement, Che's image graced flyers, placards, and murals in Mexico and in student uprisings throughout the

Figure 1: Mural with image of Che Guevara. Colección Universidad Sección: Movimientos Estudiantiles, Archivo Historico de Universidad Autónoma de México-Centro de Estudios Sobre la Universidad, AHU-NAM-CESU, Biblioteca Nacional, México D.F., Folio 4626.30.

world (See Figure 1). The icon of Che represented a conception of the New Man, characterizing the importance of the revolutionary who was not tied to the constraints of modern society, who was anti-imperialist and anti-capitalist. Of course, Che's construction of the New Man and its application to Cuba was far less important than its cultural representations in the years immediately before and after his death. In Cuba, Che wished to eradicate the use of money, and he also believed that the revolution should be exported. Che's image, while of liberation against imperialism, was also a highly masculinized one. He represented the male revolutionary—extremely theoretical and intellectual, who could rise above adversity, physical and/or emotional, to challenge and overthrow tyranny. His image and his diaries served as a rallying call for young men. Although he maintained a close relationship with his progressive mother, Che's diaries reflected *his* views, and he rarely mentioned women as part of revolutionary change.

Indeed, Che was a mythical figure. His life and diaries fueled many young revolutionaries' dreams. From Che hopping on a motorcycle to tour Latin America despite severe asthma, to fighting in Cuba, to his defiance of both the United States and Soviet camps, to dying in the jungles of Bolivia on October 7, 1967, he was the model of the devoted militant. He appealed to students across the world. Che charmed both male and female activists, but young men still had greater opportunity to live up to his ideals of Che, particularly his ideals of "The New Man." Women, according to Che, were necessary to consider, but they were not central proponents of revolution. That privilege was reserved for men. Thus, young men, like those who followed Che, were poised to be the revolutionary vanguard.[9]

Che, as well as Fidel Castro, offered to the world an example that a group of devoted fighters could face a Goliath and win. Although women were not completely included in the revolutionary process during the fighting, Castro and Che recognized that the overthrow of capitalism would free women from certain restraints. However, women's potential remained circumscribed in Fidel and Che's bourgeois attitudes. The young male vanguard had provided the potential for female liberation through revolution. It appeared almost as if female liberation was a gift from the revolutionaries to their female comrades. Thus, the Cuban Revolution, led by young, educated, urban, middle-class vanguard males who were followed and supported by their female comrades, offered a perfect model of gender relations and potential outcomes for the urban, middle class youth of Mexico City.[10] The possibilities that Che and Fidel advocated and personified were not lost on young Mexican men and women. The impact of the Cuban Revolution and the images of Che taking Havana followed by Fidel encouraged the belief that change was possible, and to bring change to fruition took many forms.

Masculine Power: The President

Che Guevara and Fidel Castro offered a new image for young, middle class, educated, and politicized men and women throughout the world. They were revolutionary yet modern, and in Mexico, the images of Guevara and Castro had a particular impact. Mexico was a country that also had experienced a revolution, and it was a country that was ruled by a government that sprang from that revolution. However, during the 1950s and 1960s, Mexico did not seem to have maintained the ideals of the revolution. New debates emerged that considered the role of the revolution and the making of presidential and political power that proved no less revolutionary than the new image for youth represented by Guevara and Castro. Certain writers explored the Mexican psyche and culture as manifested in masculinity and femininity. One of the most famous was Octavio Paz who published *The Labyrinth of Solitude* in 1950. The work probed Mexican identity and questioned the ideals of the revolution.[11]

Paz's works reflected a general idea that Mexican culture and Mexico were masculine creations. The male, particularly the president, truly exemplifies Mexico; he is the central actor, both protagonist and antagonist. Paz's work also embraced a traditional gendered approach. Women are passive constructions in a male world. They have "no wills of their own." Women are the sleeping bodies coming alive only when a man awakens them. Paz wrote, "She (woman) is the answer rather than the question, a vibrant and easily worked material that is shaped by the imagination and sensuality of the male."[12] Indicative of his time, Paz's perceptions placed women on the outside of public life securely within the private realm.

The work of Paz portrayed aspects of gender and its cultural manifestations to a broader audience. Paz did not favorably portray femininity or women during a time of rapid and political change that came during the 1950s. While women were finally becoming formally politicized with the extension of suffrage in 1953, Paz argued that women were secretive and suffering.[13] With men however, he captured the enduring image of masculinity. More specifically for Paz, the Mexican president was the embodiment of Mexican masculinity. As Paz noted and other scholars have continued to reveal, the president represented power and legitimacy in Mexico. He was both the wise and benevolent patriarch and also the unyielding and violent macho.[14] Thus, the image of the Mexican president that Paz painted for the international audience of his work seemed to be based on those men who occupied the presidential offices. Lázaro Cárdenas (1934–1940) had a quality that soon disappeared from his successors. Cárdenas was a revolutionary general, thus his machismo and power derived from lived experiences on the battlefields, not from rhetoric cast about from the Presidential Palace, in union halls, or during street battles with workers and peasants.

Following Paz's literary analysis, other authors questioned the ideals of the revolution, and in turn, the place of men in the modern world. The Mexican Revolution had been the muse for numerous novels, particularly *The Underdogs* by Mariano Azuela, but by the 1950s and 1960s, another form of writing that criticized the revolution emerged.[15] Carlos Fuentes, in his *The Death of Artemio Cruz*, issued the message that the Mexican revolution was dead.[16] Fuentes' work cited four reasons for the betrayal of the Revolution: "class domination, Americanization, financial corruption, and the failure of land reform."[17] Through the protagonist, Artemio Cruz, ex-revolutionary turned front man for a U.S. business, Fuentes depicted contemporary Mexican history. From fighting in the revolution to receiving and paying bribes, suppressing rights, and assisting U.S. intervention in economic and political affairs, Cruz reflected the history of Mexico. Cruz became the voice of the government but also of the people whether, they were the poor, strikers, or small business men.

Cruz is not the embodiment of masculinity. Rather he is stereotypically feminine. He is manipulative, indecisive, traitorous, and deceitful. While feminized, Cruz is also a foreign contagion.[18] He is a corrupt bureaucrat working more for foreign interests than for the Mexican people. Fuentes casts the PRI insider, one of the patriarchs of the revolutionary family, as foreign and dangerous, an obstruction to the ideals of the revolution. Cruz seemed to represent those men who occupied Mexico's highest position of power since Cárdenas.

The image of the PRI as an obstacle to the revolution resonated through Mexican contemporary history. Both Octavio Paz and Carlos Fuentes eloquently captured the shifts during the Mexican Revolution from the 1930s to the 1960s.[19] During these years, presidential changes brought new players into the political scene, but also left others on the margins. While heroes of the revolution were celebrated as national figures, their heirs were killed by the same people who proclaimed the beauty of the revolution. The activists of the 1960s grew up in a period of time of great economic change and progress, but also, as Paz and Fuentes suggested, a revolution that could not meet the demands of the people.

Mexico's economy grew throughout the 1940s, 1950s, and 1960s to produce what has been commonly referred to as the Mexican Economic Miracle, triggered in part by the administration and policies of Obregón, Calles, and Cárdenas. Cárdenas was and remains the image of the true revolutionary and a representative of the Left.[20] A revolutionary general, he ousted and took on the corrupt political machine of Plutarco Elías Calles that ironically followed his fairly progressive presidential administration from 1924–1928.[21] Cárdenas co-opted much of the Calles political machine and used it to assure his political authority. Cárdenas's administration ushered in a new age of reform that represented the pinnacle of revolutionary ideals.[22] He embraced the use of populism and "revolutionary rationalism," to centralize control in the executive branch, and he offered reforms that initiated an unspoken pact between the people and the executive. Cárdenas' presidency mimicked his governorship of the state of Michoacán where he incorporated workers, teachers, small business owners, and peasants into the government. He received support and the people received greater social welfare. During his presidency, the state became the arbiter of labor discontent.[23] Cárdenas also distributed land by expropriating large estates and re-distributing them among peasants; consequently, he engendered peasant support for the official party, *Partido Revoluciónario Mexicana* (Party of the Mexican Revolution, PRM).[24]

Those presidents that followed Cárdenas recognized the need to build the economy. However, they did not embrace the same socialist style of development as Cárdenas, nor were they as interested in developing a just society.[25] During World War II, Mexico found markets in the U.S. and Europe for its raw materials and goods such as chemicals, textiles, and food. Thus, its manufacturing sector grew. With goods scarce and prices high, Mexico began to produce products that had previously been imported from the United States or Europe prior to World War II. The Mexican government also implemented policies to protect this nascent industrialization. These efforts appeared successful; foreign competition was kept to a minimum and Mexico experienced 6.4 percent GDP growth from 1940 to 1960.[26] During and after the war, Mexico found itself in the United States camp. Manuel Ávila Camacho (1940–1946) enacted restrictive labor and anti-left policies to appease the Allied forces during World War II when Mexico declared war on the Axis powers. Like Cárdenas, Ávila Camacho was another revolutionary general, but he was not the populist leader his predecessor had been. Ávila Camacho used labor laws to circumvent workers' right to strike. He also instituted the law of social dissolution that was a law of sedition in which those who opposed the government could be imprisoned if they were Mexican or deported if they were foreign. The law of social dissolution, or Article 145, was used against union leaders and political dissidents during the 1940s—Mexico's own red scare.[27]

In 1946, Miguel Alemán became president. Historian John Sherman argues that with the Alemán administration (1946–1952), Mexico embraced "unbridled capitalist development" that included borrowing foreign capital to promote rapid industrialization.[28] Although there remained aspects of the government's nationalistic approach to development, foreign investment in areas of manufacturing increased.[29] With foreign investment flowing into Mexico, Alemán also sought greater Mexican investment. He had to assure Mexico's foreign and domestic investors that his administration would not threaten capital like Cárdenas' expropriation of petroleum had or side with labor in labor/management disputes. Indeed, Mexico enjoyed steady economic growth throughout the 1940s and 1950s as reflected by its GDP.[30] Alemán courted the wealthy industrialists of northern Mexico and the emerging urban middle classes. For these new enfranchised political movers and shakers, he offered investment opportunities and public works. Dollars and tourists from the United States flowed into Mexico during his *sexenio* (six-year term of office). Superhighways connected much of Mexico, new airports brought tourists into Mexico, while promoting greater mobility of Mexicans and goods throughout their country. With the expanding economy, Alemán spent lavishly on public works. In 1952, he dedicated his crowning achievement, University City where *Universidad Nacional Autónoma de Mexico* (National Autonomous University of Mexico, UNAM) was housed.

The fiscal policies of Alemán and his successors proved successful at the macroeconomic level, but many Mexicans did not benefit from the growing foreign and domestic investment. In 1948 and again in 1954, the Mexican government undertook two devaluations in order to stabilize the economy and stop the rise in prices and salaries.[31] Though positive for investors, the devaluation of 1954 contributed to inflation, but more importantly, it eroded the earlier wage and salary gains of workers and teachers. The erosion of salaries and standards of living contributed to more labor and opposition party actions.

In keeping with Alemán, President Adolfo Ruiz Cortines (1952–1958) expanded some social services and public works projects that benefited the emerging middle class, but he too encountered problems from labor and the left. *Instituto Mexicano del Seguro Social* (Mexican Institute of

Social Security, IMSS) added clinics and hospitals, thus creating greater access to medical care and offering medical professionals more employment opportunities.[32] Ruiz Cortines also initiated the construction of *Ciudad Deportiva* (Sports City) for professional sports and recreation. During his tenure, wages rose, but did not keep up with the rate of inflation.[33] Unlike Alemán, Ruiz Cortines recognized the importance of extending some benefits to the poorer sectors of the population. He expanded price controls on staples and saw to the development of more roads and extension of electricity to smaller cities and pueblos.[34] The extension of public works and social services offered modern conveniences to various sectors of the population, but industrialization and construction projects did not alleviate or end poverty. Thus, the 1950s was a period marked by a crescendo of dissenting voices, some that were new to the political arena.

As Ruiz Cortines' term came to a close, the presidential campaign heard new political voices. In the 1958 national election, women cast their first presidential votes. In 1947, Alemán did something that Cárdenas had not: he extended suffrage to women in municipal elections. In 1953, Mexican women achieved complete suffrage, quite late compared to other Latin American countries.[35] Since the era of the Mexican Revolution, women were denied the vote on the basis of stereotypical views. Men who opposed extending the vote to women asserted that women were too emotional and too capricious to vote. Or, they argued that politics were the domain of men, and men did not want women to dirty their hands with such business. More persuasive, however, was the argument that women were more conservative because of their perceived affiliation to the Church.[36] Consequently, it was probable that they would follow the whims of clergy at the ballot box.[37] In 1958, it was feared that women would vote for a *Partido Acción Nacional* (National Action Party, PAN) candidate. The Church, relying upon the old stereotypes of the past, thus encouraged women to dissent from their husbands and vote for Luis Alvarez of the PAN.[38]

Despite Alvarez's attempt to gain the first votes of Mexican women, the defeat of PRI candidate Adolfo López Mateos (1958–1964) did not occur. However, a new era of turbulence began under the new president. Sectors that Alemán and Ruiz Cortines had abandoned and ignored challenged the new president. When López Mateos took power,

21

he confronted emerging labor problems. Perhaps to turn the tide of popular discontent, López Mateos declared that he was (politically) left within the Constitution.[39] His declaration suggested that he would initiate social reforms at a far greater level than his predecessor. López Mateos meant on some level to reclaim the legacy of Cárdenas by showing that he was not like his immediate predecessors. Perhaps López Mateos hoped to engender the same populism that the Mexican people admired in Cárdenas.

During his tenure, López Mateos seemed to recapture the social vigor of Cárdenas with increased expenditures on social services, and he re-initiated a program of land distribution. During his *sexenio* (six year term), he distributed thirty million acres of land to *ejidos* (communal landholdings), and he opened other agricultural lands in the south. He distributed more land than any other Mexican president, including Cárdenas.[40] His administration also continued many of the social policies of Ruiz Cortines by building affordable housing in the Federal District, much of which was directed toward working-class and lower middle-class families. The rents were low and the mortgages were kept at low fixed rates to encourage home ownership. López Mateos established the *Instituto de Seguridad y Servicios Sociales de los Trabajadores del Estado* (Institute of Insurance and Social Service of State Workers, ISSSTE) which provided medical services, childcare, and other social services to workers—particularly state workers. He also expanded IMSS under a reform law.[41]

López Mateos' social welfare programs added to his leftist reputation, but his labor policies did not diverge far from those of Alemán. He attacked the organized left and critics of his administration. In 1962, he imprisoned one of the great Mexican muralists, David Alfaro Siqueiros under Article 145 of the Federal Penal Code, which permitted the government to imprison those who commit "social dissolution" or more simply, sedition.[42] While abroad, Siqueiros had criticized the Mexican government. Upon his return, he was imprisoned. Like Siqueiros, communists and union leaders found themselves targets of the administration. While economic growth was evident, that growth bypassed large sectors of the Mexican people. As the economy flourished, the income available to the lower classes dropped from nineteen percent in 1950 to fifteen percent in 1963.[43] Workers, one of those marginalized groups, engaged López Mateos in his greatest presidential battle.

Revolution and "Miracle" Betrayed

Even before López Mateos' election, 1958 was turbulent. On February 6, 1958, telephone workers went on strike.[44] The union demanded a fifty percent increase in salary. Telephone workers had agitated throughout the 1950s. With the 1954 devaluation and with the rates of inflation by 1958, workers insisted that their standard of living had drastically declined.[45] The telegraph workers' strike was significant for a number of reasons. First, it disrupted communication during an election year. The Mexican press based in Mexico City could not contact their stringers or journalists in other parts of the country. The strike also caught the attention of the international community because embassy officials and international businesses were cut off from their home countries.[46] The strike precipitated a year of working class unrest. While the business community was supporting the government in its negotiations with the telephone workers, other independent unions supported the telephone workers.

On February 11, 1958, the *Sindicato Mexicano de Electricistas* (Mexican Electricians Union, SME) published their support of the telegraph workers in an announcement in the newspaper *Excélsior*.[47] The SME went on to argue that the wages of the telegraph workers were inadequate compared to other workers. The support of the SME encouraged the telegraph workers to continue striking and to stay with their demand of a fifty-percent increase. On February 14, 1958, the SME sponsored "The Day of the Telephone Workers." The SME provided donations to families of the workers, collected by their spouses or other female family members.[48] The following day, the SME demonstrated its own discontent with the situation of the Mexican Miracle and announced that it, too, would go on strike on March 16 unless it received a thirty percent increase in salary, a forty-hour work week, paid vacation, and housing assistance.[49]

Communication workers and the electricians' union were not the only ones to strike. In April of 1958, the teachers' union also agitated. On April 12, 1958, the tenth national congress of the *Sindicato Nacional de Trabajadores de la Educación* (National Union of Workers in Education, SNTE) convened on the patios of *Secretaría de Educación Pública* (Secretary of Public Education, SEP). The *granaderos* (Mexican riot police) blocked the teachers' access to the SEP, so they went to the *Zócalo* (central plaza of Mexico City). En route, granaderos harassed and beat many teachers. Later in April, the teachers held further demonstrations demanding to know who was responsible for the repression they experienced, and they also demanded a forty percent increase in salaries.[50] On April 30, teachers and parents went to the SEP and refused to leave, again insisting that their demands be met.

In May of 1958, at a ceremony to honor teachers, out-going President Ruiz Cortines announced that teachers would receive salary raises beginning in June. Still, the strike did not subside. Instead, railroad and petroleum workers, students, graphic artists, and campesinos joined teachers and supporting parents on the patios of the SEP.[51] The government outlined its proposed solution guaranteeing teachers raises. On June 3, the *Movimiento Revolucionario de Maestros* (Revolutionary Teachers' Movement, MRM) accepted the deal with the government, and the strike ended June 15.

During the teachers' strike, the issue of union democracy emerged, and teachers voted for others to head the union rather than the *charro* leader Enrique W. Sánchez. The term *charro* came to be used when Miguel Alemán imposed Jesús de León, who liked to dress as a cowboy or charro, as head of the Mexican Railroad Workers' Union.[52] *Charrismo* became synonymous with corruption, government collaboration, and undemocratic practices within the union. Although Sánchez's defeat marked a dramatic change, the union's activities were marked by charrismo.

The MRM called for a demonstration on September 6, 1958, in response to the continued violence against teachers, telephone, and other workers. Again, participation came not only from teachers but from workers, students, campesinos, and parents. The march did not begin, however, because the police brutally dispersed the marchers. While some demonstrators fled, police detained others. In response to on-going demands for the release of prisoners, the Secretary of *Gobernación* (Interior) guaranteed democratic and free elections.

In November of 1958, at the Fifth National Congress of the SNTE, representatives from the Federal District demanded the repeal of the law of social dissolution as contained in Article 145 of the Federal Penal Code and the release of political prisoners as part of the platform. Other sectors of the SNTE did not wish to include these positions because the members of Section 9 of the Federal District were viewed as ultra-leftists. At the end of the meeting, Alfonso Lozano Bernal, a supporter of the

SNTE establishment, was named secretary general. This would ultimately weaken the SNTE because it split the union into factions.[53]

Other demands for greater democracy continued. Besides the SME and telegraph workers, the *Sindicato de Trabajadores Ferrocarrileros de México* (The Mexican Republic Railroad Workers' Union, STFRM) went on strike along with primary school teachers. In 1958, the STFRM was awarded a salary increase before the presidential elections. The same year that the STFRM fought for an increase in pay, the union also attempted to confront charrismo within its ranks.[54] Expressing solidarity with the other striking unions, the STFRM demanded that the government free political prisoners, pay an indemnity to families of those who were killed, and punish those responsible for the deaths of not only three STFRM union members but others, as well.[55] This union, with a membership of approximately 100,000, would continue to agitate and influence other unions.

When López Mateos entered office, he inherited the labor problems from his predecessor Ruiz Cortines. From May to June 1958, the Ruiz Cortines' administration had battled with the STFRM's *Gran Comisión Pro Aumento de Salarios* (Commission for Increased Salaries). While teachers had received an increase in June of 1958, the police and army had occupied all of the STFRM offices after a six-hour work stoppage. Demonstrations and other work stoppages occurred and resulted in clashes between workers and police.

On August 1, 1958, the STFRM held a plebiscite to see which of its factions would head the union. The one headed by Demetrio Vallejo won with 59,000 votes compared to 9,000 charro votes. Vallejo's victory reflected the workers' demand for greater democracy within the union. It also led to increased demands for higher wages and a six-day work week. Vallejo contended that if need be, the STFRM would use work stoppages that would start at two hours and increase daily. The government did not support the decision of the STFRM, and charros within the union filibustered. Thus, the work stoppage went to a referendum before all railroad workers. The charros' attempt to block the strike was indicative of the Mexican government's intervention in an independent union's affairs while trying to overturn the decision of the workers to elect Vallejo. This government meddling added to further agitation within the ranks.

Throughout the remainder of 1958 and early 1959, official union representatives denounced Vallejo, but his support was growing within the railroad union, and other independent unions also joined in support of him. On February 1, 1959, the STFRM announced that they would strike on the twenty-fifth if the railroad line Líneas Nacionales did not meet their demands including 16.6 percent pay increases and medical benefits to family members.[56] The union also insisted that the government respect the rights entitled to them by the Querétaro agreement of 1917 that is contained in section XII of Article 123 of the Constitution.[57] This article guaranteed that all owners of all industries that had over 100 workers had to provide safe, clean, and affordable housing.

The strike stalemated with charros supporting the government and Vallejo and his supporters maintaining their position. In March, repression began. The police patrolled working-class neighborhoods to prohibit workers from gathering in groups of more than three at a time. Federal employees who had contacts with workers were asked to report on their neighbors or family members. The military took control of the southeastern rail lines—smaller lines with fewer workers—and they detained and arrested 10,000 workers.[58] Leaders were arrested and imprisoned, including Vallejo and Valetín Campa, a long time union and Communist activist. The railroad workers' strike was significant because it, like the teachers' and telephone workers' strikes, foreshadowed student demands for democracy and civil rights. In 1968, Mexican students issued the same demands of the workers. The workers in the 1950s, like the students in 1968, experienced the Mexican government's continued implementation of violent repression—rather than negotiation—to suppress any opposition or independent organizations.

Struggle for self-determination was not simply a goal for urban unions, but it also extended to the countryside. Since 1943, ex-Zapatista revolutionary Rubén Jaramillo and his band of guerrillas had continued to act upon Emiliano Zapata's vision of land distribution. The *jaramillistas* demanded greater agrarian reform and protection for the existing ejidos. Jaramillo founded the *Partido Agrario Obrero Morelense*, (Morelos Agrarian Worker Party, PAOM) and unsuccessfully ran for governor of the state of Morelos in 1945 and 1952. In 1954, Jaramillo fled to the mountains in order to avoid police persecution. In 1962, he left the mountains with his family and followers to negotiate an amnesty from President López Mateos. When negotiations stalled, Jaramillo ordered the occupation of prominent politicians' land in Morelos. Shortly afterwards,

Jaramillo's body and that of his wife Apifania Zúñiga and those of his sons Enrique, Filemón, and Ricardo (PAOM activists) were found riddled with bullets.[59] Although never formally charged nor documented, the government had destroyed a peasant movement by assassinating its leaders. Jaramillo's death was another example of the brutality of the regime and the distance between the Constitution of 1917 and the Mexican reality. Furthermore, Jaramillo's agenda was to promote and continue land reform which was guaranteed in the constitution. His formation of an opposition party suggested his, as well as his followers, belief that the PRI was not representing the people of the state of Morelos, the home to Mexican revolutionary leader Emiliano Zapata.

The events of the 1940s, 1950s, and early 1960s can not be separated from the summer of 1968. Mexican youth enjoyed the economic benefits that were bestowed on their parents. However, many student activists also witnessed uprisings, and in some cases, they observed their parents in struggles against the government. Activists of the 1950s and 1960s, in turn, provided the ideological impetus for the student protesters and offered direct support in 1968. Some young men, future leaders of the 1968 student movement, joined the Communist Youth and split and formed other student organizations. Mothers of 1968 activists were the first generation of Mexican women to gain formal political rights in the form of suffrage. That battle also carried over into the 1970s when the Civil Code would be modified to outline earlier rights guaranteed to women in the 1917 Constitution.

The attempts of workers and peasants to engage in the political process as they had during the Cárdenas years were marred by power struggles and violence. Certain working-class leaders had been co-opted by the state, while other workers and peasants found themselves labeled as dangerous, and targeted for repression, imprisonment, and even execution. Men from the same social classes who had fought alongside the Mexican revolutionary heroes Emiliano Zapata and Pancho Villa, and men who had supported Cárdenas found themselves marginalized from their revolutionary government. Unfortunately for the PRI, their courting of the urban, educated, middle class was not as successful as they thought. While the PAN benefited from voter discontent because of the corruption and authoritarianism of the one party system, young urban people from the Federal District observed the struggles between men of the fields and factories and those who controlled the money and the technology.[60]

The ability of workers and peasants to engage in a political and social discourse was undermined by the powerful and centralized authority of the government and the executive, whether Alemán, Ruiz Cortines, or López Mateos. Cárdenas, perceived by many as the defender of the ideals of the Mexican Revolution since he had facilitated the co-option of workers and peasants into the revolutionary fold, was also the one who created the power structures that allowed his presidential successors to rein in his bases of power. The populist wing within the PRI, symbolized by Cárdenas, watched as unsympathetic and war-inexperienced politicians and technocrats replaced the benevolent and revolutionary ideas of their *patrón*. Witnessing the struggles between the powerless and the powerful in the 1950s marked the generation of 1968. To them, workers like Vallejo and peasants like Jaramillo seemed to embody the revolution, and yet the heirs to Zapata and Villa were imprisoned and slaughtered.

Student Perspectives on the Movements of the 1950s and early 1960s

The events and the movements of the 1950s and 1960s greatly influenced student activists of 1968, and the leaders of the earlier protest movements became icons in the student protests of the 1960s. Images of Vallejo appeared in propaganda that circulated during the movement (See Figure 2).[61] *2 de octubre*, a documentary film about 1968, opened with a film clip of peasants being massacred by government forces.[62] Students also incorporated images of themselves—men and women— juxtaposed with images of workers bound and silenced to represent how the government silenced opposition. These images and the students' attempts to reach out to workers reflected their growing awareness and recognition of the preceding movements. Student leader Gilberto Guevara Niebla stated in an interview:

> The student movement had many dimensions. On one
> hand, it was a student movement; on the other, it was not.
> The student movement was the bearer of demands that were

Figure. 2: Student-produced propaganda with image of railroad workers' union leader and political prisoner Demetrio Vallejo. Colección de impresos Esther Montero, AHUNAM-CESU, INV. 991/0043.

not only strictly student concerns but those of the society. Before 1968, the authoritarian state had brutally beaten workers also campesinos, and it had destroyed leftist opposition parties. It was in this vacuum, that students injected their demands, aspirations, and desires that were not exclusively of student interest, but also of interest to campesinos, workers, intellectuals, political parties, etc.[63]

The teachers' union and their struggles had an important impact on the 1968 student movement. Teachers groups such as the *Coalición de Profesores de Enseñanza Media y Superior Pro-libertades Democráticas* (Coalition of Secondary and Post-graduate Professors for Democratic Liberties) founded by Mexican engineer and professor Heberto Castillo joined students in 1968. Teachers had a long history of organizing for better pay, and their union endured intervention by the government. In an interview, 1968 activist Roberto Escudero responded to a question on why the teachers' union had rallied behind the students. He noted that many of the teachers involved in 1968 had been involved in previous protest movements at UNAM. For example, many had protested when Rector Ignacio

Chávez was ousted in 1966.[64] Escudero summarized this position as a cry for democracy: "I think, without sociological or economic analysis, that the reason is very simple; the students, the professors, the people, the engineers, the architects, the lawyers, the housewives, the young people who did not study, everybody was tired of this anti-democratic climate that they experienced in this country."[65]

José Revueltas, an ideologue of the 1968 movement, viewed teachers and workers' movements as the beginning of social discontent: "The 1968 movement is not an isolated historical process, but it has its roots in the lack of independence of the working class and the repression of 1958, ten years earlier, against the railroad workers."[66] The repression of the rail workers, their subsequent imprisonment, and the sentencing of Vallejo, Campa, and others to prison under the law of "social dissolution" became a rallying call for many students. In turn, the political prisoners of these early protests would offer their solidarity with students. Vallejo, who in 1968 was on a hunger strike, encouraged students and workers to join together to fight for justice.[67]

Women teachers and later activists in 1968 were also marked by the struggles of workers and peasants in the 1950s and 1960s. They, their mothers, and their sisters were the first enfranchised generation of women voters. Thus, women who came of age in the 1960s were the first formally politically engaged women. They too acknowledged the power struggles between the workers, peasants, and government. Aída González, an artist, was a teacher in an UNAM prep school in 1968. She recalled the previous movements:

> [T]he beginning of social movements, before this period
> (1968), like with the railroad workers and many others was
> the beginning of a real problem for the government because
> it was the beginning of political consciousness of organized
> groups from different parts of society. Although the railroad
> movement had its peak in 1958–1959 with Demetrio Vallejo
> leading it, I think it was part of the background of fertile
> ground that made it possible to arouse the political move-
> ments of the 1960s.[68]

Some student activists who were children of workers became radicalized by their parents. Raúl Jardón, a 1968 student leader, was the son of Edmundo Jardón Arzate, a railroad worker turned journalist for the Communist newspaper *La Voz de México*.[69] In 1958, Jardón Arzate covered the railroad movement and the 1968 student movement. In 1969, he published an early book about 1968 entitled *De la Ciudadela a Tlatelolco*.[70] Jardón's father was not the only one involved in politics. His mother was active in the *Union Nacional de Mujeres Mexicanas* (National Union of Mexican Women) which was one of the first women's groups to support the students in 1968. Jardón's experience growing up with leftist parents and witnessing many of the events of the late 1950s and 1960s contributed to his activism in 1968. His parents, along with the events of the 1950s and 1960s, were responsible for the development of his political consciousness.

Because so many students were politically aware of the struggles of workers and teachers, in 1968 students distributed propaganda that targeted workers trying to create links with the previous movements and their own. One example referred to the workers' continued struggle for a better life through the years. One example, entitled "Comrade Worker," addressed the socio-economic schism between the haves and the have-nots in Mexico. Students wrote:

> Every day, you get up to leave early to the factory; by mid-day you eat your sandwiches of beans and chile, what ever, sitting in front of the factory; by evening you leave tired only to return for the same routine. . . . You work, years pass all the same, the money never increases for you, when you gain a raise in salary, the price of food and clothing has risen too, and all remains the same for you. There is no future for your children, nor for your co-workers, you simply work, work, and work. . . .
>
> Some festival or Sunday, you go to Chapultepec or El Centro with your wife and children. You see the luxurious cars, fine clothing, and elevated prices. You see luxuries that neither you nor your children and wife will ever have . . . these luxuries are for the family of your bosses. . . . All the days you work for the family of your boss not for yours. . . . Don't you ever think about the money produced by the factory, don't you think this money should be distributed to those who

work in the factory, don't you think the factory should belong
to those who work in it. . . . We are making this movement in
popular reaction against a terrible government.[71]

The workers' struggle offered students inspiration for their own movement; however, the underlying mobilization for both movements focused on workers' and students' attempts to access power. In the case of the workers, Vallejo, Campa, and their followers discovered the limits of democracy. They were not in control of their own destinies or even their own work because the government intervened in union issues. When government attempts to manipulate union elections failed, the government brutally punished workers when they attempted to chart an independent path as if they were children. The harassment of workers in their own barrios and their subsequent imprisonment stripped them of their dignity and independence. The workers were powerless, disrespected, and dependent; López Mateos and his administration had publicly emasculated the leadership and destroyed a potential workers' uprising.

Although the telephone and railroad workers and teachers' protests were brutally repressed, their movements contributed to a shift of ideology among Mexico's youth. In the 1960s, Communist Youth activists saw how independent labor, those unions not affiliated with the *Confederación de Trabajadores Mexicanos* (Confederation of Mexican Workers, CTM) adopted a more activist approach to address their demands.[72] The CTM was an organ of the PRI rather than an independent entity that served the needs of workers. Independent unions published editorials, they held work stoppages, and they went on strike rather than simply negotiating for their demands. That led young leftists to question working within the system versus direct action. Communist Youth activist and 1968 student leader Raúl Alvarez Garín stated that the difference within the left became increasingly apparent at the XIII Congress of the Communist Party in 1960. As in the United States and Europe, the *Partido Comunista Mexicano* (Mexican Communist Party, PCM) split into various factions because of Nikita Khrushchev's denunciation of Joseph Stalin in February of 1956.[73]

Alvarez Garín contended that the old leadership demonstrated its incomprehension of events. New forces under Arnoldo Martínez Verdugo and Luis Terrazas added a dynamic element to the party. They were younger and energetic. Alvarez Garín stated, "In these moments, a large number of politicized young people aligned ourselves with the Communist Party [Martínez Verdugo and Terrazas faction] and until 1961 they pushed the possibility of reconstructing the Communist Youth that had disintegrated."[74]

With Martínez Verdugo and Terrazas in the CPM, students met in Morelia and formed the *Central Nacional de Estudiantes Democráticos* (National Democratic Student Committee, CNED). Although Communist Youth were active, the CNED was comprised of students of various ideological backgrounds, who embraced the ideals of the telephone, teachers, and railroad workers, and their purpose was to "fight for a program of reasserted democracy."[75] It was a student organization that promoted democracy, civil rights, and a more just socio-economic system. From the student committee, young people separated from the traditional Communist Party. The formation of this group reveals a youth challenge to old guard leadership and ideas. This split provided young men in particular the opportunity to develop their own leftist ideology that encompassed various theories and relied heavily upon direct action.

The confrontation between the new and the traditional left was important for a number of reasons. It offered young men and women a space to chart their own interpretations of the left and of politics and to abandon those ideas and ideologues that did not adequately represent them or their generation. The "new" left provided young men another arena to engage in political discourse outside of high school, higher education, or government sanctioned student organizations. In these organizations, young leftists did not have to yield to a party, union, or organization official who looked and sounded like their fathers. They could pay particular attention to those issues that concerned their generation, and they could develop means of protest that they found appropriate.

Student activism was not limited to Mexico City or simply student issues. Other student organizations, some affiliated with regional CNED groups, rebelled. Students in Guerrero demonstrated for better educational facilities, but some also joined armed struggle. In Puebla, Michoacán, and Sonora, students rebelled against *porros* and anticommunist and fascist students who terrorized leftist students with the government's encouragement.[76] The student uprisings in Guerrero,

Puebla, Michoacán, and Sonora met with violence when military forces brutally suppressed student unrest.[77] In August 1965, medical students launched a strike in the Federal District for better working conditions. As more clinics and hospitals were built, more students entered medical school, and many worked under difficult conditions. Students from other disciplines, such as Science, Economics, and Political Science of UNAM, joined their peers from the medical school. The departments that supported the medical students would become instrumental in the protests of 1968.

By the late 1960s, new models of activism and ideology infected Mexico. Students were influenced by the Cuban Revolution that showed a new model of revolution. At the same time, students saw a crisis brewing in Mexico. Attacks on workers, teachers, and students seemed to bolster the view that those in power in Mexico were manipulative and traitorous. The corporatist, authoritarian state no longer received obedience in exchange for reforms that were not keeping pace with demands. Mexico was changing, and criticism was growing in the streets along with expressions of culture. Mexico entered a new age, the 1960s with antiquated infrastructures that were slowly collapsing under its inability to address the weight of the demands of the people. The revolutionary family seemed to be squabbling, and a few of its privileged children entered into the debate and painted a picture of disillusionment for all the world to see.

Chapter Two

LOS CHAVOS EN LA CALLE:
The Beginning

While much of the world was rocked by student unrest in 1967 and the first half of 1968, Mexico's earlier problems with workers and teachers seemed to have eased as the Mexican nation prepared to host the Olympic Games.[1] By the early summer of 1968, Mexico City was prepared for the forthcoming Olympic Games in which the entire world was invited to experience a modern country, whether in person or by television. To the visitor or television viewer, Mexico seemed to gleam with the comforts of modern life. Upon arrival, international journalists, Olympic athletes, and their representatives found new stadiums and sports facilities for the games and apartments to house the athletes during their final months of training and during the competition. In *El Centro* (the colonial center of Mexico City), hotels had been constructed for spectators, journalists, and invited guests, and metro lines had been added to move tourists between sports venues and scenic sites.

During the spring of 1968, the Mexican government was also immersed in discussions and debates about lowering the voting age to eighteen.[2] The government as well as the Mexican people also responded to aspects of changing social and cultural mores in 1968 that seemed to be opposed to their traditional, particularly religious, practices. The birth control pill was introduced for distribution in Mexico, while the Beatles made their first appearance in Mexico. Mexico City, to all outward appearances, appeared truly modern; moreover, Mexico also seemed immune to the student and anti-war problems plaguing France, Germany, and the United States.

Chapter Two

With the glow of the new hotels and the buzz of the new metro lines, President Díaz Ordaz, Secretary of Interior Luis Echeverría, Mayor of Mexico City Alfonso Corona del Rosal, Police Chief Luis Cueto Ramírez and his undersecretary Raúl Mendiolea Cerecero encountered an unforeseen obstacle that jeopardized their world fiesta: politically mobilized young middle class men and women students. The rising tide of student disturbances that began in late July collided with the government's plans to showcase a modern Mexico that seemed responsive to change. In a period of less than twenty-four days, a secondary school student squabble snowballed into a mass social movement that questioned the revolutionary regime and publicly challenged the authority of the government. In a few short weeks, students took to the streets and demanded that the government respect their concern for social justice and democracy contained within the Mexican Constitution of 1917. In 1968, the one-party system that had ruled Mexico for over forty years came under attack. Students believed that if their rights were not respected, they were justified in their rebellion against the revolutionary government.

During the initial stage of the student movement, young men and women from across the Federal District developed a sophisticated social uprising that drew support from university professors, administrators, staff, teachers, intellectuals, left and right-of-center parties, women, and parents. In less than a month, the Mexican government's immunity to the era's rages of youth culture and student unrest crumbled before the eyes of the nation as well as arriving international visitors. The whole world was watching as young men and women transgressed physical space, class differences, and gender to organize a social movement that demanded democratic reform. Why young people took to the streets remained a staggering question that all sides attempted to answer.

The first stage of the movement reveals the gendered struggle within the revolutionary family. Like unsuspecting parents, the Díaz Ordaz administration and the PRI were caught off guard. In response, they lashed out with force against students, particularly against young men. The struggle between young men and the administration exemplified the generational and familial confrontation that took place throughout the world in 1968; in essence, it was a struggle between father and son. Initially ignored by the government, young, urban, middle-class women who mobilized alongside their male comrades discovered a political and social opportunity that emerged from the movement that had not previously existed. In turn, young people encountered something many of them had never directly encountered before and that would mark them as a generation: government sponsored violence and repression.

Mexican Barricades

On July 22, 1968, street violence broke out. The causes of the fight remain unclear. Students from two secondary schools struggled with one another in El Centro. Young men from Vocational School 2 affiliated with the *Instituto Politécnico Nacional* (National Polytechnic Institute, IPN or Poli) and another group from Isaac Ochoterena Preparatory school affiliated with the UNAM met each other and came to blows in the street.[3] Although this street battle seemed benign, it would trigger a sequence of events that led to a confrontation between youth and government forces.

Neighborhood gang members from the lower classes acted as allies of both schools in the fighting. These two gangs, *los Arañas* (the Spiders) and *los Ciudadelos* (City Boys) were most visible in the violence. Accounts differ regarding the influence of these gangs in the initial violence. Some activists and journalists argued that the gangs were the main instigators of the confrontation. Other accounts suggested that gang members convinced students from the vocational school to attack the Isaac Ochoterena Preparatory school, or alternatively that the students had gathered to fight the gang members. Whatever the actual events, nearly all accounts agree that gangs were involved and fights broke out.

On the following day, students from Vocational Schools 2 and 5 again fought students from the preparatory schools. This time, students involved in the melee encountered two hundred granaderos (riot police). The gang presence and students' confrontations with police and granaderos led to news reports and rumors that the students involved in the street battle were little more than thugs with gang ties.[4]

The initial fight may have remained just a brawl among young men, but the decision by Police Undersecretary Raúl Mendiolea Cerecero to send in granaderos to squelch the disturbance altered the event. The granaderos responded ferociously and battled with students that

Monday, July 22 and the following day. The use of granaderos to control and dissipate a student fight aroused suspicion and anger among other students because the history of the granaderos was notorious. The granaderos had been formed during the presidency of Manuel Ávila Camacho (1940–1946).[5] Their first mission was to suppress a strike at a munitions factory. The granaderos had then remained a repressive tool of the Mexican government. Indeed, granaderos served as an instrument of manipulation whenever a crisis— particularly a labor dispute—emerged that posed a perceived challenge or threat to the government. The granaderos repressed the telegraph workers' strike of 1958, the railroad workers' strikes of 1958 and 1959, the teachers' strikes of the 1950s and early 1960s, and student protests in 1964 and 1965. Independent labor unions continually questioned the very constitutionality of the granaderos.

Student activists as well as international observers in Mexico at that time viewed the July 22 and 23 street fights as the starting point of the later mass movement.[6] The summoning of the granaderos to repress a student squabble escalated the confrontation and drew in new participants. In the following days, newspapers generally accepted the government's rhetoric that the students involved in the struggle were thugs and gang bangers. This of course demonized the students and justified the beatings by the granaderos and police. The *Federación Nacional de Estudiantes Técnicos* (National Federation of Technical Students, FNET) which had close ties to IPN, other vocational students, non-autonomous institutions, and to the *Secretaría de Educación Pública* (Secretary of Public Education, SEP), planned a protest march for July 26, 1968, to protest the beatings and efforts to defame the students. The FNET demonstration was scheduled to start at the plaza de La Ciudadela in the Casco de Santo Tomás and continue to the Zócalo at the center of the city. The demands issued by the FNET focused on halting the repression of IPN vocational school students.

Across the city, the left-of-center *Central Nacional de Estudiantes Democráticos* (National Center of Democratic Students, CNED) along with a coalition of student groups from UNAM gathered to protest the growing escalation of the United States' war in Vietnam, but more importantly, to commemorate the fifteenth anniversary of Fidel Castro's attack on the Moncada army barracks.[7] While the FNET demonstration was supposed to end before the CNED march, the two groups actually converged close to the Zócalo in El Centro. The crowd numbered about five thousand. Both groups had obtained permits for their protests from the Federal District offices for the same day, Friday, July 26, thus both marches were legal. However, the police were called in again and violence erupted.

On Saturday, the newspapers described a riot that supposedly had been orchestrated by the students. The government version of the July 26 marches described the FNET student march as orderly; however, when it met with the second march led by students from the "extreme left," violence erupted.[8] Allegedly, some students broke downtown shop windows and looted jewelry stores. These students, mostly young men, faced the police in the streets of Tacuba and 5 de Mayo.[9] By the morning of July 27, students had barricaded the streets close to their schools with buses. The police viewed these barricades as a dangerous provocation and decided that more reinforcements were necessary to combat the students.[10] As more armed police and granaderos arrived, students armed themselves as best they could. Mysteriously, in the garbage cans that lined the avenues, students found rocks that they hurled at the police.[11] A more violent clash between three thousand students and two hundred granaderos and police took place, and as on July 22, Police Subdirector Mendiolea coordinated the actions of his men.

Although newspapers generally reported the government's version of the events—that student violence forced the summoning of the granaderos—eyewitnesses disputed these claims. Aída González, a young teacher in a UNAM prep school, was in the downtown area that day. She and her sister decided to see a show at the *Palacio de Belles Artes* (Palace of Fine Arts) and spend the day in the center of the city. She recalled this particular day differently from the official record because she says that she saw granaderos and porros (government-sponsored student agitators that were used in student struggles) looting and breaking windows.[12]

Another eyewitness, student Mario Ortega Olivares recalled that once he entered the Zócalo, the granaderos had arrived and began to beat the students. Ortega said that "A granadero arrived and gave me a club to the head and I left running. Thankfully, the people in the shops in the area protected us...someone put me in an elevator and later we fled after the police had left to attack our comrades..."[13] Young men had fought government-supported porros and granaderos in the streets of

Argentina, El Carmen, and San Ildefonso, among others. Students protesting police brutality in the city were victimized again.

Leftists, Foreigners, and Students: Masculinity and the Enemy

From that day forward, the movement coalesced. The street battles of July 26 set a tone. Both FNET and the UNAM student groups had acquired the licenses needed to hold a march, and both student groups attempted to protest in an orderly fashion. The FNET students were protesting the very thing that they fell victim to: police violence. The CNED and UNAM students, many from the left, found themselves singled out for criticism. They were described as "extreme left," and "Communist." One newspaper, *El Universal*, made a point to report that a student carried a placard that read, "*Che no ha muerto. Vive en nosotros*" (Che is not dead, he lives in us). Less than a year before the student uprising, Che Guevara died in Bolivia at the hands of CIA financed Bolivian soldiers on October 9, 1967. Mexican newspapers, like other newspapers throughout the Americas, announced his death. Guevara's untimely death exporting the revolution abroad further added to his image for young activists. He had sacrificed his life for his ideals becoming a martyr for the revolutionary concepts of the age and an icon for the left.[14]

The myth and martyrdom of Guevara was important for the students, but the students' use of his image provided the press and the government support that the students were controlled by foreign influence. Moreover, in the days that followed the July 26 street battles, the press characterized all young politicized males, particularly from the left but also of the status quo, as dangerous. Thus, young men from the middle classes who diverged from their roles as students found themselves under increasing attack.

On July 27, 1968, police chief Luis Cueto Ramírez argued that the police had used necessary means of force to control the students. The next day, the newspapers declared that seventy-six communist agitators had been detained.[15] In an attempt to control what they saw as a dangerous situation, police raided the offices of the *Partido Comunista Mexicana* (Mexican Communist Party, PCM) and apprehended various members of the PCM, journalists of *La Voz de México,* and members of the *Juventud Comunista Mexicana,* (Communist Youth, JCM). The left-leaning newspaper *La Voz de México* had a difficult time countering the stories of the mainstream newspapers because its offices had been ransacked. Along with the attacks on the PCM and *La Voz de México,* Communist Youth leaders Rubén Valdespino, Arturo Zama, and Félix Goded had been detained.[16] The destruction of the Communist Party offices and the detention of Communist Youth members led to a growing involvement by the Mexican left in the student movement; PCM and JCM members offered their solidarity to students and circulated in their own publications the names of people who had been taken prisoner.[17] The arrests of communists and students further galvanized students who were members of leftist organizations. *La Voz de México* continued to report on the events of 1968.[18]

The police justified their attack on the PCM headquarters by insisting that foreign influences were contributing to the student unrest. In considering the attack on the Communist party headquarters, it seemed that the government manipulated nationalism. Moreover, the government deemed protests that questioned or challenged the status quo or embraced "foreign" ideas as traitorous. Thus, it is important to note how newspapers presented the list of those detained from July 26 to specify individuals who were members of the JCM. Arturo Ortiz Maravan was listed as "director of the Communist Youth," and Gerardo Unzueta Lorenzana as "first secretary of the Central Committee of the Communist Party."[19] The newspapers provided names of others who were detained by authorities, particularly those who were not Mexican citizens and who, according to information provided by the newspapers, had all entered Mexico illegally. These names included Raúl Patricio Pobleta Sepúlveda, a Chilean who supposedly had passed into Mexico illegally while posing as a journalist; Wilfrido Rosado, a Puerto Rican who entered Mexico on a false passport; and Mika Seeger who accompanied Rosado whose actual name was reported to be Alejandro Pérez.[20]

In the wake of the arrests of "76 Red Agitators" and the invasion of their offices, the Communist party issued a manifesto saying that the government was using its organization as a scapegoat.[21] This manifesto was part of the PCM's effort to defeat what it called "a sordid campaign" that the government was waging against the traditional or the student left. This campaign focused blame for the violence of July 26, 1968, on the three organizations.[22] The PCM went on to insist that it, as an opposition party, employed political methods of dissent rather than anarchism. The manifesto attempted to divert attention from the party by casting blame on the United States' Central Intelligence Agency (CIA). The CIA was also blamed by the Mexican government for the civil unrest in the streets. Like the government's interpretation of the Communist Party, the CIA was another possible foreign influence on the students. The PCM also criticized the Mexican government for violating freedom of the press by its invasion and occupation of the *La Voz de México* offices, and it called upon the workers and the people to support them.[23]

The manifesto of PCM did little to mitigate the continued perceptions that the students were incited to rebellion by some foreign agent or group. The government-supported press, however, jumped on the government's rhetoric bandwagon that assured the republic that young men were being led astray by foreigners and communists. In the first few weeks of the movement, the press portrayed the students as street thugs, gang members, or overindulged spoiled brats. The newspaper *El Sol* reported that although there may have been a few Mexican "leftist" students involved, the majority of the chaos was provoked by foreign communist agitators who were in Mexico illegally.[24] The newspaper *El Sol* continued to report that the illegal, foreign agitators were followers of Fidel, Che, and Mao, "and all the apostles of hate and anarchy."[25]

The frenzy over charges of foreign interlopers—perhaps looking for another May in Paris when students and workers rioted—and communists' agitating the students became mixed in the public's mind with the belief that young men were impressionable and violent. With the international reports that Parisian students organized and participated in a nation-wide strike only months before the outbreak of student battles in Mexico City, perhaps the government feared a similar event could happen in Mexico. Through the press, the Mexican government continued to insist that the student agitators were controlled by foreigners who came to Mexico to disrupt the Olympics or by communists who wished to embarrass Mexico internationally. These attitudes played out in editorial cartoons.

In a political cartoon published in the newspaper *El Universal* on July 29, two sloven young men hide behind a shield that is reflecting an image of a well-groomed, if not stunned, student with books in his hand

ESTUDIANTE

"Cuántos crímenes se cometen en tu nombre..."

Figure 3: Student activists as professional agitators and traitors to the nation. "Cuántos crímenes se cometan en su nombre," in *El Universal*, July 29, 1968.

(See Figure 3).[26] In this representation, the young student's good reputation is being tarnished by outsiders using him to shield their exploits. The young men maniacally grinning at the chaos they have concocted from behind the shield are unshaven and sport longish hair. One young man wielding a club wears a shirt that reads "Professional Agitator," and the other student with a scraggly beard wears a shirt that reads *Vendepatrias* (Traitors). Beneath an image of the hammer and sickle, papers stacked at their feet identified with the words "Propaganda." The caption reads: "How many crimes do they commit in your name?" Thus, the "foreign" students are traitors and communists. The Mexican student is contrasted as studious and patriotic, while the "others" engage in dissent and violence. The real student respects his elders and himself, as evidenced by his clean-cut appearance.

In the July 31 edition of the major daily newspaper *Excélsior*, caricaturist Marino published an editorial cartoon entitled "Yo Acuso (bis)

Figure 4: Who is responsible? Marino, "Yo Acuso (bis) (I accuse you)" in *Excélsior*, **July 31, 1968.**

(I accuse)" in which two students are denouncing one another with the same phrase: "*El es el culpable* (He is guilty)."[27] Again, juxtapositions of good versus evil and citizen versus foreign interloper takes place. One student is clean-cut, carrying a book, and wearing a sweater with a "U" for *Universidad* on it (See Figure 4). The other young man has long hair and a beard. He is wearing a vest and hippie-type clothing. On his arm, he wears an arm band with an image of the hammer and sickle. Again, communism and foreign influences upon youth culture are portrayed as having provoked student unrest. Thus, student activists are only thugs doing the bidding of the left in its desire to embarrass the Mexican government in its shining international Olympic moment.

In these two editorial cartoons, caricaturists portray a face-off between young men who are imprinted with emblems of popular culture and defied the bourgeois sentimentality of manhood constructed by Díaz Ordaz and the Mexican revolutionary family. The young men who are clean cut, well-dressed, and carrying books are portrayed as "true" students and "true" Mexicans. In contrast, those young men contaminated by foreign influences are responsible for the violence. The images depicted certain young men as traitors, communists, and professional agitators. In essence, they represented male deviance and criminality that the Mexican government associated with young male activists in the United States and France.[28] Indeed, the cartoons questioned the nationalism of the young men. How could these young men support the ideals of the Mexican Revolution when they were contaminated by foreign influences? Thus, the government rhetoric was intertwined casually with the sort of message suggested by these cartoons: the students were being incited by some foreign influence, whether French students, Fidel Castro, or the Communist International. Some other force or agent was influencing the constructions of Mexican masculinity. Those agents of deception and change had to be challenged to preserve the revolutionary family. What is also intriguing about the editorial cartoons is that middle class masculinity of the 1960s is one of restraint. A twist to the brutal side of revolution, young men who do not conform to the government interpretation of revolutionary progress and modernity are violent, not restrained, dignified, and clean-cut.

The portrayal of students as left-leaning was already common in the national news. Months before the emergence of the student movement in Mexico City, the CNED had been on the government's radar screen for subversive activity. The Mexican government targeted the PCM, JCM, and CNED for the obvious reason that they comprised the formal left, but also because the PCM and the CNED were particularly visible because of their political activism throughout 1968. As a result, beginning in January of 1968, communists found themselves targets of government repression. In January of 1968, the PCM protested the arrest and detaining of two professors from Chilpancingo, Othón Salazar and César

Nuñez.[29] Some communists fled Mexico in response to the growing level of repression triggered by the approaching Olympic games.[30]

As the official party was targeted, student organizations also found themselves under federal and state government scrutiny. In January of 1968, the CNED working with the *Federación de Estudiantes Universitarios de Sinaloa* (Federation of Sinaloan University Students) planned a march for February to protest repression against students in the provinces. The theme *"Marcha por la Ruta de la Libertad"* (The March for the Path of Liberty) passed through cities famous as centers of Mexico's struggle for independence in Dolores, Guanajuato and on to Morelia, Michoacán.[31] Almost immediately, the CNED ran into problems that included being denied the right to pass through a town. The PCM claimed that both state and federal governments had conspired against the CNED and students. The communists argued that the federal government instructed school directors to threaten students with expulsion if they attended the march. Furthermore, newspapers undertook a smear campaign against the student leaders; a campaign very similar to the one that occurred in the summer of 1968. Thus, the CNED was already fully acquainted politically with the Mexican federal and state governments some seven months prior to the July 26 march.

Growing police violence and the orchestrated press campaign fueled students' growing outrage and desire to organize. UNAM and Poli students gathered at the Poli campus to combat the police on Sunday, July 28.[32] This was unprecedented. Students from Poli and UNAM had rarely joined together for anything except sporting competitions. These students came from two different worlds. UNAM hosted Mexico's top research institutions and scholars in University City nestled in the comfortable southern suburbs. Future politicians and business leaders actively recruited from the ranks of its student organizations.[33] UNAM had gained autonomous status in 1945, yet its long history of student activism continued.[34] In relationship to Mexico's socio-economic divisions, UNAM was the academic temple of the elite. Poli, on the other hand, was a technical school housed in the midst of the middle- and working-class barrios lying to the north of the old colonial center of Mexico City. From its ranks came technical and middle management professionals. Although the student population was diverse, many students from Poli were the children of skilled workers and the emerging middle class who, due to the Mexican economic miracle, were for the first time able to send their children to an institution of higher learning. Poli was the ticket to the middle class; UNAM was the confirmation of having arrived. Students gathering from across the city and from different backgrounds revealed that their demands were not institutionally bound. Instead, the students thought that by coming together they would be able to combat the growing violence and perhaps become a force for change.

With students from UNAM and Poli gathering to discuss the implications of police violence, the streets of Mexico City were already heating up. Secondary and vocational students engaged in on-going street battles on July 29 and July 30 against police, granaderos, and the military. A police report document from Campo Militar Numero 1 reveals that by 11:00 P.M. the night of July 29, 1968, the military had orders to remove students from the streets in the center of the city, and to take control of Preparatory School 1 of the UNAM.[35] As police and government forces moved into the historical district in light armored tanks and vehicles, students blockaded avenues and confronted police and granaderos in street fighting, With the military surrounding and barricading streets in the center district, other students sought shelter in Preparatory School 1, San Ildefonso. Military officials later claimed that the students occupied the building and refused to leave, even attacking the military and police with Molotov cocktails.[36] With the students holed up in the school, the military later claimed that they initiated negotiations with the students. When the negotiations broke down, the military fired an explosive bazooka round at the baroque doors of the school.[37] After forcing their way into the building, the military and granaderos occupied the school. They detained 126 young men and collected 10 Molotov cocktails, 2 cans of gasoline, five bottles of nitric acid, and a bottle of ammonia. They also found a box of propaganda from the PCM.[38] By 2:00 A.M., the military had taken control of four preparatory schools and one vocational school.

Newspaper reports of the event estimated that four hundred students were injured and approximately one thousand detained. These newspapers did not list any dead. Officially, the Mexican government claimed that no student had died during the unrest of July 29–30. Student-produced reports told a different story. They argued that both students and bystanders had been killed during the two days of fighting, and that the victims were mostly those who had sought shelter in the school. The names of the dead were circulated unofficially by student groups, along with the names of students and activists detained on July 26, 1968.[39] Student-produced materials questioned how anyone could survive behind those baroque doors blasted by a bazooka round.

The attack ignited student outrage against the government's actions. On the morning of July 30 and continuing through August 1, preparatory and vocational students encountered military and police units occupying areas around their schools. The on-going presence of armed forces around the vocational and secondary schools contributed to further outbreaks of violence.[40] When the police and military fired on the children of the emerging middle class and skilled workers, the government ignited a tumult of rage. Until these events, students had merely organized demonstrations to express their concerns over police brutality. After the attack on San Ildefonso, students began to organize themselves specifically to combat the government's use of force. They also sought to end the occupation of their schools and the campaign of disinformation being waged in the press by the government. Students circulated flyers criticizing the military and the police and questioning the government's policies. They demanded that the Mexican government serve the people, and more provocatively, they began to reclaim their own schools.[41]

By the end of July, young men found themselves depicted as enemies of the nation. Although some of the activists were leftists, the violence against young people mobilized more of them to join their fellow students. In turn, young men and women set out on a course to build a movement that defied student organizations of the past and further challenged the Mexican government, but also the students themselves.

STRIKE!

In the wake of the violence, students at the secondary schools affiliated with UNAM feared further violations of school autonomy. They organized guardias to protect the schools, but indeed these small groups of students inadvertently engendered tremendous social and cultural change.

The guardias had begun to appear immediately in the wake of the government's attack on the preparatory and vocational schools. These ad hoc units each were comprised of eight to ten students who volunteered to remain in the school building during the night to ensure that it would not be taken over by police or military forces. The students in guardias were unarmed. They hoped that their physical presence alone could deter police and/or military occupation of the schools. While students in the guardias occupied and defended the schools, other student groups provided support and assistance. Activist Lucy Castillo recalled in a 1993 interview: "When they [students] took voca 7 [vocational school 7], we went to reinforce that group. Various brigades of the faculty went and we stayed all day."[42] Thus, students organized brigades to supply students occupying the building, thus facilitating the guardias' ability to hold the schools.

Many young women encountered obstacles to their participation in the guardias. To be a member, one had to be physically present in the school. That meant sleeping at the school without parental supervision. The presence of members of the opposite sex created difficulties for young women from "good" families. That reality sharply clashed with the cultural expectations about young women's behavior and capabilities. Carmen Landa stated that the young men in the guardia at her school simply assumed that women would not join. Landa was from a family with a long history of participation in political activism. Her father and mother had supported the Spanish Republican cause during the Spanish civil war. The Landa family then fled Spain and settled in Mexico when Francisco Franco triumphed. Landa's father became a mathematics professor in Mexico. As a young woman in the midst of the protest movement in 1968, Landa wanted to join the guardias. Her parents and her male comrades at her secondary school rebuffed her initial efforts. She continued to press her desire to join the guardia, finally gaining acceptance from her male peers in the end because she was the only student who knew how to operate a mimeograph machine. Because she would only teach other students in exchange for a position with the guardia, she was grudgingly admitted.[43]

As her male comrades had predicted, Landa, like many other women activists, had to battle her parents over her participation. Landa recalled having horrible fights with her parents over her role in the guardia. On the evening she was scheduled to stay at her school, her parents did not want her to go. She told them that she must go because she had a commitment. Landa described what she recalled: "[My parents] taught me that you should be responsible in whatever you take on. You have to be brave if you are involved in a group. So, we had a big fight. Of course, that year I learned that you could fight with your parents and still love each other. We had terrible, terrible fights."[44] In the end, her father, a professor at UNAM, relented and convinced her mother that Landa should be able to keep her end of the agreement and participate in the guardias.

Landa remembered that her service in the guardia helped her feel more comfortable and engaged. While occupying the school, students discussed ideology. This gave Landa the opportunity to discuss her family's Spanish Republican background and her own support of anarchism. Landa and her student comrades sang traditional Mexican folk music and the music of emerging international icons of the youth and counterculture movement: Bob Dylan and Joan Baez. Together in the occupied buildings threatened by police, young men and women did not have to struggle for leadership recognition or the microphone to speak. Instead, they could establish friendships with each other, united in a common cause. In the guardias as well as the general meetings, students were able to talk about the protests, but also about issues common to youth: music, ideology, parents, and dating. But, in the guardias, these intimate settings permitted women greater contact with activists, and as Landa commented, young women felt more comfortable and accepted in a smaller space. Young women were more likely to speak in these groups, and many found that with a more intimate audience, their ideas and thoughts were better received.

Landa, like other women who joined the guardias, had to negotiate and then subvert gender constructs held by her peers, her parents, and herself. Since she was the only child from a "good" family, the family's honor, as well as her own honor, were of a concern. Although her parents agreed with her political ideals, her parents also feared how she would be perceived in this unsupervised and sexually charged setting. To gain her parents' permission, Landa used politicized arguments to convince her parents that her participation was needed and significant. Landa battled her parents, but she also struggled with her male comrades. Embracing traditional ideas about gender, her male peers assumed that young women would not be permitted to participate by their own families. Landa not only had to combat paternal authority, but after gaining their permission, she struggled with her male colleagues. She subverted the male authority of her peers by withholding her skill to run a mimeograph machine to break through the gendered barriers of the guardias.

In the guardias, students transgressed deeply held Mexican cultural mores about honor, sexuality, and gender to become active in the movement. While Landa's memory of her experience in the guardias remains positive, she was more fortunate then others. She recalled that many of her female friends never gained their family's support to participate in the guardias or in the movement. Landa mentioned that a few of her friends stayed at her home during these events because their parents had kicked them out of the house for violating family rules. Historian Julia Túñon Pablos recalled that some women who participated in the guardias were stigmatized by other students who felt that female guardia members had most likely been sexually active.[45] Young, urban, middle-class women who joined the guardias were gender rebels. Their transgressions defied strict gender codes that the middle-class in particular were expected to uphold. Perceived as public and perhaps sexually active, women in the guardias were the embodiment of the dangerous *chica moderna* (modern girl) who was influenced by foreign and negative concepts of modern life.[46] Their revolt against middle-class gender ideals caused problems between young women and their families.

Young men and women that aligned with one another in their guardias, student groups, and *Comités de Lucha* (Committees of Struggle) laid the infrastructure for the movement. The July 29 and July 30 attacks on San Ildefonso and the other schools were the impetus to create a new organization to coordinate the city-wide student protest and strike. The city had been under military control, and numerous students were injured or murdered. In the days following the San Ildefonso incident, the movement heated up. As young men and women formed informal associations such as the guardias in response to the fighting, students from IPN and UNAM, two competing campuses, aligned themselves with one another as well as with the students from the National Agricultural School and the National Teacher's School. Public meetings took place in which students addressed the issues that they thought needed to resolved immediately. By August 1, 1968, students from various schools gathered at Poli to issue their first set of demands. Students in assemblies organized by academic departments or schools forged these demands. Typically, arduous debate lasted for hours during which young men dominated the meetings discussing what was to be done. At times, young women spoke, but for the most part, they were only present and did not lead the assemblies. Yet they, too, were caught up with the growing excitement of the period and movement as exemplified by Landa who joined a guardia in the first few days.[47]

From these initial assemblies, the first set of demands were released to the press and published on August 1, 1968. The demands included respect for democratic liberty; the termination of certain police officials from their positions; disbandment of the granaderos; an indemnity for the families of injured or murdered students; release of all student prisoners; and abolition of Article 145 of the Penal Code (an article of sedition).[48] These demands, first articulated in August, would become the basis of the Six Point Petition that circulated later in September. Along with the demands, talk turned to a possible student strike. Student strikes, in fact, began on the campuses of Poli and UNAM. The strike then spread to the provinces where students protested in solidarity with the Mexico City students.

As the demands and a strike action were discussed, certain sectors of the student population remained aloof. In these early meetings, some students claimed that FNET was trying to hold on to some vestige of control of the movement, even though it was being denounced by the newly formed *Comité Coordinador del Movimiento de la Huelga del IPN* (Central Coordinating Committee of the IPN Strike). Poli student leaders challenged student groups that seemed to be a road block to the movement, particularly FNET. Although FNET organized the July 26 protest march, its ties to the government deemed it a potentially dangerous ally for student activists. Representatives from UNAM and Poli first demanded that FNET be dissolved.[49]

The divisions among students grew from a general suspicion that the government would infiltrate the movement. That fear remained a constant throughout the turmoil of 1968. Some students affiliated with UNAM and Poli charged that members of FNET had called for the police and granaderos' intervention. These student claims about FNET were partially substantiated by reports published in the newspapers after July 26 in which journalists juxtaposed the orderly demonstration of FNET with that of the chaos created by leftist students.[50]

FNET reacted by arguing that its enemies from UNAM and Poli had themselves been infiltrated by radicals and old leftists.[51] Having organized the July 26 march to protest police violence, it denied responsibility for the presence of police and granaderos. It also published statements substantiating its claims that student activists had been incited by radicals and old leftists. The organizations' credibility was undercut by its reliance on government statements that blamed the Communist Party and leftist students for the disturbances.[52] By August 3, FNET made its position clear by arguing that the Mexican government was a "victim" of a national and international conspiracy. FNET went on to offer its support of the approaching Olympic games.[53] These positions confirmed students' suspicions that FNET was not a sympathetic voice, but instead an instrument of the government. From late July on, the student group remained a critic of the student movement, and student activists came to lump FNET with right-leaning student groups. The student-led purge of right-leaning groups from the movement and leadership reflected a growing concern and awareness of potential government infiltration in the movement.

The meetings in late July and early August and the purge of FNET mirrored the social movements of the 1950s and 1960s. The discussion was predominantly a masculine discourse between young men. In the meetings, young men demonstrated their willingness to chart their own political goals, and their readiness to challenge governmental authority and infiltration. As workers had resisted government-appointed charro union leaders during the railroad workers strikes of 1958–1959, students severed the power of FNET, a government arm, from the student uprising.

With students embroiled in an internal struggle to define the movement, divisions also began to emerge at upper levels of national and political power. These divisions also reflected the gendered constructs of power and political negotiations. In response to the attack on San Ildefonso and the detention of art students affiliated with UNAM, Javier Barros Sierra, the rector of UNAM, held a public meeting on August 1, 1968 to discuss the concept of autonomy and the government acts that had violated university rights.[54] Barros Sierra's move to open a discussion reflected a growing concern on the part of the upper administrative level of UNAM. But more importantly, the mobilization of Barros Sierra complicated the issues of masculinity, youth, and the enemy of the revolution.

Figure 5: March by led by Javier Barros Sierra from University City, August 1, 1968. Colección Universidad Sección: Movimientos Estudiantiles, AHU-NAM-CESU, Folio 4626.17.

Barros Sierra held the prestigious appointed position of rector for *Partido Revolucionario Institucional* (Party of the Institutional Revolution, PRI). At one time, Barros Sierra had been considered a potential PRI candidate for president. He was well-respected in the party and his call for the meeting added to the credibility of the students' protest.

Following the meeting, Barros Sierra led students and faculty from Poli and UNAM in a march. On this rainy day, they marched from University City toward their planned destination of the Zócalo (See Figure 5). Marching north on Insurgentes Boulevard, the demonstrators ran into units of the National Army at Felix Cuevas Boulevard that separated the Del Valle and Napoles districts. Newspapers later reported that community and district chiefs of both Del Valle and Napoles feared outbreaks of violence and the destruction of their businesses and private property, and both had requested police protection.

Rather than continuing on Insurgentes as planned, the march turned east, heading toward Coyoacán in order to return to University City. Although the National Army turned back the demonstrators, the newspapers reported that the marchers remained orderly. Journalists also noted that the jubilant atmosphere among protesters had not undermined the tranquility of the march. For example, María Luisa Mendoza reported on the "dignity" by which the students demonstrated their citizenship.[55] A journalist for *El Universal* wrote: "An example of order and sanity that will pass into the history of the student movements was the gigantic demonstration that happened yesterday, approximately one hundred thousand students marched in defense of university autonomy, civil liberties, and law."[56] Photos published in newspapers showed Barros Sierra and upper administrators and faculty leading the march.[57] Barros Sierra, like his colleagues, was mature, somber, and professionally dressed. Thus, this high-ranking government official did not behave like a dupe for the CIA, PCM, or Castro. Barros Sierra was a prominent Mexican politician, not some young man caught up in the youth culture of the 1960s. Although Barros Sierra was not of the generation that would ultimately lead the mass social movement of 1968, he helped ignite the movement and gave it respectability.

The August 1 meeting and march were pivotal to the movement. When Barros Sierra joined the students, he validated their purpose and demands. In interviews conducted for the twenty-fifth anniversary of the movement, activists spoke about the importance of Barros Sierra in continuing the movement's objectives.[58] After August 1, the movement was not simply a student movement; it was a growing social movement demanding respect for civil liberties and political rights.[59] News coverage of this remarkable event reflected a small, but important, shift in perspective. To the media, Barros Sierra and other administrators and professors who joined the students established a new dynamic between students and non-students. No longer seen by the media as bored and over-privileged thugs, the students, now joined by university officials and faculty, were described by journalists as "dignified" and "orderly."

Barros Sierra's public support of the students was not the only novelty in the expanding politicized whirlwind that encircled the movement. Opposing Barros Sierra and the students, Fidel Velázquez, leader of the *Confederación de Trabajadores de México* (Confederation of Mexican Workers, CTM) became a spokesperson for the government's position.[60] Velázquez echoed the government's and FNET's criticism of the students. He said they "were controlled and directed by professional agitators the shade of color that obey foreign commands to disrupt public order and to undermine the authority of the government of the Republic of Mexico that is only paying attention to the necessities of the people."[61]

Velázquez attempted to reassert the paternalism of the revolutionary state that claimed to meet the needs of its people. For the students, the government-affiliated CTM appeared to be another agency of repression, but they continued to try to reach out to workers. While the official statements of the confederation continued to condemn the students inferring, that the Communist Party and foreigners were to blame for the unrest, other opposition parties joined the debate as tentative allies of the students. Opposed to Velázquez, the right-of-center *Partido Acción Nacional* (the National Action Party, PAN) criticized the Díaz Ordaz's administration's use of force, but the PAN also denounced student violence to further their demands.[62]

With the CTM supporting the government and male leaders of the Communist and right-leaning parties and left-leaning independent labor groups publicly condemning the government and supporting the students, women also added their distinctive voices. On August 2, 1968, the *Unión Nacional de Mujeres Mexicanas* (National Union of Mexican Women) published a condemnation of the actions of the government and police against the students. The union wrote:

> Mexico is living in an alarming and tragic moment of unrelenting violence and repression by the public forces against hundreds of students, democratic personalities, political leaders, and the citizens in general.
>
> The granaderos, soldiers, secret agents, and police, have, in their barbarous acts, attacked, detained, and assaulted a large number of men and women.
>
> As Mexican women, as mothers, as sisters, as wives, as members of the National Union of Mexican Women we express our indignation, our pain, and our protest before a situation that through its course in these past days has become worse. This gravely unstable and disruptive climate has intensified. . . .
>
> Mothers, Mexican women: We call on all of you in our country to hold your own protests and support the various outstanding groups, organizations, and personalities that have expressed in defense of the students and constitutional guarantees.

We exhort you to energetically and quickly lift your
voice through letters, telegrams, or manifestos directed to
the authorities of the Republic to condemn the violence,
defend our children, and for the return to normal life.[63]

The Union reveled in its exalted status as mothers, sisters, and wives to engage in a criticism of male Mexican authorities. As women—tied in one way or another to activists, but not themselves activists—they supported aspects of the students' demands such as the release of those detained and the removal of granaderos from streets and schools. While appearing to be concerned about the movement only on the basis of familial and maternal relationships with the activists, the Union was actually subtly subverting traditional gender constructions. The Union used the rhetoric and vocabulary that the general public felt most comfortable with: that women in traditional feminine roles as mothers, sisters, and wives deplored the violence. The Union called upon women to take action, not as political actors, but rather as mothers who must defend their children. In this context, women employed maternal instinct rather than political consciousness as a motivating factor as they joined the students. However, while the Union's rhetoric was ornamental and utilized maternalistic sentiments, members adopted a public stance both in criticizing the president and inviting other women to join them in their defense of the students.

Though employing traditionally gendered language as a means to engage in political dialogue, the Union was not simply a group of mothers and housewives who stepped out of the kitchen to engage in political dialogue at a national level. The Union had ties to a political party, the Communist. In 1963, the PCM had tried to rebuild its membership, and had supported the establishment of the Union in order to encourage women's activism. The Union was formed the following year.[64] Many Union members were the politicized wives of party members.[65] In turn, they often attempted to influence the PCM to address women's issues.

With students on strike, professors and teachers protesting, the rector of UNAM holding public discussions, opposition parties criticizing the Mexican government, and mothers of activists calling on women to support the students' civil rights, President Díaz Ordaz had to respond to the proliferating crisis. He feared that his plans and work could be undermined by a student protest witnessed by the thousands of visitors who were arriving daily in Mexico City for the Olympic time trials. On August 1, 1968, Díaz Ordaz published a statement from Guadalajara addressed to the nation calling for harmony and an end to the violence. In it, he stated:

> Peace and calm must be restored in our country. A hand has been extended; it is up to the Mexican citizens to decide whether to grasp this outstretched hand. I have been greatly pained by these deplorable and shameful incidents. Let us not widen the gap between us; let us all refuse to heed the prompting of our false pride, myself included, naturally.[66]

In his speech, he directed his comments to the people of Jalisco. Offering a brief history of the struggle that led to modern Mexico and acknowledging that problems continued in the country, Díaz Ordaz as the patriarch of the Mexican revolutionary family, appealed for national unity on the basis of nationalism. He did not single out students for criticism; instead, he asserted the capabilities of the Mexican leaders and nation to meet the needs of the people. And though Díaz Ordaz did not criticize students, he also never mentioned them explicitly. Instead, he discussed how he was pained by the embarrassing disruptions in the Federal District. Rather than specifically addressing the student protests, Díaz Ordaz relied upon a revolutionary rhetoric of nationalism, he stated, "With the blood and lives of our heroes, with the sacrifice of thousands of lives through the years, we have built this country that has many painful problems and poverty, but it is our country..."[67] In the president's comments, the problems of Mexico seemed inconsequential, as if they were happening on the west bank in Paris rather than awaiting him in the Federal District. Nevertheless, Díaz Ordaz viewed his gesture as a generous reaching out to students, who in his perception, defied his authority by continuing to organize.[68]

While the "outstretched hand" of the president was intended to pacify the students, the opposite happened. The August 1 march headed by Barros Sierra, faculty, and teachers reflected a growing collaboration between students and other sectors of Mexican society. Thus, Díaz Ordaz's paternalistic gesture was offered too late to hinder the university march. Furthermore, Díaz Ordaz's approach seemed too distant for activists who wanted his attention.[69] Teachers and professors were keenly aware of their students' demands and their grievances for political action. Some faculty and teachers had also been present at the initial skirmishes. The continued violation of university autonomy further ruffled the feathers of those affiliated with secondary schools and institutions of higher learning.

Since the street battles of July 29 and 30, professors had continued to express their concern over violations of university autonomy and civil liberties, as well as the continued use of violence by the government. Faculty and students of the National School of Biological Sciences sent a telegram to President Díaz Ordaz protesting the violence of late July. Their letter denounced the "anti-democratic" atmosphere and blamed officials, rather than students, for the violence. The telegram stated: "We affirm that the police, the army, and the government are completely responsible for these acts." The letter went on to state that it supported a dialogue between "the authorities and the affected parties so that a solution could be reached."[70]

Professors from the National School of Economics also challenged the government in an open letter printed in *El Día* on July 30, 1968. This signed letter demanded respect for university autonomy and also supported student demands. The professors insisted that those students detained and imprisoned should be released and they called for the punishment of those responsible for the violence. The letter was signed by seventy-four members of the school with the lead signature by Ifigenia M. Navarrate, the director of the school.[71]

Other letters to the president followed claiming solidarity with students. Professors and researchers from the prominent research institution El Colegio de México signed a declaration protesting the repression of the students.[72] In another signed statement, the professors from the school of Political and Social Sciences at UNAM protested the violence and demanded a repeal of Article 145 of the Federal Penal Code, which was essentially a law of sedition.[73] The professors from the school of Social and Political Sciences stated:

> We call to all those affiliated with the university, students,
> professors, administrators, and staff to reinforce the unity

and maintain the just in defense of autonomy, and we
demonstrate that we continue to struggle for all the means
in our range for the reestablishment of university autonomy.
    At the same time, we are making a call to all the people
of Mexico to support us in the defense of university autonomy, for it is an essential part of the defense of our historically hard fought liberties and guarantees.[74]

Faculty attempts to voice concerns were given urgency through discussions of a student strike. First discussed at Poli, and then circulated
by student activists elsewhere, the idea of a strike spread like wildfire. The
public declaration of the strike as well as the students' demands propelled further mobilization. With the declaration of a strike at Poli that
was joined by UNAM, Poli students held a march on August 5 from their
campus to the Casco de Santo Tomás where much of the fighting on July
22 and July 26 and again on July 28–29 had taken place. Poli students had
asked Dr. Guillermo Massieu, General Director of IPN, to head the march
as Barros Sierra had. Massieu declined, but a march with an estimated
one hundred thousand faculty and students took place nonetheless.[75]

Newspapers reported that five speakers took the podium at the meeting, and that the demonstration was orderly. Genero Alanís from
Vocational School 5 and Raúl Alvarez , from the School of Science, Physics,
and Mathematics of Poli both spoke about the 1956 invasion of their campus. Along with Alvarez, José Tayde, from the National School of
Agriculture in Chapingo, criticized the repressive forces. Alvarez also criticized Article 145, and Tayde spoke about the deaths of students.[76] Gilberto
Guevara, from UNAM, and Fausto Trejo, professor from Poli, both focused
on unification of the students from across the city.[77] It was at this march
that the students issued an ultimatum to the government: release all political prisoners in 72 hours or they would call a general strike.[78] The government responded that there were no political prisoners in Mexico.

Consejo Nacional de Huelga

In response to the violence and the government's recalcitrance to negotiate with students in the face of the public ultimatum, students moved

to institute a city-wide strike. Since nascent strike and student organizations at various campuses were already in place, students from across the city democratically elected representatives for a National Strike Council (*Consejo Nacional de Huelga*, CNH), which formed on August 8, 1968, to oversee the city-wide strike and serve as a leadership body for the movement. Like the guardias, both men and women served on the CNH. In some cases, women represented schools and departments that were predominantly male.

The CNH was composed primarily of students from UNAM, National Preparatory Schools, IPN, Vocational Schools 5 and 7, Prevocational School 2, and the National School of Agriculture (Chapingo). Schools that focused on education also joined: the National School of Teachers, Superior Normal School, and Specialized Normal School. Students and faculty in private institutions joined their public school peers: El Colegio de México and Iberoamericano (a private Jesuit university). Other state and national schools joined including Autonomous University of Puebla, the Autonomous University of Chihuahua, and the National School of Anthropology and History.[79]

As in most political organizations, the CNH mirrored the practices of Mexican society. Young men dominated; approximately ten members of the CNH were women out of the estimated 230 official members.[80] CNH member Adriana Corona argued that there may have been upwards of five hundred activists on the CNH, a number that includes representation from the provinces.[81] Thus, the movement had spread beyond the borders of Mexico City. Corona's estimates rely upon the fact that at CNH meetings and events, council members were accompanied by friends or lovers who worked on the strike and in the movement. Other activists worked with the CNH distributing information, whether from student organizations, labor, or the left.[82]

Scholars have questioned the CNH's organization. Historian Donald Mabry wondered whether the large membership of the CNH was "foolhardy" because its size may have undermined its ability to meet and organize.[83] Other authors and some participants claimed that the large numbers of representatives were necessary to ensure that all leaders could not be identified if some were detained.[84] Moreover, students distrusted individual leaders and representatives because of the ability of the government to co-opt student leaders into the PRI or into the bureaucracy. Since the PRI recruited future members from the students who won in UNAM student struggles—these politicized struggles launched the political ambitions of many young men. Consequently, the CNH organizers wanted a widely dispersed and representative organization to combat the traditional practices that plagued student politics.

From personal experience or from observation, student activists were keenly aware that the Mexican government had a record of detaining opposition party members, and that the government was willing to detain student activists as well. Some of the most prominent activists on the CNH who later became theorists of the movement were affiliated with the left: Eduardo Valle, Marcelino Perelló, Carlos Sevilla, and Raúl Jardón. Yet, in Jardón's own estimates, only about 27 of the 128 documented members of the entire CNH had affiliations with the left prior to the movement.[85] They came from various organizations on the left. But more important for understanding later events, it is significant to note that leftist activists were the minority on the strike council. Some members were PRI sympathizers. Thus, while leftist activists played a key role in the movement and they were elected to the CNH, they in no way had control. Because of the diverse ideologies of student leaders, a much more moderate influence prevailed in the strike council's decisions despite the depictions of the CNH in the Mexico City newspapers.

The organization of the council ensured that diverse student voices were part of it. For people to win seats, they had to be elected by their schools or departments. Thus, all members were elected democratically from various departments and schools. The Comités de lucha of the schools and departments facilitated the voting for representatives on the CNH. The council was therefore an umbrella organization that developed after the movement emerged. The Comités de lucha were the initial tools of the movement, and those activists in the Comités were responsible for organizing on the campuses and transmitting the ideas and programs of the council. By holding elections for the CNH, students who may not have otherwise been selected won elections. This included the election of female representatives from traditional male fields of study.

Although enrollment of women in universities had increased in the 1960s, young men still dominated most of CNH representative ranks from the institutions of higher education. The exception was traditional areas of women's interests such as teaching, social work, dentistry, and nursing.[86]

One of the most controversial elections to the strike council was that of UNAM law school representative Roberta "Tita" Avendaño. Avendaño had to struggle in order to become the CNH representative from her school. In an interview in 1988, she stated that, "The School of Law had been governed by the PRI, it entered on the side of the PRI, with tremendous power and great orators. My comrades attacked me. They said the school should be represented by a man."[87] However, Avendaño persevered. Another woman, Mirthokoleia González Guardado was also elected as a CNH representative from the Wilfrido Massieu Industrial Technical School at IPN. González Guardado, a student activist with PRI affiliations in 1968, joined the movement because she sympathized with the students' demands. She, too, was from a school that was predominantly male, but she also proved that women could represent students in predominantly male fields: "I was the only woman that participated in the school and moreover, they elected me to be their representative to the CNH..."[88] Being one of the few female activists from Wilfrido Massieu school, González Guardado became the council representative.

The elections of Avendaño and González Guardado were particularly important at the time to many women who were involved in the movement. Both were elected to the CNH from male-dominated fields of study, and neither had any documented leftist involvement prior to 1968. While the elections of both women were significant in themselves, Avendaño emerged as a recognized movement leader. María Alvarez, a 1968 activist from *Escuela Normal Superior* (Superior Normal School) recalled in a radio program in 1993: "I also want to mention that among the most notable participants in the movement was La Tita Avendaño and that Tita was originally a *normalista* (teacher) and was the representative for the School of Law."[89]

Male activists also recognized her influence and leadership. José López Rodríguez recalled how he heard Tita speak on September 13, 1968, in the plaza: "It was fascinating to arrive at the plaza of the Constitution and to see how all the students sat together there on the ground waiting for the moving words of la Tita, the great leader."[90] The women elected to the CNH were also exceptional in other ways. The majority had earlier been active in other organizations. María Eugenia Meste, for example, was from the School of Philosophy and Letters and an activist in the *Liga Comunista Espartaco* (Spartacus Communist

League, LCE). Some women came to the movement from religious activism such as School of Dentistry representative Marcia Gutiérrez who had been an activist in Catholic student organizations.[91]

With the student-based leadership in place and two successful marches behind them, faculty across the city organized their own committees and coalitions of support. On August 5, the faculty at Poli had established the *Comité Coordinador de Maestros de IPN Pro Libertades* (Coordinating Committee of IPN Teachers for Liberty). This group offered their solidarity to the striking Poli students. The Poli professors echoed previous sentiments from the faculty of various departments. They publicly denounced the violence and echoed the students' demands to respect democratic liberty and abolish Article 145. The Poli professors also offered their solidarity with and support of professors at UNAM.

The organization of the Poli faculty undercut IPN Director Massieu's attempt to have students return to classes. As reported in the newspapers, neither Massieu nor any of the other administrators of Poli attended the Poli faculty's meeting.[92] The committee of teachers exposed the dissent between the institute's administration and the faculty on the campus. Without the faculty, the possibility of students returning to class greatly diminished in the wake of the solidarity statements.

By August 8, teachers, professors, and researchers from various institutions formed the *Coalición de Profesores de Enseñanza Media y Superior Pro Libertades Democráticas* (the Coalition of Secondary and Postgraduate Professors for Democratic Liberties, hereafter referred to as the Coalition). Led by engineer Heberto Castillo, the Coalition was comprised of faculty and staff from Poli, UNAM, and their affiliated institutes and national schools, as well as Chapingo, Poli's technical and vocational schools, various UNAM preparatory schools, and the Association of Administrative workers at UNAM.[93] As with other faculty-led initiatives, the Coalition supported the Six Point Petition, but the Coalition added:

> Moreover, as unconditional defenders of Mexican culture,
> we protest the aggression against human and citizen rights
> that in these past days has taken the forms ranging from the
> violations of students' rights, to movement throughout the
> Republic, to the apprehension of people for only being pro-

gressive, to the intimidation of recognized political groups
such as Communist.[94]

The professors' public support of students was instrumental to the
student movement's success. In assessing the general strike, students
certainly needed faculty support. If the professors had not joined the
students, the strike would not have been effective because classes would
have continued with or without the participation of activists. As the CNH
served students' needs, the Coalition served as an umbrella organization for the faculty. Schools and departments still individually supported students in their schools and departments, but the Coalition offered
an opportunity for teachers, researchers, and professors to organize
across the city over an issue that was outside their traditional local areas
and disciplines.

As with the Barros Sierra earlier march on August 1, faculty support
through the Coalition now legitimized the movement. It could no longer
be viewed as youthful flirtation with social activism. In a few short days,
what had been a street squabble was slowly becoming a sophisticated city-
wide social movement that was spilling over into the provinces. By joining
the students, the faculty brought university administrators and staff into
the strike. If there were no students to sit in the classes and no professors
to teach the classes, there was no reason for staff to show up either. In the
wake of the organization of the Coalition, statements were issued from
administrators and staff who supported students and their strike.[95] By
August 9, seventy schools were on strike. With the faculty on board, the students were now in a position to organize beyond educational institutions.

At this juncture, fifty-five prominent Mexican intellectuals and artists
added their voices to the movement. Providing an overview of the situation since July 26 in a public statement printed in the newspaper *El
Día*, intellectuals and artists criticized the government's use of violence
against students and Mexicans, and after analyzing the situation, they
supported the students' struggle for democracy:

> Because the government acts as the framer of the law rather
> than on the margins of it, because the government settles for
> repressive and unconstitutional mechanism, the students'
> struggle for democratic liberties . . . the liberty of political

prisoners; for genuine university reform; to liberate Mexico
of its dependence and secular misery.[96]

The letter was signed by artists such as David Alfaro Siqueiros, writers such as Raquel Tibol and Carlos Monsiváis as well as academics such
as Alonso Aguilar M., Angel Bassols Batalla, and Victor Flores Olea, and
medical doctors such as Ismael Cosío Vallegas and Isaías Cervantes.[97] In
the letter, intellectuals, professors, and artists challenged the government's contention that the Communist Party or some other foreign
influence, FBI or CIA, were behind the violence though some, such as
Siqueiros, were prominent Communists. Mexican intellectuals decried
the government's allegations that these influences created chaos and
disorder so that nationalistic pride would unite the people against the
students and pave the way for the Olympics. Instead, intellectuals argued
that the students were the ones who were struggling for the dignity and
rights of the Mexican people, not the government.[98]

With growing support from various sectors of the civil as well as
political society of Mexico, students began to relish their newfound sense
of power. As the clock ran out on the students' demands for dialogue
and other concessions, Alfonso Corona del Rosal, the regent of the
Federal District (Mexico City), sent a public letter to IPN Director Dr.
Massieu.[99] Perhaps Corona del Rosal hoped to assist in Massieu's efforts
to return students to the classrooms at IPN; however, the letter was perceived as a vehicle to undermine the student strike. In the correspondence, Corona del Rosal addressed the students. He argued that he was
unable to respond to the students' demands to terminate key police
figures without following proper procedures in the police department.[100]
In response to the students' demands for indemnities to the families of
those murdered or injured, Corona argued, his department needed to
have precise information regarding those individuals who had died or
were injured in the riots. He stressed that all the demands could not be
acted upon without further investigation.

By August 11, the CNH had clearly positioned itself as the leader of
a mass student movement. More significantly, it had finally provoked a
public dialogue with the government though the government's
response had been to a university official. In considering Corona's letter, his response maintained the authority and power of the PRI and its

leadership. Corona chose not to speak to the students, because he could possibly exert more influence in Poli by using the political hierarchy. The government may have been provoked to respond to the students, but it responded only to those who had recognized authority like Massieu.

On the same day as the publication of his letter to Massieu, Corona addressed a government sponsored-demonstration of ten thousand people in Lázaro Cárdenas park. Corona took the opportunity to directly criticize the students and to justify the government's actions in order to maintain peace. Returning to the government-preferred mantra that outside agitators and supporters of the "Cuban Revolution" were responsible for the violence, Corona declared that the government was simply maintaining peace. In his speech, he disputed student claims that the police and army had killed young people in the street battles since July 26. He argued that "There has not been one death."[101]

The following day the CNH issued a public statement disputing Corona's letter and speech.

> The *Consejo Nacional de Huelga*, the representative of more than 150,000 students on strike, considers it necessary to clarify before the public and students and professors of the country, some points that derived from the letter of Lic. Corona del Rosal, chief of the Federal District, to Doctor Guillermo Massieu, director of the National Polytechnic Institute, which have been interpreted by the national press as a response to the students' petition.[102]

The CNH countered statements made by Corona by publicly restating their own demands. The idea to form a commission to investigate those who were responsible for the violence was part of the students' initial petition. They criticized the fact that Corona had addressed himself to Massieu rather than the students from universities, technical schools, normal schools, and private institutions. Consequently, the CNH response reflected an understanding of the power dynamic that Corona had deployed. The students were not to be swayed. At the conclusion of the letter, the CNH invited people to join them for the march to be held August 13, 1968.[103]

The First Mass March

The first edition of the *Gaceta: Boletín Informativo del Comité Coordinador de Huelga* (*Gazette: Information Bulletin of the Strike Coordinating Committee*) at UNAM, reflected how the CNH envisioned this first mass meeting.[104] Students would march organized by schools and departments; Poli was to lead, followed by the national university, and then other schools involved in the strike. The CNH had organized "accommodation brigades" which would attempt to assist and protect students. These informal groups had emerged during the Barros Sierra-led march on August 1 when some students had formed a protective line between marchers and police. Now, these groups were formalized and recognized. The CNH had also arranged communication via walkie talkies and made sure that the doors of the churches would remain open to offer sanctuary if violence broke out. Finally, the council had arranged for the *Centro Universitario de Estudios Cinematográficos* (University Center for Cinematic Studies, CUEC) to film the march.[105] The themes for this march were Mexico's socio-political situation and the legality of the means of force that the government was using to break the movement.[106] The organization and focus of the students reflected their growing political sophistication in a brief period of time.

The Coalition issued a statement on August 12 outlining its position and its expected role in the march.[107] In the statement, the Coalition reiterated its support of the students' demands and expressed solidarity with the movement. It vowed to participate in the strike and to make exam arrangements for students.[108] The Coalition also supported other, more controversial, demands and ideas. It denounced certain student groups such as FNET and "fascist groups" like *Movimiento Universitario de Renovadora Orientación,* (University Movement for Renovated Morals, MURO) and *Frente Universitario Mexicano* (Mexican University Student Front, FUM).[109] Lastly, spokespeople also reiterated their group's conviction that the student movement was not simply a movement of student agitators from IPN and UNAM.

The first mass action was held on Tuesday, August 13, 1968 at the Plaza del Carillión in the Casco de Santo Tomás. From there, the students planned to march to the Plaza of the Constitution (Zócalo) in front of the national cathedral and presidential palace.[110] The morning of

August 13, newspapers carried the announcement of the march. Since Poli students were actually debating returning to classes, FNET attempted to block the march. The FNET continued to officially exist as a representative of Poli students, and it saw the march as an "act of provocation against the Mexican government." However, the newspaper *El Sol* reported that twenty-one of the twenty-six schools affiliated with IPN wanted to continue the strike.[111] Despite FNET efforts, the strikers persevered.

As students, professors, teachers, and movement advocates gathered in the Casco de Santo Tomás, the meeting opened with a public reading of a letter by political prisoner and journalist Victor Rico Galán. Rico Gllán had been imprisoned for allegedly organizing a guerrilla group.[112] His letter expressed his admiration for the student struggle, but he also positioned the movement in a historical context. He argued that the movement for the political prisoners was a movement for all oppressed. He stated: "To liberate us will be to liberate the force of all the oppressed masses, to open the channels of their development and their organized struggle."[113] He cautioned students to contemplate that for every one of the eighty-five political prisoners in Lecumberri prison, there were countless peasants, workers, and other political prisoners throughout Mexico. He wrote:

> Political prisoners do not suffer more legal abuse than ... the
> Mexican campesino suffers under the power of the cacique,
> agrarian authorities, large landowners, corrupt leaders....
> political prisoners do not suffer more legal abuse than that
> suffered by the Mexican workers exploited by *patrones*, open
> management conciliation committees, charro leaders, gun-
> men, and cops.[114]

Alongside the workers and peasant struggles, Rico Galán placed the student and medical students' uprisings against the government in the same context as the struggles of workers. Rico Galán identified the student movement as part of a continuing struggle in Mexico.

As outlined by the CNH, the demonstration was orderly with students marching in their respective schools and departments. Professors and teachers affiliated with the Coalition led the march from the Casco de Santo Tomás. The 150,000 to 200,000 demonstrators wound their way from the Casco de Santo Tomás past the Hospital of the Green Cross, to the Plaza of the Constitution, about five kilometers away. Military units and police lined the streets, and most of the shops had closed early to avoid trouble. Newspapers later reported that the march was orderly and peaceful as the students insisted that the government address their Six Point Petition.

Upon arriving at the plaza, students paraded in front of the presidential palace with placards that challenged the very legitimacy of the government. Perhaps learning a lesson from the revolutionary family's patriarch, activists questioned the authority of the president and his administration by engaging in a discourse of male deviance just as the government had done in the press. The protesters' use of imagery and language ridiculed the machismo of the granaderos and police, denounced the PRI and Díaz Ordaz administration as the true traitors, and attempted to reclaim revolutionary rhetoric for the people.

Students carried placards and distributed flyers and posters that depicted the granaderos and police force as gorillas. In Mexico, the use of the image of the gorilla signified a government thug. Activists in the march disparaged the young men who served in the granaderos, depicting them as mindless drones who cracked heads on command. Thus, the students reviled and challenged the granaderos, young men much like themselves. One student protester carried a poster showing an ape wearing riot gear and holding a gingerbread man on a stick with a U on its chest (See Figure 6). Crumbs fall from the ape's mouth suggesting he has just devoured another "student." The caption reads: "Persuasion is our job."[115]

Obviously, peaceful persuasion was far from students' conceptualization of the granaderos. In the depiction, the granadero was an uneducated beast who devoured the students because he was told to do so by his superiors. Unlike the male student activists, the granaderos appeared out of touch with youth culture and the struggle. In the class antagonism between the students and the granaderos, the granaderos gained immediate power over the students from their arms and their job. However, the students had greater power potential because of their education, and in some cases, the social positions they held that could lead to a government or business position. The students' war of rhetoric on the granaderos was full of gender and class biases. Many of the young men in the granaderos did not have access to higher education, nor

Figure 6: Student-produced propaganda: "Persuasion is our job." Colección de impresos Esther Montero, Colección de impresos Esther Montero, AHU-NAM-CESU, INV. 994/0044.

would they ever have the potential for power that young educated men held. In turn, the portrayal of the granaderos by the students as idiots and imbeciles reflected the students' own class prejudice.

To dramatize the deaths and disappearances of students in earlier demonstrations, a group of young men marched carrying a casket on their shoulders shouting "*El Ejército incinerado los cadavers!*" (The Army burns the cadavers).[116] Other student placards read "*Ante la agresión de la reacción, la resistencia popular!*" (Before the reaction of aggression, popular resistance); "*Respeto a la Constitución!*" (Respect the Constitution); and "*Los verdaderos agitadores son el hambre, la ignorancia, y la injusticia.*" (The true agitators are hunger, ignorance, and injustice).[117] Although the students' position was not widely distributed in the press, photos and news clips of them and their placards provided the movement with publicity that had not previously existed. In front of the presidential palace, young people implored their government to provide social services and education, and to respect the Constitution. If these needs went unmet, they called for popular resistance from the Mexican people.

Five speakers who addressed the protesters in the plaza offered their analysis of the movement and the socio-political situation of Mexico. The first to address the crowd was Felix Raymondi from IPN. He explained: "The people support us against the repression and to make institutions more democratic against gangster-like organizations. From the tragic consequences of the railroad workers, teachers, telegraph workers, the students of Sonora, Morelia, Tabasco, UNAM, and IPN, today you yield the fruit of their efforts."[118]

José Tayde, a student leader from the National Agricultural School of Chapingo, spoke about Mexico's 20 million hungry people and 10 million illiterate people. Mexico, he stated, was a nation where only one small group had the power to impose "their truth and their law."[119] Eduardo Valle, a CNH representative from UNAM, reflected on the past seventeen days (beginning with July 26) of struggle between the students and "the charros of FNET." He asserted that the students struggled for liberty.[120]

Fausto Trejo, from the Teacher's Coalition, offered one of the most important points to emerge from the August 13 march. He stated that "This movement (demands) that the Constitution and democratic liberties be respected."[121] This was one of the few explicit and direct references to democracy up to that point in time reported upon during the movement. Students and their proponents believed that they were struggling for a more democratic form of rule despite the government's depictions of their movement.

The following day, some journalists reporting on the event noted that some of the students had been aggressive and confrontational. Journalists pointed to "brigades" of students who used megaphones to coordinate chants deemed offensive to the armed forces and to the police. The coffin that had "The Army burns cadavers" painted on its side was offensive to officers.[122] That statement would result in Secretary of Defense Marcelino García Barragán attacking this claim of students' deaths. He stated: "The Secretary of Defense categorically denies that there were deaths that resulted from the confrontations between students and soldiers."[123] He went on to claim that the military had nothing against the students and that many officers had children at the UNAM and IPN. García Barragán further attempted to minimize the army's role arguing that the army of Mexico is not that powerful as in other countries; consequently, the Mexican people enjoyed peace and stability compared to other countries.[124]

In examining the interview with García Barragán, there was an attempt to obstruct the goals of the students by portraying the government, represented by García Barragán as the defender of the ideals of the Mexican revolution. He was introduced in the article as a Mexican revolutionary hero. While critical of the movement, he viewed the students as one of his children, even if they were wayward. Unlike the students, García Barragán was also portrayed as a paternal and national figure. He was concerned with maintaining the goals that he had fought for during the revolution. Having put his life in danger as a young man, he was the living embodiment of Mexican democracy.[125]

Building upon García Barragán's reassertion of paternalism and revolutionary posturing, the caricaturist Carreño played with this same theme. In the newspaper *Novedades*, Carreño depicted a granadero father returning from work armed and in his riot gear sitting down and relaxing (See Figure 7).[126] His son, wearing a Poli pullover, waves to his father saying "*Quihúbole papá!*" (What's up, pop?). His father replies, "*Hola hijo, gusto de verte en la casa*" (Hi son, it is a pleasure to see you at home). Thus, the granadero father represents García Barragán's reflection that the military and police do not hate the students because these young people are actually their sons and daughters. Tellingly, the son in the cartoon enthusiastically greets his father, who is gently reasserting his authority in the household. Perhaps, as García Barragán inferred, all that the students needed was a firm paternal hand of guidance. Carreño may have been contributing a tongue-in-cheek commentary of young people's subversion of parental control. As the son gleefully greets his beleaguered father, he seems to be dashing out the door, possibly to a march or meeting. The father, who has not seen his son in a few days, seems content to kick off his boots and relax while his Poli-student son heads out to the streets to encounter his father's comrades bedecked in their riot gear.

Indeed, the government's attempt to assert a symbolic paternal authority fell on deaf ears. The student march of August 13 had invigorated the movement and attracted more support. The struggles over definitions of democracy and power and the clashes over generational

Dibujos de CARREÑO
FAMILIARIDAD

–Quihúbole papá.
—Hola hijo, gusto de verte... en la casa.

Figure 7: Student activist son with *granadero* **father. Dibujos de Carreño Familiaridad,** *Novedades*, **August 15, 1968.**

and gender structures would further intensify after August 13. The students' nascent vision of democracy slowly intruded even into the state-supported press. By mid-August, the anti-movement tide had already begun to turn. The students' voices, ideas, demands, and opinions began to appear in the newspapers that reported on the speeches given by the five male speakers on August 13.

The daily arrival of more foreign journalists in Mexico to cover the Olympics gave activists a broader audience. Newspapers began to reflect the change of attitude toward the students, first by displaying the opinions of foreign journalists. *El Universal*, in its column "El Mundo Hoy, " printed: "An English paper commented, 'The organized cleptocracy of Mexico is seriously threatened. Finally, the citizens have awakened from their lethargy.'"[127] The French newspaper *Le Monde* also commented on the Mexican students' demands for greater democracy.[128]

While not applying terms such as "cleptocracy" or inferring political or social lethargy, Mexican newspapers shouted the success of the first march. *Excélsior* reported: "Few mass demonstrations have been seen in the capital of the Republic other than that of the students held yesterday."[129] The students, with the support of professors, teachers, and administrators had begun to show their growing influence and power. Success in Mexico City promoted organization elsewhere. The day following the march, students in Cuernavaca, Puebla, and Durango organized to support the emerging student uprising in the capital city.

In the twenty-one days leading up to the August 13 march, young men and women from across the city had created the infrastructure of a mass social movement rapidly. They formed guardias, *Comités de luchas*, and they formed the *Consejo Nacional de Huelga*. In turn, they questioned and struggled internally with constructions of gender, class, politics, and social injustice. They debated the capabilities and potential contributions of the movement and its leaders. Some women from the middle class defied traditional gender roles to serve on the CNH and to join the guardias. In turn, young people from the middle classes joined together to voice their political dissent and challenged their leaders who viewed themselves as champions for the middle-class. No longer were student demands focused exclusively on student-related issues. Young men and women questioned the constitutionality of certain codes such as Article 145. They challenged the authority of government officials like Corona de Rosal, Cueto Ramírez, Mendiolea Cueto, and Frías. Young men and women transgressed political and social terrains all in view of an arriving international press corps and community.

The August 13 demonstration represents an escalation of a war of words and the ability to define concepts of freedom and democracy. Young people took to the streets and organized the march thus publicizing their demands and requests for public dialogue. In a few short days, the students' public image evolved from foreign-influenced thuggish spoiled brats to a united voice promoting reform. In the following weeks, that successful model of a mass demonstration would be elaborated upon and further formalized. Students saw allies in professors, teachers, intellectuals, and workers, but they also saw allies in mothers and fathers as initially expressed by the *National Union of Mexican Women*. Building upon a growing coalition that was further developed in the following weeks, later marches would use similar methods, with the CNH coordinating at the top along with the Comités de lucha organizing at the department and school level. The "brigades" of students who acted as agitators during the August 13 demonstration would be formalized, and students would select representatives to engage in a public dialogue with the government. One of those chosen would be Marcelino Perelló.

Chapter Three

LOS DUEÑOS DEL MUNDO:
The Mobilization of the People

Exalted in the press, the August 13 protest had been a tremendous success. By their sheer numbers, the students and their proponents demonstrated their unity and their growing power and influence in the Federal District. Student activists had sought and found support from various sectors of Mexico City and the provinces. By mid-August, seventy schools had joined the strike and university, college, and high school staff and faculty had taken up the student cause as well. Opposition parties like the Communist Party and the National Action Party offered their support, and prominent intellectuals and artists further propagated the message of the students. Young men and women in Mexico City had developed a sophisticated social uprising in a period of mere weeks, and the movement was spreading to other states. To the youth of Mexico, they appeared to be on the brink of bringing forth profound social changes both in the Federal District and the nation despite the government's hostile public rhetoric and on-going physical attacks.

Throughout late August and into September 1968, the students escalated their mobilization. In retrospect, those five weeks, August 13 to September 15, were the pinnacle of the popular movement. Although their access to the government-controlled press was limited, students actively sought new methods to spread their messages. By circulating and publicizing their demands, they hoped to force the government into an open debate that would address their demands. The National Strike Council (CNH) and the Teacher's Coalition implored the government to enter talks. In anticipation, the two groups also selected representatives to serve as chief negotiators for the movement when and if the Díaz Ordaz admin-istration relented to public pressure for dialogue. One of the student rep-resentatives was Marcelino Perelló, the child of Spanish émigrés and a CNH representative from the national university's school of Mathematics.

This elevated level of activism in August led scores of young men and women to immerse themselves in the movement. By taking their demands to the streets, students transgressed social, gender, and polit-ical barriers that they had never had before. At the same time, the move-ment and the publicity it generated thrust the problems of Mexico into the national and international news. That growing attention contributed to a heightened questioning of the approaching Olympics scheduled to open on October 12, 1968.

Although the marches were successful, the movement was not without dissension. Differing student factions emerged and continued to engage in street violence and confrontations with police. Publicly, young men and women fronted a mass social movement that questioned their politics, their society, and their culture. In turn, male and female students negotiat-ed with one another regarding their respective roles in the movement. Young men continued to be public figures, but women rebelled against their assumed traditional roles. Through their activism, women ruptured circumscribed gendered social expectations that were imposed on young women by the family, culture, and society to be subservient, compliant, and enclosed.[1] As men and women charted new roles for themselves, they also united over their demands for change. Students' insistence on public dialogue with the president and the state was an attempt to try to negoti-ate with the president and his administration for a more democratic coun-try that they believed, naïvely or not, that they could bring to fruition.[2] The continued demand for public debate and political reform challenged cer-tain constructions of power at both the personal and national levels, but the student activists still recognized the authority of the president.

The Lightning Brigades

As early as August 1 during the Javier Barros Sierra led march, brigades of students organized to protect demonstrators from police and to distrib-ute propaganda at the marches. Initially ad hoc in their formation, the lightning brigades took on a new and more defined role after the August 13 march. Alongside the guardias, the lightning brigades served a political purpose by spreading the ideals of the movement. The brigades had tremendous impact on questioning political and social thought. The brigades confronted proscribed gender relations because young men and women were instrumental in their organization, work, and success. Officially formed on August 16 when the CNH recognized those brigades that existed and announced the development of 150 brigades to be formed in all of the institutions that were on strike.[3] The brigades, like the guardias, offered young men and women a more focused and intimate way to participate in the student uprising.

In some brigades, students organized according to their skills. For example, there were medical and legal brigades. Others were formed by the Comités de lucha in schools and departments solely with the purpose of spreading the propaganda of the movement. When the CNH and Comités de luchas issued statements, the brigades, usually comprised of six to ten students, took to the streets to spread propaganda and to organize solidarity as outlined by the CNH and Comités de lucha.[4] The brigades were to participate in assemblies, intervene in demonstrations by chanting and spreading propaganda, hold meetings in factories, supermarkets, cinemas, sports facilities, businesses, bus stations, and any place where people gathered. The brigade members were to focus on students, parents, workers, or any person or group that may have been or become sympathetic to their cause.[5] If a group or individual was not sympathetic to or was simply unaware of events, the brigades were to educate them about the movement.

The CNH distributed areas to the Comités de lucha because these groups were located in the *facultades* (colleges), departments, and schools. Thus, the comités had direct contact with many students. The comités then turned to the brigades. Edgard Sánchez, an activist in the School of Chemistry at UNAM became active in the movement through the brigades. He was impressed by the CNH's organization of the brigades by *colonias* (neighborhoods) and by the organization of the various Comités de lucha. He argued that comités and brigades were responsible for most of the city. He stated: "When a group of my friends and I joined the [political] brigades of the Comité de lucha, we were assigned the colonia behind the airport to spread information."[6]

The brigades served their designated areas by disseminating the messages from the CNH and the Comités de luchas. At times, problems emerged because students in the brigades were sent to areas that they were not familiar with. Thus, well-dressed middle- and upper-middle-class students found that people in working-class neighborhoods were not particularly interested in—and at times were hostile to—the students and their rhetoric. The students also had to learn that when well-dressed young people commandeered a bus and shouted Marxist, Maoist, Anarchist, or other political philosophies in working class neighborhoods, they did not garner respect. The resistance that the students encountered in working-class neighborhoods resonated with the government's portrayal of students as opponents to nationalism and the Mexican Revolution. In part, students were to blame for their icy receptions in these areas. By donning their clothing—symbols of the elite or the foreign counterculture—and spouting doctrine about a way of life they had never experienced, in this way they reflected their inability to bridge the class divide.

Students may not have been successful in realizing all aspects of the brigades' objectives. However, they did learn lessons about civil disobedience and organizing, and they also learned valuable lessons about the city. The brigades moved clandestinely through the urban landscape going to parts of the city that its members did not know, even areas where their parents had forbidden them to enter. Thus, young people developed relationships beyond their families. In the brigades, they worked together in close-knit small groups that traveled together to unknown areas.

In a short time, students learned which methods worked and which did not. In an interview published in a 1968 edition of the *North American Congress on Latin America* (NACLA), an anonymous student leader from the Faculty of Social and Political Science described the profound effect and importance of the brigades:

> The formation of the brigades has been the tactical form the
> struggle has taken in the face of aggression. Through our
> experience with them we know that it is possible to continue
> the struggle in a decided way[....] Some of the brigades have
> developed such an awareness of the situation that they
> themselves are formulating their slogans and flyers and they

> have set themselves long-range plans.... The politicalization
> that the brigades have achieved has been effected by means
> of round table discussions, seminars, assemblies, and studies
> they have been carrying out—a political awareness that has
> been in turn transmitted directly to the public in general.[7]

Beyond structured study groups, students in the brigades learned from their experiences in the neighborhoods what methods were the most successful. Thus, they adapted to their surroundings and the experiences they acquired in their assigned areas. Over time, students learned that the information and language that circulated in the assemblies and Comités de lucha had to be modified once the rhetoric entered the streets. Brigade members modified and adapted their language and their interactions by using street theater, pictorial depictions, and less jargon. From the beginning of the movement, the students were ostracized from the mainstream government-controlled press. As mentioned in the NACLA interview, the brigades were the propaganda tools of the CNH and Comités de lucha throughout August and September. The individual units propagandized the messages of the movement's leaders, but each unit added their own ideology and thoughts through flyers and slogans. Flyers were produced by college as well as high school students. Some propaganda appeared very professional, while others simply portrayed the state of the movement or addressed the violence. In direct statements, Comités de lucha many times relied on simple and direct language to convey their struggle and condemn the violence. Many of these statements opened with phrases such as "*Al pueblo de México*" (To the Mexican people) or "*A todo el pueblo de México*" (To all the Mexican people), and went on to briefly discuss events, issue invitations to marches, or contradict government statements.[8]

To move about the city, some brigade members commandeered buses. Once they arrived at a site, they sometimes simply passed out their statements and flyers at major intersections. If a driver was not willing to take a flyer, the students tried to place it through an open car window.[9] Other times, students addressed people in a public area, reading the demands of the movement or discussing the issues. Some students did not find reading to be effective, thus they became more creative. They wrote slogans and painted and printed flyers and posters that criticized or sought to humiliate the government, granaderos, and Díaz Ordaz.

Some groups employed guerrilla theater in the streets to spread their message. As an excerpt in Elena Poniatowska's book *Massacre in Mexico* revealed, brigade members staged a confrontation between a young person and a more mature adult.[10] Margarita Isabel recalled how these performances were staged in public places to depict the students' struggle. She explained that an elderly woman would buy a newspaper at a newsstand, and acting in her role, would comment "Those crazy students are born troublemakers. Just look at this, will you? When there are so many Mexicans like me, people who simply want to live in peace and quiet and not make trouble for anybody! What in the world do those students want? They just want to stir up a fuss, that's all! I'm certain they're Communists. . . . "[11]

The student participant would then respond to this prompt. Isabel elaborated on her response: "I'd stand there in my boots and mini-skirt listening to her, and then suddenly I'd turn to her and burst out, 'Listen, señora, you're going to have to explain what you mean because what you are saying is nonsense. What are you trying to insinuate?'"[12] From that point, the two political actresses raised their voices and further escalated the debate. Isabel recalled that she would then have the opportunity to explain the six demands to the gathering bystanders who would turn on the "señora" who portrayed the government dupe for the day. In these interactions, the young person was always right.

Isabel and other "actors" used this and other forms of guerrilla theater scenarios as a means to spread the movement's propaganda. This script, in turn, reflected a cultural and gender shift among the students. In evaluating the above scenario, Isabel described her clothing, boots and mini-skirt reflecting the youth culture of the 1960s. Her physical appearance was representative of the alluring youth culture, but also of the representations of communists and enemies of the state as portrayed in editorial cartoons. Isabel not only donned the emblems of youth cultural resistance, in the script she publicly challenged an older adult. Isabel, a young woman, engaged in political discourse before an audience of adult men and women. Through her spoken words and actions, she as "the hippie" or "Communist" convinced the people that she and the students were the just ones. Not only was Isabel a hippie and a woman engaging in public political discourse, she defied perceptions of appropriate behavior for young women and youth in general.

In this scenario, Isabel defeated the señora who was the representative of the government and state.

Like Isabel, the young men and women who worked together in the brigades took their work very seriously. Like the guardias, the brigades had few members. In these smaller groups, women felt more comfortable in speaking, and they were able to contribute more. Similar to guardian activist Carmen Landa, women brigades members found the brigades less intimidating. Vida Valero Borrás, a brigade member, like guardia member Landa, expressed that in the smaller groups they were able to discuss theory in her brigade and publicly.[13] Women veterans of the movement have asserted that the larger groups intimidated them and others. Many feared they would not sound intelligent, or they would be ridiculed in large public forums. In the brigades, women debated people in the streets and buses where they were able to apply their knowledge and skills. In these street performances, debates, and speeches, women had the opportunity to debate and engage in political discourse in a public venue perhaps honing their skills for later involvements.

Women in the CNH, brigades, and guardias found opportunities in a time of crisis. History reveals that there are always rebels in times of crisis who challenge perspectives of "correct" gender behavior such as in the brigades and guardias.[14] By claiming public roles, women challenged the ritual practices of feminine gender that relegated their duties to the unseen private realm.[15] In the brigades, women were public, and they were loud. They yelled slogans, they engaged in hostile debates, and they viewed themselves as political actors who had something to say and who deserved to be heard. Consequently, a few women rose to the ranks of formal leadership by representing their school on the CNH, while others saw themselves as revolutionaries, adding a feminine twist to the image of Ernesto "Che" Guevara, the young Cuban revolutionary figure. Vida Valero Borrás claimed in a 1997 interview that while she was in one of the lightning brigades she wore a vial of cyanide around her neck. Although she laughed about her actions, she said that in 1968 she thought that if she was captured, she would never be taken alive. That was how serious she took her work and commitment in the movement.

Although there were exceptional women who challenged gendered expectations in the movement, negotiations about roles in the brigades remained particularly tenuous. In many cases, the brigades reflected the general society's views of gender roles. In the movement and among the activists, certain work was deemed appropriate for women, and other, more public work, was deemed appropriate for men. As one woman replied when asked if men accepted the women in the movement, she replied "Sure, as maids and secretaries."[16] Of course, women performed many tasks traditionally reserved for women. They made coffee, ran the kitchens, and performed secretarial tasks. Marta Lamas, a student and LCE activist in 1968 recalled that she served the movement by driving brigade members from place to place, action to action.[17]

Mostly, women did perform traditional women's work usually with little or no recognition. And yet, this work, at some level, contributed to a growing awareness of its importance. Raúl Jardón, a CNH member from the National Preparatory School and JCM activist, argued that the work that women performed, such as occupying and running the kitchens at UNAM, was instrumental in allowing students to hold UNAM until September 18, when the military invaded University City. He explained that had the women not formed kitchen brigades to provide food, the students would have abandoned the movement because of lack of food and resources.[18] Women's traditional work—for example cooking—enabled students at UNAM to continue their occupation of the campus.

While traditional women's work was important to the momentum of the movement, young women sometimes found their attempts to engage in direct action limited because of the traditional gender expectations of their male comrades. Perhaps derived from masculine notions of honor, male student activists argued that the street actions, where young men confronted the police, were too dangerous for women. This clash between traditional ideologies and women's desire to be active contributed to women actually subverting their male comrades' imposition of traditional gender roles. When men in a brigade wanted to encourage the women to perform traditional roles, some women resisted. Isabel Huerta was one of the members of the political brigades of the *Escuela de Ciencias Politicas* (School of Political Science at UNAM). She recalled, "The *compañeros* wanted to send us to the kitchen, but we wanted to dedicate ourselves to learning to propagandize and to do what they were doing."[19] Like guardia activist Carmen Landa who withheld her knowledge of a mimeograph machine, Huerta insisted upon defining her own role by joining a political brigade despite the attitudes of her male peers.

Eduardo Valle, a CNH activist, offered insight into how male activists viewed their female comrades. In one instance, women attempted to join a demonstration by hiding on a bus en route. Once Valle and his male comrades discovered the stowaways, they insisted that they get off the bus. The women replied to Valle "that Che Guevara allowed women to fight in his brigade." The women finally departed the bus, only to sneak back on. Ultimately, they went to the action, but they traveled covertly in the back of the bus later.[20] Both Huerta's and Valle's stories demonstrate that women and men were conflicted over their roles as activists. Consequently, they negotiated with each other. Other times, when young men were too entrenched in traditional ideology, women challenged prevailing gender constructs openly. Some women were not content to simply contribute to the movement in traditionally feminine ways as set out by their male comrades. Many women, such as Huerta, wanted to be out in the streets. She was not content, nor were others, to stay hidden in the kitchen.

Other women found that through the brigades, they discovered new roles and meanings to their lives. Mercedes Perelló had been active in the LCE. Prior to the movement, she had participated in actions at factories and with workers to develop working-class consciousness.[21] When the student movement began, Mercedes, a student at UNAM, was unwilling to accept the obstacles to participation that had been erected by her male comrades in the LCE when they organized workers. There, in a mass student uprising, young, educated, middle-class women took political and social messages to the streets. They engaged in public debate and interacted with people beyond simply handing out flyers to weary workers exiting a factory after a long day's work on the line. This public involvement had a profound effect on women, and contributed to a growing political and social consciousness that resulted in personal liberation for young women that grew during the movement and the years beyond.

Parents: Protagonists/Antagonists

Latin American historians have noted the centrality of the family as the most important social and cultural institution.[22] Both historians of Mexico and 1968 activists concur that the metaphoric revolutionary family of Mexico served as the basic socio-political institution of the ruling

Figure 8: Student-produced propaganda targeting mothers. Colección de impresos Esther Montero, AHU-NAM-CESU, 991/0041.

party.[23] The president was the patriarch of the national family (and the PRI), while the national family was comprised of individual families that benefited from revolutionary ideals. The family, then and now, remains the center of social activity in Mexico, plus it serves as an instrument for the acculturation for children. The influence of the family as an important socio-political and cultural institution was not lost on activists in 1968. Students responded to the significance of the family through a number of means. With the CNH, comités, brigades, guardias, and the Coalition in place by mid-August, they targeted families of activists.

Student leaders began to view their parents as potential allies. After the August 13 march, students from the National Preparatory School 8 circulated flyers inviting parents to participate in assemblies with students.[24] Students from the Faculties of Law and Medicine of the UNAM also invited parents to meetings. In some cases, parents formed their own organizations in solidarity with students such as the School of Medicine's *Unión Cívica de Padres de Familia* (the Civic Union of Parents). Once organized, parents encouraged other parents to attend marches, boycott the press, and support their children.[25]

Student-produced propaganda encouraged parental participation, and at times, appeared to threaten parents with drastic consequences if they did not participate. In one poster, the students played upon every parents' most dreaded fear: the death or disappearance of their child or children. An image of a woman wearing a traditional *rebozo* (shawl) over her shoulders and head has one arm raised and the other gripped in a fist (See Figure 8). A masculine hand with stripes at the cuff, representing a military officer, threatens the "mother." The caption reads, "Yes, señora, your son is dead, but think hard about this, if you open your mouth, you will lose your other children."[26]

The image exhibits the interconnections of subtle gendered intricacies of power and resistance. The masculine "hand" of the government is chastising the mother while at the same time threatening a grieving woman. Considering the image, the stern hand of government that was only trying to guide errant children, is now the menacing arm of repression. The mother's raised arm seems prepared to block a disciplining blow, while her clenched fist appears to demonstrate her continued struggle. The traditional rebozo and anguish in her face makes the mother image appear similar to that of the suffering Virgin Mary, the essence of femininity. She is both the suffering and devoted mother, but also a defiant proponent of the students' cause.

Student lectures and propaganda as well as the continuation of violence did rally some parents to support their children. Parents offered support by going to meetings, and assisting with tasks such as copying student flyers or propaganda. More importantly, they permitted their children to participate.[27] Once organized, parents issued public statements of solidarity with their children. Leaders of the parent organizations also became known since they spoke publicly in favor of their children and the student movement. Agustín González, a representative for the *Asociación de Padres de Familia de Estudiantes de IPN* (Association of IPN Students' Parents) was quoted in the press as stating that "parents must support their children and remain at their sides during the struggle." Angel Martínez de Ovando, member of the *Unión*

Cívica de Padres de la Familia de UNAM (Civic Union of UNAM Parents) stated that "every time the government invokes the nation and the Constitution, it continually violates them both.[28]

As the movement continued to grow, the *Union de las Mujeres Mexicanas* (Union of Mexican Women) demanded that the president stop the violence that persisted throughout July and August. They published letters to President Díaz Ordaz framing their petitions in traditional, and therefore acceptable, gender rhetoric. One correspondence stated, "Yes, we have been offended by the words and actions, threats, unjust detaining, but not in one case have the ones responsible been the students, our compañeros, our children, our brothers; those who have shot and beaten us have been the army and members of the repressive forces . . ."[29] As mothers, the letter stated, they rejected the violence against the students, and they offered their solidarity with them. Union members protested alongside their children, and after October 2, they continued to demand answers about those who disappeared.[30]

The CNH, as the directing body of the student movement, recruited parents and courted parents to broaden the movement's base of support. Mothers and fathers were supposed to protect their children from harm; consequently, they were perceived as natural allies. In one flyer, a mother asked all mothers of political prisoners or disappeared and all "Mexican women" to demonstrate with the students in demanding the release of the imprisoned activists, the return of the bodies of those killed in demonstrations, and the indemnification of families of murdered students.[31] This statement was unsigned, and it may have been student-produced. In another statement issued in August 1968, a Comité de Lucha stated that the government was concocting lies about student violence and implored parents to join students so that more would not be killed.[32]

Parents were also courted by the government for bases of support. While the students saw parents as potential allies, the government saw parents as their best ally in containing the students. Parents were the key to student participation since parental authority remained central. If they prohibited their children from taking part in the demonstrations in the street, then there would be fewer protests and protesters. If parents joined their children, the number of protesters would continue to increase.

Supporters of the Díaz Ordaz administration recognized the power that parents could wield over their own children and over all Mexican youth more generally. Thus, parents of activists became a target of both encouragement and criticism. In the early stages of the movement, government officials refused to recognize that Mexican youth were the instigators of the movement. That stance preserved the paternal honor of the family and the nation since the activists were foreign. Moreover, it ensured an illusion that Mexican parents were not condoning the behavior of their children against the nation. As the movement grew, it became more difficult for the government to claim that it was a foreign led movement, and to ignore that some parents marched alongside their children. As parents and other adults joined the movement, critics of the students attacked errant parents who permitted their children to march in the streets, wear their hair too long, or their skirts too short. Many parents of activists agonized over their children's involvement in the movement.[33] Those parents who opposed the student agenda formed their own organizations to counter pro-student parents. In turn, those parental groups encouraged parents to forbid their children to go to marches and demonstrations.[34]

Although student leaders reached out to parents, some students found their parents to be hostile to their participation. Women, especially, had trouble because of constructions of gender in Mexico. Adriana Corona reported that many young women had to confront their parents to participate in the movement. Corona, one of the few women elected to the CNH, represented Preparatory Six of UNAM; consequently, she was still high-school age in 1968. Corona recalled that: "Women started to participate equal to men. We said, half and half, but it was not equal because the majority of women had to [endure] questions in the home: where are you going, with whom are you going."[35] Although Corona was aware that many of her female peers struggled with their parents to join, she clarified why she had fewer problems. "I was always free because I worked from the age of fifteen, and this gave me a different negotiating position. In reality, my family was not very large, a brother and my mother, because at this time my sister was living in England. Consequently, I did not have that other type of [parental] control."[36]

Corona gave voice to many of the goals for women to be treated equally in the movement, but her experience as a fairly independent young woman contrasted with the reality of many of her peers. In the past, the first studies on gender in Mexico usually focused on the dichotomous relationship between males and females.[37] Much of this work has centered on issues of female honor. The women of the family were essentially responsible for the honor of the entire family. Men were the more public figures and were permitted greater freedom in *la calle* (literally the "street," the term also refers more generally to anything outside the home). From this traditional perspective, young women who were engaged in the student movement may not have been a threat to the state, but they were a threat to the culture of Mexico because their actions were in opposition to accepted gender standards.

By the 1960s, concepts of female honor were changing, but traditional structures still existed even in more socially progressive households. Mercedes Perelló offers an example of how a mother dealt with two children, one male, one female, in a politically volatile time.[38] By 1968, Mercedes and Marcelino's father was deceased. Although Mercedes recalled that her mother was proud of her activism, she did think that Marcelino enjoyed greater freedom because he was a man, but also because he had been injured in an accident as a boy.[39] Both her actions and those of her brother brought hardship to their family.[40] During the movement, Mercedes and Marcelino's younger brother encountered problems with the police. After 1968, the Perellós' mother fled Mexico because of constant harassment. She returned to northern Spain where her son would also spend part of his own sixteen year exile.[41]

Thus, the role of young men and women depended frequently on whether their parents condoned their participation or not. Obviously, young male leaders encountered opposition from parents who feared for their safety. For young women, however, the burden of gender and sexuality led parents to play upon young women's precarious position in Mexican culture, thwarting their daughters participation in the student movement. Moreover, the crimes of children could suggest a lack of parental control and lead to criticism.

If parents could not be relied upon to establish order, other adults were recruited to exercise some parental influence over youth. In 1968, Lilia Granillo was attending a Catholic girls' secondary school. She recalled that the nuns continually threatened their students by insisting that the male activists were violent and dangerous.[42] The nuns discouraged their young charges from joining the movement or from even interacting with potential activists. Granillo's boyfriend at the time was an activist, and she continued to date him, not heeding the nuns' warnings. She and her classmates found it difficult to participate because they were not permitted by the nuns to hold the assemblies necessary to organize.[43]

Young women's and men's roles in the movement became construed as sexually dangerous as well. As the young male activists had been characterized as dangerous, so, too, were young women. Their use of clothing and their engagements in public political discourse rankled government observers and the press. Those responsible for the honor of young women thus attempted to rein them in to ensure the maintenance of traditional gender constructs. However, the brigades and the guardias relied upon young women. Young women wanted to join the movement, and many did so regardless of parental disapproval.

Talking About a Revolution

As young women and men navigated the treacherous terrains of gender and parental relations, the political nature of the movement intensified with the growing demand for public dialogue. A few short days after the lightning brigades were formed, the CNH directed them to spread the Six Point Petition, and the demand for public dialogue between the representatives from the government and from the movement.[44] The Six Point Petition, as it came to be known, was first developed in the early days of the movement first at Poli. Ultimately, the Six Point Petition read as follows:

> Liberty for all Political Prisoners.
> Dismissal of police chiefs General Luis Cueto Ramírez,
>   Raúl Mendiolea, and Armando Frías.
> Abolition of the corps of granaderos, direct instruments
>   of repression, and the prohibition of similar corps.
> Abolition of Article 145 and 145 bis of the Penal Code,
>   juridical instruments of repression.
> Indemnification of the families of the dead and injured
>   who had been victims of the aggression since July 26.
> Determination of the responsibility of individual govern-
>   ment officials implicated in the bloodshed.[45]

The petition reflected the students' desire to create a modern nation in which the ideas of the Constitution of 1917 were respected. Along with respect for the law, students wanted the government to recognize its responsibility in using repressive measures. Marcelino Perelló referred to the petition as a "flag" that mobilized the people.[46] Rufino Perdomo, a CNH member described the demands in an interview:

> What did the students demand? Freedom for political pris-
> oners; cessation of the repression; suppression of the
> granaderos; suspension of the political bosses; and indem-
> nification for the injured and their families. It was a student
> movement that did not really make student demands.
> Therefore, it was a movement that was steered to liberalize
> and democratize the society. It was a mass social movement
> that transcended the walls of the schools and converted
> itself into a movement for democracy in this country.[47]

Points two, five, and six specifically addressed the violence students had endured since the beginning of the conflict. Activists continued to insist that student demonstrators had been injured or murdered by government forces. By including these points, the students challenged authorities' use of power. Furthermore, they wanted the government to show good faith in light of the students' demands by determining who the key players in the police ranks were in the violence. Points one, three, and four had their legacy in the workers' strikes of the 1950s. To the students, the inclusion of these demands reflected the Mexican government's continued violation of its Constitution of 1917. They called for the disbanding of the corps of granaderos because its mere existence was unconstitutional according to the students. The Mexican Constitution permitted only the police to exist under the jurisdiction of the Judicial Department.[48] As discussed in Chapter One, during the presidency of Manuel Ávila Camacho (1940–1946), the corps of granaderos was founded to suppress a strike at a munitions facto-ry.[49] The purpose of the corps had been repressive from its inception. The corps had also been called in to put down the telegraph and rail-road workers' strikes, and the teachers' and students' strikes in the 1950s and 1960s.

The students also suggested that Article 145 of the Federal Penal Code was also unconstitutional because it allowed the government the right to arrest and detain demonstrators in any movement. According to them, the existence of Article 145 violated freedom of speech and assembly as guaranteed in the 1917 Mexican Constitution. Indeed, Article 145 led to the imprisonment of those who criticized the government, and the government invoked the article to hold Demetrio Vallejo, leader of the railroad workers' union, and Valetín Campa, a Communist Party member, as well as other labor activists and students. Furthermore, Article 145 was implemented against activists and their comrades in struggle.

In assessing the students' demands, they were by no means revolutionary, but simply an appeal for greater democracy as mentioned by Perdomo and Perelló.[50] The circulated demands served to galvanize mass support. The numerous brigades circulated visual representations on placards of the Six Point Petition during marches and in as many public spaces as possible. The image of Vallejo on a placard or circulating in printed propaganda countered the Mexican government's claim that it did not hold political prisoners (See Figure 2). Vallejo had been imprisoned since the early 1960s for his role in the 1958–59 railroad workers' strikes. Held in Lecumberri prison, Vallejo, like Rico Galán and Valetín Campa, served as an image of the brutality of the state and its authoritarian practices. The use of Vallejo's image as a political prisoner called upon spectators to question why Vallejo, a well known figure because of his union activities, was still in jail ten years after the railroad workers' strike.

Other student propaganda expressed rage at the violence they encountered and government violation of the laws. Much of the propaganda targeted the granaderos, emphasizing their violence and lack of constitutional sanction. As Díaz Ordaz remained publicly removed from the student strife, certain student images tried to tie Díaz Ordaz to the granaderos. In one image calling for the determination of those responsible for the bloodshed, Díaz Ordaz's profile is superimposed over the gorilla-like image of a granadero (See Figure 9). Images such as these reflected the brutality of the government forces, but reiterated that students were the ones struggling for human rights and dignity, not the government.

With the brigades, CNH, and Comités de lucha circulating the Six Point Petition, throughout the city, the idea of public dialogue emerged

Figure 9: Student-produced propaganda with image of President Díaz Ordaz. Colección de impresos Esther Montero, AHUNAM-CESU, 991/0010.

LA FIERA DEL 68 TIENE SED DE SANGRE!

as a central student demand. Previous discussions of talks between the government and students emerged in early August, but in the wake of the successful August 13 march, student leadership felt more comfortable dictating how, where, and in what format the talks would take place. By August 18, the CNH invited members of the government to a public debate. No representatives from the government attended; however, Corona del Rosal offered to establish a commission comprised of students, faculty, and government officials. That compromise seemed to provide the students a potential path of reconciliation with the revolutionary family, if they were willing to accept it. In spite of the offer of a commission to study the students' demands, the CNH and other leaders did not allow the promise of a commission to mitigate the growing strike. With Corona del Rosal's offer on the table, the students held their meeting on August 20 without government representation to address why the public and open dialogue was essential to the students' goals. Students, as well as workers, had grown accustomed to privately negotiating with the government. In the end, however, the agreements were generally squelched or the spokespersons co-opted. The students wanted access to a public forum demanding all discussions and dialogue be public. This demand was unprecedented in Mexico.

Despite the lack of government engagement, the students and the Coalition held several meetings to outline how the public dialogue would take place. On August 21, the Coalition took out an announcement in the newspaper *El Día*, and publicly approached the government with the idea of a dialogue. The students and their proponents demanded that the dialogue take place in some public space, such as *Ciudad Universitario* (University City, CU), Belles Artes, or some other public space, and that representatives from the press, radio, and television be present along with spectators.[51] With the circulation of the demands and the growing clamor for dialogue, on August 22, Secretary of Interior Luis Echeverría contacted the movement leaders and stated that he was willing to talk.[52]

With talks between the government and the student leadership beginning, problems surfaced within the student movement. The initiation of negotiations and how those negotiations would take place led to fractioning and suspicion within the movement. Many students feared that the student leadership would become co-opted by the government, or that the CNH would betray the students and engage in private talks with the Mexican government. Other students disavowed the idea of public debate and demanded greater mobilization. Some factions were not interested in talks, but in a more confrontational and violent stage. Other students, wanting to end the violence and afraid of escalation demanded that the upcoming August 27 march be cancelled. They sought to prevent antagonizing the government while the CNH and Coalition negotiated the details of the public dialogue. In turn, the CNH and the Coalition held an assembly on August 25 to elect ten or twenty students for a commission to meet with the government. In that same meeting, the council and Coalition also decided to hold the march on August 27, hoping that the talks would begin August 28. The brigades, in turn, moved throughout the city spreading the word about the August 27 march.

On August 27, newspapers carried announcements inviting all the Mexican people to "participate in the great popular demonstration in defense of democratic liberties that will take place today leaving from the national Anthropology Museum at 4:00 in the afternoon and will end in the Plaza of the Constitution." Many heeded the invitation. By 2:15 P.M., buses from UNAM and IPN arrived at the museum transporting student activists; but by 4:00 P.M., eighty-seven different groups comprised the march. These included students, teachers, the *Coalición de Padres y de Maestros* (Coalition of Parents and Teachers), workers, people from the provinces, and street vendors. Protesters numbering 400,000 to 500,000 took the activists up on their invitation and joined them to march down Paseo de la Reforma boulevard.

Students were organized by schools or academic departments. Labor activists, artists, intellectuals, professors, and parents also joined the march down Reforma Boulevard under the watchful eye of government and police forces. Students carried placards with images of Mexican independence and revolutionary leaders: Hidalgo, Morelos, Juárez, Zapata, and Villa, as well as the more modern icons of Che and Vallejo. Upon passing the U.S. Embassy, a newspaper reported that the students yelled "Assassins! Assassins!" and "Cuba si, yanquis no!"[53] By 6:35 P.M., the first wave of demonstrators entered the Zócalo (See Figure 10). There, they found that activists had parked buses from IPN to create a stage for the speakers. By 7:30 P.M., the Cathedral was aglow with lights and its bells had chimed as the demonstrators gathered. The meeting opened with Isasias Rojas, who had been detained and incarcerated for a time, reading a protest poem. Following Rojas, various students, professors, and parents took the microphone to discuss the demand for dialogue and freedom for political prisoners. Roberto Escudero of the CNH represented UNAM's School of Philosophy and Letters. He declared that the movement was a popular one for democracy. Worker Enrique Ruiz discussed the impact of the movement on workers' on-going struggle against charrismo. Luis Tomás Cervantes Cabeza de Vaca, CNH member from Chapingo, advocated liberty for all political prisoners. He was followed by Coalition members Heberto Castillo who demanded public dialogue, and Fausto Trejo who implored "a cleaning of the government using the Constitution as the broom."[54] One student read a letter from Demetrio Vallejo, who was on a hunger strike and supported the strike and the students.[55]

Another student read a letter from political prisoner and journalist Rico Galán who responded to the forthcoming public dialogue. He told

Figure 10: August 13 march to Zócalo in Mexico City. Colección Universidad Sección: Movimientos Estudiantiles, AHUNAM-CESU, Folio 4626.27.

the students that the representatives who were to negotiate with the government must remain more united and strong than ever before because the government would try to undermine them. Turning his attention to the crime of social dissolution, Rico Galán wrote:

> The struggle against the crime of Social Dissolution is a
> struggle against the terrorist and arbitrary application of the
> Penal Code against any group that politically organizes
> against the prevailing regime. It is true that since July 1962,
> there have not been new accusations of social dissolution.
> But also, other crimes have been used for the same purpose
> with the same end result, to impede an independent or
> oppositional organization. In that way, all political entities
> that do not agree with the government are deemed "danger-
> ous associations..."[56]

One of the last speakers that day was Sócrates Amado Campos Lemus, a CNH member who served as the master of ceremonies. Campos Lemos proposed a vote to see if the students wanted to stay and to occupy the Zócalo until 10:00 A.M. to force the government into a September 1 dialogue. September 1 was the day that the Mexican president traditionally addressed the nation. It was later rumored that Campos Lemus proposed this vote without consulting the other members of the CNH. Regardless of whether or not Campos Lemus acted independently, his audacious initiative was greeted by thousands of students igniting lighters that glowed their support. Those students and teachers who occupied the plaza numbered three thousand to four thousand. At 9:45 P.M., students still in the plaza, raised a red and black flag of revolution alongside the Mexican flag. Symbolically, the raising of the flag signified that they had taken the plaza. The festive atmosphere was shattered when the department of the Federal District used bullhorns to announce that the students were in violation of the law, and they had five minutes to vacate the plaza or they would be forcibly removed.[57] At 1:00 A.M., August 28, Army troops and police entered the Zócalo and removed the activists still in the plaza.[58]

Although the police did forcibly clear the Zócalo of protesters, the march was a great success. Student leaders estimated the number of participants had been close to one million. The newspapers recounted the strength of support for the students by referring to the applause and shouts of support for the students that came from the buildings and the sidewalks.[59] However, many newspapers leaped upon the damaging evidence that the students had rung the cathedral bells and had hoisted a red and black flag over the Zócalo. In essence, it was claimed that the students had desecrated the Cathedral and the Plaza of the Constitution, the heart of the Mexican Church and government. To add to the smoldering flames of anti-nationalistic activities of the young people, the pro-government newspapers focused on the image of Che as proof that the students were, and had always been, under a foreign influence. The press also cited that the students chanted anti-Olympic and anti-government slogans as they passed through the streets. Thus, the students were thrust back to the early days of the movement by the media. They were doing the bidding of some foreign power; they were anti-Mexico; they were dangerous.

Unfortunately, media attention on the red and black flag and ringing the cathedral bells overshadowed the success of the march. Recalling the August 27 march, Marcelino Perelló in a 1993 radio interview with Radio Educación spoke about the size of the march and the excitement of its participants. Perelló recalled that upon arrival in the Zócalo, the plaza was already full of demonstrators. However, hoisting the black and red flag caused conflict. Perelló stated: "Some guys flew the red and black flag, and the government used this as a pretext to organize a staged demonstration of all the government office workers and bureaucrats to make amends for the flag."[60]

Both Perelló and CNH leader Gilberto Guevara Niebla saw the August 27 march as the height of the movement. In a interview later, Guevara Niebla remembered:

> The August 27 march was a very important day in the devel-
> opment of the events of 1968; I think that movement arrived
> at its apogee on August 27 and afterwards it continued to
> develop in another manner, more as a political defense. With
> great emotion, we remember the silent march, but from an
> objective point of view, the movement was on the defensive
> because from August 27 the authorities had started to raise
> the conflict to a level where the movement had difficulty
> acting with much success...[61]

The government staged a counter-demonstration in the Zócalo to dispute the success of the students utilizing government employees and young people. The newspaper *Novedades* reported that Gonzalo Cruz Paredes of the *Instituto de la Juventud Mexicana* (Institute of Mexican Youth) took the stage and claimed, "All of us here, Mexican people, have come here with great civic pride..." The press declared that the crowd yelled "*Viva México, Viva la bandera nacional!*" and shed tears while singing the national anthem.[62]

While the press declared the patriotism of the Mexican people, activists recalled a different reaction. Disgruntled because they were forced to take part in a counter-demonstration, the government employees chanted: "BAA!!! We are sheep!! BAA!!"[63] While the government forced bureaucrats out of their offices and into the streets, groups with ties to the state began to show dissent against the government. Professional business people issued a statement published in *El Día* with regard to their frustration at the government's continued violation of "individual guarantees that are consecrated in the Mexican Constitution."[64]

Other counter-demonstrations continued through the end of August and the first weeks of September. *Movimiento Universitario de Renovadora Orientación* (University Movement for Renovated Morals, MURO) and the *Coalición de Organizaciones de Defensa de los Valores Nacionales* (Coalition of Organizations for the Defense of National Values) held two counter-demonstrations, one in the Plaza de Torros (bullring) and another in the Basilica of Guadalupe. At 12:45 P.M. on September 9, the *Coalición de Organizaciones de Defensa de los Valores Nacionales* burned a replica of Ernesto "Che" Guevara, stating that he represented all guerrillas.[65] These demonstrations revealed the effective use of propaganda to portray the students as Cuban-influenced guerrillas who wanted to overthrow the government, and as a dangerous contagion that could effect the entire country if not contained. The students' demand for democracy was never mentioned by the government or by its supporters.

The march and the ringing of the cathedral bells also propelled reverent Catholics to demonstrate. The government and other associations assumed the role of protectors of the church. Because students rang the bells of the Cathedral, allegedly without permission, the government declared the sanctity of the Church had been violated. Following such portrayals of students, groups like the *Mujeres de Acción Católica Mexicana* (Women of Mexican Catholic Action) demonstrated on their knees asking pardon for the students and all Mexicans.[66] As some secular groups rushed to defend the sanctity of the church, some factions in the church actually supported the students. The bishop and priests at the Cathedral confirmed that the students did not do anything wrong, and that in fact the students had sought and were given permission to ring the bells. Other priests added their voices in support of the students. On September 9, 1968, thirty-nine priests issued a statement deploring the use of violence against the students and demonstrators and the rumors and media manipulation. They went on to declare that they were united with the students and agreed with their hopes of establishing a just society.[67]

In the wake of the counter-demonstrations and negative publicity, the movement faced new and greater violence. Prior to August 26, the military had stated that it had no intention of violating university autonomy; however, attacks occurred again at Vocational [school] 7 in the Tlatelolco housing complex in the Plaza of Three Cultures on August 28.

With the continuing street fighting, key members of the movement found themselves under scrutiny, and that scrutiny was focused on more senior members of the movement who were targets of the military and government. On August 29, 1968, Heberto Castillo, leader of the Coalition was brutally attacked by police in front of his home. From his hospital bed, Castillo issued a statement demanding respect for the Constitution.[68]

With more violence, the effects of negative publicity, and with the government backing away from further dialogue, the CNH had to regain momentum after August 27–28. The council publicized that no public meetings would be held until September 1. Although it did not expect to engage in a public dialogue on September 1, the council hoped some exchange would occur. However, the CNH insisted that a public dialogue must take place, and it implored the government to end the violence. Despite the government mounting a greater offense against the students, statements of solidarity with the students continued to be published. In August, students had gained even more support. During the August 27 protest, railroad workers, petroleum and electrical workers, and parents marched with the students.[69] These groups, as well as telephone workers, the Communist Party, and other student and teacher groups offered their support in published statements.[70] On August 31, 1968, the Assembly of Intellectuals, Artists, and Writers denounced government violence and urged the Díaz Ordaz administration to engage in public dialogue with the students. The group also criticized the on-going media bias toward the movement.[71]

The growing momentum of support behind the students was difficult to ignore despite the negative propaganda generated in the press. With other sectors of the society adding their voices to the demand for public dialogue, it seemed that on September 1, Díaz Ordaz would address the possibility of dialogue during his annual speech. Instead, the students' hope to have some opportunity to engage in a discussion were dashed on September 1, 1968, when Díaz Ordaz delivered his annual address to the nation. His address seemed to threaten an increase in violence that would follow in the month. He stated: "We defend as men that which we must defend: our homes, integrity, life, [and] liberty."[72]

While his speech was touted by the newspapers as offering an attempt to end the student conflict in a peaceful way, the headlines screamed a different message: "I will defend Mexico and face the consequences!" and "All energy if it is necessary!" In his speech, Díaz Ordaz referred to Article 8: Section IV of the Mexican Constitution that permitted the use of all "military force for the security of the country."[73] He went on to deny that there existed any political prisoners in Mexico. With regard to Article 145 of the Federal Penal Code, he stated that, as the executive of the nation, he could not dissolve these laws, but he admitted that his position enabled him to initiate the process to do so. Thus, he proposed presenting this option to the Congress, the only agency empowered to form a committee and make a decision.

Besides dismissing the students' demands, Díaz Ordaz's speech suggested that he would do little to change the government's policy toward the students. The president embraced a procedural and bureaucratic stance toward the students in the midst of a growing social crisis. The students, like all citizens, had to navigate governmental bureaucracy and mechanisms. There would be no special treatment for the young people. In the press, Díaz Ordaz was hailed as a defender of the Mexican Revolution and the republic. Facing a mass social movement before the eyes of the international press corps, Díaz Ordaz adopted a stance that had served Mexican leaders in the past. The patriarch of the revolution did not have to negotiate with his children. His words, however articulate and eloquent, were admonishments. The president reclaimed his paternal and patriarchal authority over the nation, but specifically over the students. Díaz Ordaz wielded his executive privilege. Perhaps he was warning the students that he would do everything in his means to defend the nation, but also his honor and reputation.

The students, however, ignored this public chastisement and continued to organize hoping to achieve the modern nation they dreamed about. Brigades swarmed throughout the city passing out propaganda and holding meetings. CNH and Comités de lucha of the various campuses continued to hold meetings, print statements, and ask for more support. Meanwhile, attacks on students were unrelenting. Campuses were invaded, and brigade members continued to be detained and arrested.

In response to the intensifying situation, on Monday September 9, Barros Sierra asked students, faculty, and staff to return to their responsibilities at the university since the public dialogue looked as if it might take place because the offices of the Secretary of Interior seemed to be moving toward dialogue. Other educators beseeched the students to return to classes as well. Barros Sierra and the faculty probably understood the growing danger of the situation, and they most likely understood the veiled words of the executive. The Olympic opening ceremonies were quickly approaching, and the rector and some faculty realized that they had to get the students off the streets—not for the sake of the Olympics, but for their own safety.

The students, however, had other plans. On September 10, the *Comité Coordinador de Huelga de UNAM* (Coordinating Committee of the UNAM Strike) rejected Barros Sierra's demand. To some of them, the man who had formalized the movement earlier had now turned on them. Students felt betrayed, and some suspected Barros Sierra had succumbed to the pressures of the federal government and his party. The CNH formally stated that the strike would not come to an end until the government and students met in a public dialogue. In turn, Barros Sierra announced on September 11 that if the strike continued, he would be forced to resign from his position as rector.

At that point, the CNH was mired in internal debate and controversy. It appeared that the Mexican government was slowly undermining the students by pressuring Barros Sierra and by the bureaucratic minutiae over who in the government would engage in a public dialogue and who had the power to respond to the request: the president, the secretary of interior, or the Mexican Congress. The two sides debated their next tactic: Marcelino Perelló wanted to speak directly with the president and bypass bureaucratic intricacies rather than follow the chain of command. Perelló, and others who supported him, were uncomfortable with the dictates of the Mexican government in which the public dialogue would take place between the students and Luis Echeverría, the secretary of interior. Perelló's idea to directly address the president was adopted, and the CNH formally asked Díaz Ordaz for a public dialogue before the opening of the Olympic Games.

On September 10, 1968, the letter from Perelló was sent to President Díaz Ordaz. The letter stated:

> Based upon Article 8 of our Constitution, the National Strike
> Council sincerely request that you fulfill the request for pub-
> lic dialogue that would carry a definitive solution to the
> conflict, our demands, and the student strike....

> We would like to remind you that the contracted agree-
> ment of our nation to host the XIX Olympic Games obliges
> us both to accelerate a definitive resolution to the problem
> that will enable us to carry out with great success this most
> important sporting and cultural event.[74]

Although Díaz Ordaz was quite specific in his September 1 speech and in his official communiqués, the students still held the hope that they could engage government officials to play by their rules. Perelló stated:

> The government proposed official public dialogue under
> the Secretary of Gobernación (Interior) by mid-August, and
> this ran the risk of becoming the classic compromise in
> which a great part of opposition movements had been
> incorporated and assimilated into the system. To accept the
> dialogue by the terms proposed by the government at that
> moment was equated to falling for their trap. If we accepted
> and negotiated a conventional dialogue with the govern-
> ment, we ran the risk that the movement would be assimi-
> lated by the government . . . [75]

The CNH letter reveals that the students still hoped to hold a public dialogue with the Díaz Ordaz administration, but they also feared co-option and exploitation. Countering negative propaganda, the CNH signaled student nationalism to show that they, too, supported the Olympics. However, their reference to the approaching games as a reason to resolve the dispute seemed to be a veiled threat. If a resolution was not attained before the opening of the games, the strike would continue. Fearing co-option, Perelló, the CNH, and the Coalition still hoped that they could engage in a dialogue that would not undermine their ideals and authority within the movement. Their hopes, however, were dashed.

Three days later, the students received their reply, addressed to Perelló. Díaz Ordaz's secretary, Dr. Emilio Martínez Manatou, responded in two brief paragraphs reiterating the Díaz Ordaz September 1 speech that made Luis Echeverría responsible for this discussion, not the president. Thus, the CNH found themselves in the same position they were in in early August; nothing had changed. The Mexican government officials continued to dictate who would engage in the debate and how the debates would take place.

The students did not back down. From their prior experiences, they were aware of how other groups had been co-opted and manipulated by the government. They also knew of students and labor groups that had been betrayed by the same people who now sat across from them at the negotiating tables. The students, hoping to enter talks to construct a modern nation, found their attempts to engage in a debate were continually rebuffed. In an interview, Perelló discussed his amazement at the political astuteness the students exhibited. He elaborated:

> Then, our response was particularly brilliant. Still I am surprised at how a bunch of twenty-year-old *escuincles* could even think these things. The reaction of public dialogue, and the response that we generated, we had demanded the dialogue, but we did not want the dialogue to be inscribed by the traditional marks of shady deals and brief settlements that had characterized the negotiations between the government and opposition parties in this country.[76]

With the Mexican government resisting a student-dictated procedure for the debates and continued attacks on student activists and proponents of the movement after August 27, hopes for a dialogue dimmed. Students turned to the only alternative that seemed to work in pressuring the government and promoting change. The CNH called for another demonstration to be held September 13, (See Figure 11) to protest the violence and to demand dialogue. One flyer declared:

> The popular student movement continues. The apparent state of calm that one encounters in the city of Mexico is the result of repression against the student brigades by the authorities in their desperate attempt to distort the events and to avert the truth that the students bring to the people. Perhaps the press, the radio, and the television have confused you, but you have been a witness to the direct trajectory of our movement and of its just demands."[77]

ANTE EL SILENCIO COMPLICE
DE LOS LEGISLADORES, EL SILEN-
CIO ACUSADOR DEL PUEBLO.

GRAN MARCHA DEL
SILENCIO
Viernes 13 de Sept. 16 hs.
Museo de Antropología
— C.N.H.

Figure 11: Student-produced propaganda inviting people to the Great Silent March. Colección de impresos Esther Montero, AHUNAM-CESU, 991/0038.

Once the announcements circulated in the newspapers and on the street about the march, opposition efforts began in earnest. An organization called *Uniones y Sociedades de Padres de Familias de la UNAM and IPN* (Parent Unions and Society of UNAM and IPN) had flyers dropped by helicopters across the city. The flyers called upon parents to forbid their children from attending and warned parents that the military would be present.[78] The purpose of the flyer was to instill fear in students, their allies, and parents. By September 13, the Olympic Games were scheduled to open in a month. By mid-September, greater numbers of international journalists and visitors were in the Federal District to cover the games but also the protests. Although the government had been direct and forceful in its reply to the students, the young people were not backing down.

Los dueños del mundo: The Mobilization of the People

The Great Silent March, as the September 13 demonstration became known, reflected how the students had learned from their earlier mistakes as activists sought to deny the press further ammunition for questioning movement goals. Prior to the march, the CNH circulated statements asking activists and others not to use images of Ernesto "Che" Guevara and Ho Chi Minh. The CNH called upon students to use images of Mexican heroes to challenge the idea that student activists were foreign-led and manipulated. To ensure that students did not chant anti-government slogans or other slogans that could have been deemed offensive to the government and the press, the march was to be silent exhibiting non-violence. The march also built on a legacy from the past. IPN students had used silent marches in the 1950s as had the medical students in 1965.[79] In one statement, the CNH called:

> People of Mexico: Do you understand the significance of silence? Of course. Our silence is evidence of one part the degree to which we have attained organization and unity, and for the other part, our silence must be interpreted as unanimous repudiation of the injustice and violence unleashed by the government against the Mexican people. March alongside us as a symbol of protest because they have trampled your rights.[80]

Flyers circulated throughout the city specifically calling on various sectors to join the students for the march. In one flyer, the students targeted the bureaucrats of Mexico City: "Compañero Bureaucrat: The students ask your attendance at the Great Silent March that will take place on September 13 departing from the Museum of Anthropology at 4:00 in the afternoon. . . . Your attendance in this event is voluntary"[81] The students hoped to challenge the anti-students demonstration that the government held on August 28. Furthermore, through August and September, the students received letters from comités de barrios (neighborhoods) in the Federal Districts, particularly those barrios in which the police and granaderos were occupying the areas and harassing the people.[82] The CNH, Comités de lucha, and the brigades invited workers, parents, community leaders, intellectuals, all the Mexican people to join them on September 13.

The march of September 13, 1968, remained a pivotal event in the history of the movement. At 3:00 P.M., students and their supporters marched from the National Museum of Anthropology and History to the Zócalo, arriving at 5:15 P.M. They ended with a mass meeting in the Zócalo.[83] The Great Silent March was a successful event for the students. For many activists, it was the pinnacle of the movement. CNH activist Eduardo Valle recalled:

> The silent march is a great moment of discipline, valor, and the capacity of the civil society to confront the state. The silent march was surrounded by warnings that the government was going to massacre us. And I remember when I arrived with Raúl, Gamundi, and another compañero at the Museum of Anthropology at the designated hour, we were alone, suddenly, a immense river of people. . . . And, the affection of the people, the discipline, the silent march was the best moment of '68."[84]

Like the August 27 march, students met each other in the park where some put white tape across their mouths to broadcast their silence. Once the event began, the demonstrators marched in absolute silence out of Chapultepec Park. Luis González de Alba, a CNH member, recalled that as the students left the park, a helicopter flew "dangerously low" over the demonstrators.[85] The march continued out of the park, past the U.S. Embassy. This time, there were no anti-U.S. chants. The march moved passed the Monument to Independence and under the eyes of the statue of Cuauhtémoc, the last Aztec emperor, passing through the business districts. One student recalled that the only words one heard were from the people observing the march and offering their words of solidarity.[86] González de Alba wrote. "All of Paseo de la Reforma, the sidewalks, side streets, the buses, monuments, even the trees were covered by multitudes of people. . . . The silence was the most impressive thing about the crowd. If the other shouts, cheers, and chants of the other marches gave an atmosphere of a party, the austerity of the silence was similar to a solemn ceremony."[87]

The march turned off Paseo de la Reforma onto Avenida Juárez, Cinco de Mayo, and then on to Plaza of the Constitution. González de Alba wrote:

The people were in the windows, on the balconies, on the
sidewalks, on the statues, and on the tree branches. Now
we could hear their exclamations, their shouts of encour-
agement, and their applause. Again, the Zócalo was full.
Sheets, banners, large images of Villa and Zapata, none of
Carranza and Obregón. When our contingent entered the
Zócalo, the meeting began. Each speaker discussed the Six
Point Petition. At nightfall, we broke the silence with the
National Anthem. On our feet with torches aglow we
finished the march and the meeting."[88]

The march had a profound effect on the student activists for a
number of reasons. The use of non-violence and a silent demonstration of strength challenged media and government views that the students were being foreign-led and out of control. The massive turnout
for the march also inspired both the students, and other dissident
groups in Mexico City. Student activist Manuel Moreno Rodríguez
described the silent march as the most important demonstration
because even though the president had threatened the people during
his September 1 speech, more students, more people, and more workers took to the streets.[89]

The silence that students adopted represented a form of protest. To
the students, the Mexican government continually silenced the Mexican
people through its political machinations. The government remained
silent when asked for dialogue, and the powerful members of the government instructed others to speak for them, whether newspapers, secretaries, or granaderos. The students used the silent march to reclaim
public spaces such as Chapultepec Park, museums, Paseo de la Reforma,
monuments, and the plaza for the people. The march also ironically
reclaimed their voices. Although the activists were silent, others spoke in
support of them. Government officials had to hear the ever-growing din
of solidarity that the students generated with each demonstration.

The march also signified an important event in terms of gender relations. Roberta Avendaño was selected to explain the Six Point Petition. In
a 1988 interview, Avendaño, remembered being surprised by her selec-
tion to address the crowd on the day of the Great Silent March. Male
activists also recalled her influence and seeing Tita as a movement

leader. José López Rodríguez recalled how he heard Tita speak on September 13, 1968, in the plaza: "It was fascinating to arrive at the plaza of the Constitution and to see how all the students sat together there on the ground waiting for the moving words of la Tita, the great leader."[90]

In the past marches and demonstrations, men had presented the demands and discussed the movement. Women, while present at the marches, did not have a public voice. On September 13, Tita emerged as a great and fondly remembered leader of the movement. As she explained the petition, other women heard her voice, and her politicized message. Here was a young woman, like themselves, who was talking politics. Avendaño spoke before thousands of people in front of the presidential palace and the national Cathedral. She, as a young woman, became a public voice of the movement who explained political and social implications of the student movement and the Six Point Petition. She was young, educated, and in a man's world. She was, for all purposes, the modern woman who transgressed gender barriers seeking to participate in politics and public life.

The Great Silent March displayed growing support for the students, and the students ability to transcend traditional Mexican politicking. Some newspapers commented on the diversity of student support, while others criticized the students by providing space to their detractors. A photo, published in the government-supported *El Universal*, captured some of the goals of the CNH. A señora in mourning clothes carried a copy of the Mexican Constitution in her hand while marching alongside a "hippie" who is carrying a Mexican flag. In the background, demonstrators carried an image of Demetrio Vallejo (See Figure 2). The photo was taken as the demonstrators passed the Monument to Independence seeming to reflect the movement's broad based appeal. In this snapshot, a widow has left her home to march alongside the students. Her appearance appears representative of support among more mature women. She is in black—mourning—and yet she holds the Constitution in front of her as she marches alongside a young man with longish hair, a heavy chain and cross hanging from his neck, and hip-hugging dungarees. The woman is a matronly mother figure supporting "her children," while at the same time a patriotic citizen. The young man at her side, did not seem threatening. He could even have been her son.[91]

The effectiveness of the march demonstrated that the students still had a tremendous amount of power. The following day, Luis Echeverría's office issued a second response to Perelló and the CNH's September 10 letter. Jorge Heredia Fernandez, replying for Echeverría, viewed the reference to the Olympics as the students threatening to further disrupt the games. Once again, the government fell back on their usual response demanding use of the proper channels to resolve any conflict. This time, however, the government viewed the students as a potential threat to the quickly approaching Olympic Games. Building on Díaz Ordaz's September 1 speech, they directly rejected the implicit student threat reiterating their right to host the games unmolested. The student attempt to enter directly into negotiations appeared to have failed again, and again the students dismissed the potential threats issued by the government. To the students, the September 13 march was a tremendous success. Nothing seemed capable of stopping their momentum.

Two days after the Great Silent March and a day after the response from Echeverría and his office, the students continued to ride the momentum of the Silent March. On September 15, Mexican independence day did not go unrecognized by those in the movement. As Díaz Ordaz walked onto the balcony of the presidential palace to issue the usual presidential *grito* (call) commemorating the Grito de Dolores by Father Miguel Hidalgo y Costilla that began the Mexican war for independence, students gathered at UNAM. They arrived to *Ciudad Universitaria* (University City, CU) the night before despite the fact that the urban bus lines had suspended service to CU.[92] Artists, writers, campesinos, teachers, residents from the close communities, students, and teachers gathered for a day of festivities that included music, poetry readings, and other performances. The party continued late into the night and after the national ceremony had ended. Little did the students know that the fiesta for independence in CU would be the last for the movement.

Chapter Four

ES UNA PROVOCACIÓN:
The Destruction

From the presidential palace overlooking the Zócalo, President Gustavo Díaz Ordaz called the names of the great Mexican leaders commemorating the *Grito de Dolores* at midnight on September 15, 1968. In the southern part of the city, UNAM students gathered for a mock wedding ceremony performed by Heberto Castillo who had recuperated from his injuries. The mock wedding poked fun at Mexico's traditional views of marriage in the wake of the growing youth movement. After the ceremony, the students called for a grito, and Castillo was more than happy to oblige them on that festive day.

The Great Silent March and the counter-grito proved to the movement's detractors that the students continued to have wide support. In the past two months, a minor student squabble had escalated into a genuine social movement in the capital city of Mexico. Although there had been setbacks since the August 27 protest and growing counter-demonstrations, the students seemed to be on the brink of instigating mass social change. The momentum of the uprising did not seem to flag despite continued criticism, attacks, and violence. The students' desire to participate in the designing of a modern nation propelled them into the streets of the Federal District.

From August 27 to September 13, the students demonstrated to the government that they were the vanguard of a popular movement that challenged the business-as-usual attitude of the governing groups. Published statements of support and growing numbers of demonstrators in the student-led marches reflected the broad-base of support the

117

youth enjoyed. With the opening of the Olympics quickly approaching, President Díaz Ordaz and the other members of his government desperately needed to gain control of an increasingly embarrassing situation. The eyes of the world were upon Mexico, a country that appeared to be incapable of controlling its own children despite its trappings of modernity. Although the September 13 march was a success, the level of violence had been escalating through August and September. Consequently, the students' designs for a bright new future and public dialogue were dashed only five short days after one of their most successful demonstrations.

By September 17, the students had relented and agreed to written negotiations with the government. Activists still believed that they could bring forth profound change and modernize the country, and they continued to organize despite threats from the government. Even their acceptance of written negotiations was too little too late. In the early morning hours of September 18, 1968, University City was swarming with government forces organized to re-take the national university. As this was accomplished in a few short hours, the students lost one of their main bases of operation. In a few weeks following this defeat, they would lose their larger political struggle.

Despite some efforts, the young people never overcame negative perceptions of themselves and their peers that circulated across the city, and then spilled beyond the Federal District into the provinces. Students, and young people in general, found themselves the targets of brutal physical and written attacks that led to drastic consequences for activists and young people in general. Mexican young people were increasingly viewed as a dangerous liability for the Mexican government and its plans for the Olympics. The students never could have gained a political or military victory against the government, but they were slowly winning a national and cultural battle with their marches that brought support from sectors of the civil society beyond the schools and universities. Because of this rising influence, the student-led social movement had to be stopped.

The Mexican government's response to the students in the end suggested the scale of the gender and generational schism that had appeared. This had been bolstered by a growing suspicion of international youth culture and modernity among Mexico's political elite. As an outcome of modernity that opened Mexico to cultural, social, political, and economic influences from beyond the borders of the country, the government found that it could not as easily control or manipulate youth culture or its followers as it had in the past.[1] Since the government seemed to be moving closer to a public dialogue, young people misread and misjudged their social and political influence. The government's use of the language of modernity in the context of revolutionary democracy and humility was only a cloak for an authoritarian state. The government's effective use of violence destroyed the collaborative spirit of the movement and contributed to the youth's further questioning of authority, whether political, social, or cultural. Young people clashed with their elders over responsibility for the violence and the ownership of rhetoric. Students also began to clash with one another over whether to continue the movement. What had been an encompassing mass social movement crumbled before the eyes of young activists, many of whom had engaged in their first political and social actions.

San Miguel de Canoa:
The Harbinger of Things to Come

Despite the apparent strength of the student movement in September, Mexican officials did not fear a loss of control because their traditional centers of power, the army, police, and the PRI, remained their staunchest advocates. It was these centers of control, not the students, who in the end held the reins of power. Still, the Díaz Ordaz government never planned to treat international athletes and journalists to a modern city rife with social and political conflict. Although students expressed outrage at the money that was being spent to host the games, the students also publicly stated that they were not opposed to the games.[2] And yet, the Díaz Ordaz administration, in addition to its government-sponsored press portraying student activists as foreign-led Communist or CIA and FBI dupes, argued that the young people were trying to humiliate Mexico before a global audience.

In response to ongoing negative propaganda, students continued to publicly dispute the assertions of the Mexican government that foreigners dictated the movement's action. In an interview with Marcelino Perelló, a journalist asked "Are there foreign hands in the movement?"

Perelló replied that the only foreigners in the movement were police agents. He further elaborated that it would be easy for the police to infiltrate the CNH due to the organization's large numbers.[3] Young male activists were still perceived as the enemy in the press. The image of young male student activists as deviant and threatening circulated through the government controlled press and seeped beyond the boundaries of the Federal District into the provinces. A harbinger of potential reactionary violence was manifested in a small mountain town called San Miguel de Canoa in the state of Puebla.

Far from the main center of student political activity of the student movement, two thousand townspeople attacked and lynched five young men the day after the Great Silent March on September 14, 1968.[4] As reported in the Mexican national press, the young men who were attacked had worked at the Autonomous University of Puebla and had decided one day to take a camping and hiking trip in the mountains surrounding the city. A storm stranded them in this small mountain pueblo.

In San Miguel de Canoa, the negative images of students as represented in the national press and in the government's pronouncements combined with the idea that urban youth were also anti-Catholic by the devout because of their alleged desecration of the cathedral in Mexico City that circulated in the Mexican press.[5] As outsiders to the small town, the young men seemed to embody the image of the male student activist of the capital. Thus they were a dangerous contagion of communism, youth culture, anti-Catholicism, and anti-nationalism. The lynching of the young men in Canoa was an event that revealed the fear of the student movement that circulated in the press. It reveals how portraying young male activists as the nation's enemy created a level of paranoia and fear throughout the country.[6] The language of the government that circulated in a press unsympathetic to the students fed the paranoia. The townspeople assumed that the young men from Puebla were sympathetic to the student uprising in Mexico City, to communism, and therefore enemies to the Mexican nation and the Catholic Church.[7]

When the young men became stranded in the town by the storm, they went from house to house asking for a place to stay for the night. A campesino, Lucas García offered to take them in. As the young men settled in at the García house, they heard announcements over a microphone proclaiming that a group of Communists had attempted to fly the black and red flag in the plaza. Because the young men were strangers in a small town and they had requested housing, the townspeople "knew" immediately who the Communists were. A group of about two thousand people armed with knives, machetes, and guns went to the house of García. García attempted to defend his home and his young guests, but he was killed by the crowd.

The townspeople lynched Ramón Gutiérrez, Jesús Carrillo, both employed at the Autonomous University of Puebla. They also lynched Odilón Sánchez Islas from Mexico City who was visiting his girlfriend. Julian González Baez, Roberto Rojano Aguirre, Pascual Romero Pérez, and Miguel Flores Cruz escaped with their lives, but Flores Cruz later succumbed to his injuries at a hospital.[8]

In the case of San Miguel, the townspeople had not had any contact with students or young people involved in the movement to balance the rhetoric that they heard from the Church pulpit or when the priest read to them from the newspapers. Although the young men attacked in San Miguel de Canoa were not students and were not involved in the protests, the townspeople had perceived them as a threat. According to the newspaper *Excélsior*, the townspeople reported that they thought the "students" had tried to fly the black and red flag in front of the Church as student activists had allegedly done in Mexico City.[9]

Instead, government rhetoric and the alleged student assault on the Cathedral on August 27 and 28, as interpreted by the San Miguel parish priest Enrique Meza was all that the mostly illiterate townspeople knew of the events in Mexico City. In this context, they feared the young men. To the townspeople, the young men epitomized the contagion of communism, anti-Mexican identity, and youth culture. Thus, as student activists in the Federal District became targets of the Mexican government propaganda, so, too, did the young men from Puebla.

The incident in San Miguel de Canoa vividly displayed the Mexican government's power to define who or what is Mexican. It also reflected the ability of the government and the educated minority in rural areas to rally the people to destroy those who had been designated "others" to preserve what they deemed "Mexican," "good," or "respectable." This attack on innocent young men showed the supremacy of the government and the lack of power of the students in and beyond the Federal District. In 1968, the attacks in San Miguel de Canoa did not seem to be related to the Mexican student movement, but the attacks can not be separated from the fact that the townspeople attacked the young men because they assumed they were activists from the Federal District. Young men as dangerous, young women as transgressors, and an authoritarian government who postured as modern were on a collision course that would rock the country.

Taking UNAM

The government's struggle to take control of the major campus began on September 18, 1968, at 9:40 P.M. when fourteen large transports, ten small troop transports, five light tanks and ten thousand soldiers were posted outside University City. (See Figure 12).[10] Under the command of General José Hernández Toledo, soldiers and armored vehicles blocked the main arteries to and from the national university including Avenida Insurgentes, Avenida Revolución, and Avenida Universidad. Students in the guardias and those occupying UNAM buildings observed the movements of the army and thought at first that the army was simply continuing its policy of intimidation.[11] Since the students had grown accustomed to having the army around, their initial appearance outside the campus did not seem too shocking. Yet, some students did attempt to warn others on campus attending meetings and working in the building. Twenty minutes later, one of the worst fears of the students came to pass.

Shortly before 10:00 P.M., the army sent a column in full riot gear through the gates of UNAM. The invasion had begun. Chaos gripped the activists. Some were able to flee the area into the surrounding neighborhoods. Once inside UNAM, the military forces began to conduct a building-by-building search removing all the inhabitants they found. The newspaper *El Día* reported on the event and photos show that students and bystanders who were detained were forced to come out of the buildings with their hands on their heads (See Figure 13). Later, the prisoners were told to sit on the ground where armed soldiers guarded them to ensure that they did not attempt to flee. By 10:30 P.M., the military had occupied many of the departments and colleges as well as the esplanade. The only evidence telling people outside UNAM that something was wrong at CU was when at 10:25 P.M. Radio UNAM ceased operation without warning.

Figure 12: Armored vehicles close to University City. Colección Universidad Sección: Movimientos Estudiantiles, AHUNAM-CESU, Folio 4601–4614.

As the invasion unfolded, journalists flocked to University City to cover the story. There, many reporters were witnesses to the invasion, but the reports of actual events and newspaper coverage vastly differed. Some journalists stated that a military spokesperson had fed them the story that they were to print. Consequently, the newspaper *El Día* reported: "The soldiers showed the journalists a box of empty soda bottles stopped up with pieces of cloth that were supposed to be Molotov cocktails. The journalists did not see any other types of arms during our stay in the university."[12] *El Universal* claimed that soldiers had found boxes of Molotov cocktails. Journalists José Falconi, Leopoldo Mendivil, and Miguel Reyes Razo reported that the military had also found subversive propaganda attributed to the *Partido Comunista Mexicano* (Mexican Communist Party, PCM).

The invasion of UNAM targeted student activists and their supporters, but it caught many bystanders and residents of University City in its snare. In an interview, Esteban Bravo recalled the invasion. He and his brother had gone to meet their father who was en route to the university to pick them up and bring them home. Bravo's father called their attention to the arrival of the army that was moving down Avenida

Figure 13: The invasion of UNAM and the detaining of students,
September 18–19, 1968. Colección Universidad Sección: Movimientos
Estudiantiles, AHUNAM-CESU, Folio 4601–4614.

Insurgentes. The family tried to return to their car, but the army detained
all three of them.[13] Bravo recalled watching as the military conducted a
room-to-room search of the buildings on the UNAM campus. As the soldiers moved through the buildings, they found unlikely "activists" at the
CU. In the *Facultad de Economía* (School of Economics) building, the
Comité de lucha was hosting a parents' meeting at the time of the attack.
Thus, sympathetic parents were detained along with the students. Of
course, the military also found people who were usually there at night—
custodial workers, broadcast journalists for Radio UNAM, as well as students and their families who lived in the neighborhood.

By midnight, the army demanded that all journalists and photog-
raphers leave the campus. Shortly after midnight, the army began to
place the detained into military vehicles. Some of the prisoners were
taken to Lecumberri prison while others were taken to local facilities.
Estimates of the numbers of detainees ranged from the government
figure of 500 to eyewitness Esteban Bravo's estimate of 800, to the
North American Congress on Latin America's (*NACLA*) anonymous
source who claimed 3,000.[14] By 3:45 P.M., the army was in control of

University City. All journalists, students, professors, and staff had been cleared from the campus. UNAM had fallen with little resistance.

The Secretary of Interior Luis Echeverría working with the army had made the strategic decision to invade UNAM. Throughout the summer of 1968, UNAM had been a center of student activity where students enjoyed the support of the faculty, administration, and staff. On the campus, activists had access to office equipment and protected space that was necessary to organize. To undermine the movement and weaken its ability to coordinate actions, the campus had to be wrested from the students. The government justified its actions by claiming again that the university was a center of subversion, not of education.[15] From the student perspective, the government showed its willingness to use its strength and to violate its own laws by entering UNAM. In fact, the invasion violated university autonomy. This was the first invasion of UNAM in forty years.[16]

The government's choice of General José Hernández Toledo to lead the invasion was also telling. Hernández Toledo was not new to university and college invasions. He had led other university occupations of the University Nicolaíta in Morelia, Michoacán in 1966 and of the University of Sonora in Hermosillo, Sonora in 1967.[17] The invasion of the national university was a warning to students and a sign of unprecedented force. Since their other warnings had gone unheeded, the Mexican government issued a comprehensive threat in the form of the UNAM invasion. Its narrow purpose was to deny a central space for students to organize. More importantly, the invasion also demonstrated the power of the Mexican government, and its ability to assert its authority despite the support the students may have enjoyed in the Federal District. Throughout much of the summer, the students seemed not to have understood the danger of their situation. Since the Olympics were scheduled to open three weeks after the invasion, the government felt it had to act. The political elite had grown tired of the student movement and was prepared to end the protest without meeting students' demands.

The following day, angry reactions to the invasion erupted. Playing the role of a distant father, Díaz Ordaz was absent from much of the public discussion regarding the invasion. Instead, the offices of Luis Echeverría responded as did the Secretary of Defense, Marcelino García Barragán. Echeverría issued a statement claiming that the government was justified in the invasion because the buildings occupied by students in the university were the "property of the nation and destined to be used for public service."[18] Echeverría argued that the buildings on the UNAM campus had been occupied and used illegally since the end of July, and that the buildings were not being used for their main purpose: academics.[19] He insisted that the students had exercised their right to make public demands, but they had done so in a manner that was "antisocial and possibly dangerous." Again, the government relied on the mantra that the students were dangerous, so they in turn had acted to protect the Mexican people from a dangerous contagion.

The office of the Secretary of Interior also stated that the government was within its constitutional rights to forcefully remove individuals who did not have any right to be on the campus because they were not students. Echeverría argued that the invasion that violated UNAM's legal status was necessary to safeguard the autonomy of the university from the dangerous usurpers who threatened the purpose of the institution.[20] Again, the students were portrayed as foreign dissenters.

Bolstering Echeverría's stance on the invasion, Secretary of Defense García Barragán explained during a press conference on September 19:

> In accordance with the expressed reasons, the army took the University: there were no violent incidents; the students surrendered with little resistance. The army has no interest in maintaining the university installations for an extended period of time, and it will immediately surrender it to the legitimate authorities when they come forward.[21]

García Barragán insisted that the military in no way wished to hold the university; it intervened only to return UNAM to its "legitimate authorities." The general's statements contended that the students' lack of resistance reflected their desire for control. Furthermore, he stripped the students of their legitimacy. They were weak in defense of their ideals and base of operation; consequently, they were illegitimate political actors.

After issuing his statement, García Barragán then took questions from the reporters. Some of his answers focused on the condition of university buildings. The general reported that students were found armed with Molotov cocktails, and they had alcoholic beverages such as cognac and beer in their possession. Furthermore, the general argued that the students had vandalized the buildings, and that the Procurador General was making an inventory of the damages.

Both Echeverría and García Barragán characterized the students negatively in their comments. Echeverría saw the students as dangerous in the sense that they were jeopardizing the nation and the laws that governed and protected Mexico. The invasion was necessary to protect the university from the very people who directly benefited from it: the students. To García Barragán, the students were hanging around UNAM, reading communist literature, drinking beer and cognac and building arms from the bottles they emptied only when they were not too preoccupied vandalizing the buildings. In both sets of comments, the students, like children, cried out for discipline; and the Mexican government was the one to provide it. Why else, the official suggested, did the students so readily surrender? According to the official statement made by García Barragán, the tanks, armored vehicles, and soldiers had little to do with the surrender of the buildings.

The remarks of Echeverría and García Barragán did not temper criticism of the use of the military. Indeed, many people did not accept the government's formal explanation of the events. The same day that the secretaries of interior and defense held their press conferences, critics of the government's policy denounced the invasion in the newspapers. Condemnation came from both the political left and right and from within the university and outside. The proponents of the students were particularly vehement in their rage. In newspapers, editorials protested the use of force against the students and the university.[22] The university rector Barros Sierra condemned the acts of the Mexican government while unions, students, and professors echoed his sentiment. Barros Sierra's declaration to the press stated:

> The military occupation of University City has been an
> excessive act of force that our house of higher education
> did not deserve . . . I have repeated that the University did
> not give rise to the student movement. The attention and
> solution to the problems of the youth requires under-
> standing before violence. Surely, you could have employed

other methods. Mexican institutions and our laws and traditions derive from more appropriate instruments than
armed force.[23]

Barros Sierra found himself in a very difficult position. He was a PRI insider, yet he also had to defend the institution that he led. He admonished the government for its harsh response by advocating negotiations between students and government officials. Barros Sierra called for reason and respect to prevail against injustice, and he also demanded the reinstatement of the university. Closing his remarks, he said, "We hope that these horrible acts that confront us do not affect the irreplaceable democracy of the Republic."[24]

The invasion of University City sparked politicized criticism against the government. The right-of-center opposition party *Partido Acción Nacional* (National Action Party, PAN) denounced the actions of the "revolutionary" government arguing that it supported the Mexican Constitution and the autonomy of UNAM.[25] While Díaz Ordaz remained aloof from the events and was not present at the press conference with other government officials, he became the target of criticism. The Assembly of Intellectuals, Artists, and Writers criticized the action in a full-page letter to the president published in *El Día* where they stated that the invasion violated the Constitution. Citing Article 1, the assembly contended that the invasion violated constitutional rights because it suspended individual guarantees by the unlawful arrest of people, thus publicizing the fact that some had been detained arbitrarily and illegally. The list of protesters included some of the most prominent names in Mexican society: directors such as Jorge Fons, painters such as Leonora Carrington, and cultural critics such as Carlos Monsiváis. The number of intellectuals who added their names to the public letters issued by the Assembly grew to two hundred after the UNAM invasion.[26]

Other groups also publicly deplored the actions of the government. The National Union of Mexican Women that had previously voiced their support of the students as mothers protested "the rupture of legality and constitutional order" of the country. Members criticized the violence of the government and viewed its actions as bordering on "fascist style terrorism." The Union closed its letter by calling on other women to join with them:

> Calling all women students, professionals, employees, work-
> ers, housewives to unite to form committees to defend the
> democratic rights and liberties of the Mexican people that
> have been violated by the repressive forces.
>
> Mexican women, defend your home, your sons and
> daughters, your parents, and your siblings. Meet with your
> companions and friends, with your neighbors, with the
> mothers of your children's schoolmates; with women of your
> neighborhood, office, factory, or school. We must all unite to
> demand the return of constitutional legality, respect of indi-
> vidual rights, an end to the repression, the immediate libera-
> tion of detainees, and the satisfaction of the students' and
> popular demands. Solution to the problem, not repression.
> Dialogue yes, bayonets no![27]

In the earlier months of the movement, the Union embraced maternal arguments and politics, but after the invasion their tone changed.
This above letter reflected the ideological background of the Union. Still
using their feminine roles, the Union issued a politicized call to all women
to "defend democratic rights and liberties." If women were unsure how to
organize, the Union spelled out basic grassroots methods for political
novices such as using informal meetings to discuss political issues. The
above quote reveals that the Union was something more than a group of
mothers and wives driven to join the students to protect them. The Union
showed its political astuteness by reaching out to other women who may
have been unsure how to express their support for the students.

More groups added their voices to the public condemnation.
Professors and employees from UNAM, Poli, Iberoamericana, and El
Colegio de México denounced the invasion and demanded the immediate removal of troops from UNAM. The presidium of the Communist
Party issued a declaration expressing indignation about the invasion. A
group of professionals also published a public letter of protest to the
president on September 21, 1968, in *El Día*. They, the assumed beneficiaries of the government's policies, challenged the defenders of the professional classes. The professionals wrote: "We protest the violation of
individual guarantees that are established by the Constitution of Mexico,
employed by the armed forces to obstruct the demonstration of ideas

and the liberty of association as well as to unilaterally resolve the social problems that eventually will be posed by the various sectors of Mexican society."[28] This group of professionals also denounced the violence used against the students, stating that students had a right, as students, to worry about the problems of the country and the right not to be treated as delinquents. The response of the professionals created a dilemma for the government. This was the group who had benefited most from the policies of the Díaz Ordaz administration.

Although a storm of denouncements came from various sectors of Mexican society, the government also found its supporters. The *Confederación Nacional Campesina* (National Peasant Confederation, CNC), *Confederación de Trabajadores Mexicanos* (Confederation of Mexican Workers, CTM), *Confederación Nacional de Organizaciones Populares* (National Confederation of Popular Organizations, CNOP), three sectors of the PRI, issued a statement of solidarity with the government and support for its actions at UNAM. The CTM, the CNC, and the CNOP included representatives from teachers, neighborhood, and transport organizations proclaimed their support of the government's policies to the Mexican people.

> The three largest sectors of the PRI, representatives of the majority forces of the country: agrarian, labor, and popular express... their support and confidence in the government of the Republic that had to decide that the army must occupy the campus of University City since it had become, for various weeks, a center conducive to agitation, anarchy, attacks on institutions and society with a deliberate intention to subvert social order.[29]

The three great sectors went on to echo Echeverría and García Barragán's statements that the invasion was necessary to maintain UNAM's autonomy in order to ensure that it could continue to serve its prime purpose, education. They, the CTM, CNC, CNOP, and other organizations recognized the rights of the students to "dissent, criticize, and struggle" for their ideas; however, they insisted that the students must engage in their struggles within the confines of the Constitution. Thus, the three sectors congratulated President Díaz Ordaz for reestablishing order and respect for the laws. In assessing the statement, what remains striking was that the CTM, CNC, and CNOP represented groups that had lost economic clout in the nation, but these groups were utterly dependent on the PRI and the president for their continued existence. Consequently, the relationship between the federal government and the leaders of those three groups continued to bolster the image of the state as an inclusive entity following the revolutionary ideals that toiled to maintain law and order.

Of course, students and eye-witnesses did not view the invasion of UNAM as a vehicle to ensure respect for the laws. Prisoners later released from the detention centers explained their experiences to journalists. The military had apprehended people not only on the campus of the national university but also in surrounding neighborhoods. In the days following the invasion, the government arrested people whom they assumed were leaders on campus. On September 19, Castillo, Professor Eli de Gortari, and activist Marcue Padrinos were captured in Mexico City by members of the Mexican secret service.[30] Consequently, the image of the student as dangerous was expanded to include those who were guilty by their associations with students, or in some cases, their living or working in proximity to the students and to UNAM.

The following day, students clashed with police. In turn, the press criticized student violent resistance. In *El Universal*, a photo accompanying a story about a clash between students and granaderos portrayed the "armed and dangerous" students. In the photo, the newspaper noted and circled the hands of students who were clasping rocks. Not noted by the journalists or by the newspaper, was that the students were wielding rocks against police clad in riot gear, and most likely armed with weapons.[31]

Along with the continued battles between students and military forces, sympathetic strikes in the provinces broke out despite the reassurances that García Barragán gave the press that the invasion on UNAM had not triggered solidarity protests at other autonomous universities.[32] Students, faculty, and staff at the University of Nuevo León protested the occupation of the national university. In Toluca, students demonstrated their support of the Mexico City student movement in the streets. In Quertaro, students protested the occupation of UNAM in front of the Municipal Palace. In Mérida, Francisco Repetto Milán, rector of the University of Yucatán, led a public demonstration protesting the invasion. In Cuernavaca, student brigades circulated the news of a strike, while the Autonomous University of Baja California and seven schools of the University of Chihuahua went on strike.[33]

On September 25, amidst the growing strikes in the provinces, Mexico City newspapers proclaimed the news that UNAM Rector Barros Sierra had resigned. His letter of resignation reiterated his plea that violence against the students must cease. He wrote: "The problems of the youth may only be resolved by the route of education never by force, violence, or corruption. This has been my constant rule of action and the object of my complete dedication, in time and energy, during my time as rector."[34] Barros Sierra went on to state that he had been a victim of personal attacks and defamation. He condemned the invasion and the continued occupations of campuses, and he again criticized those who did not attempt to understand the students or his pleas for peaceful solutions.

Street battles between granaderos and students escalated when the army moved in to occupy IPN. Students affiliated with Poli fought granaderos in the Nonoalco-Tlatelolco housing complex where, it was reported, that the students confronted tear gas and arms with Molotov cocktails which they flung at the troops and used to burn two "official vehicles."[35] For hours, the students and granaderos struggled. The students intercepted fifteen to sixteen buses that were passing through the area. They erected barricades with the buses to block the roads leading into the housing complex. In those areas that were not blockaded, students punctured the tires of official cars. The battle between students and granaderos led to the death of a granadero and to the injury of three police officers. Bystanders and residents of the housing complex were injured, as were students. Nineteen students, two of whom were women, were listed as detained in the newspaper.[36]

Once in control, the army then decided to blockade and occupy Tlatelolco itself using nine tanks and five hundred troops to restore order. U.S. intelligence reports stated that once the troops took the Casco de Santo Tomas building, they found "an 'arsenal' of forty pistols, small caliber rifles, shotguns, knives, bicycle chains, pipe lengths, and over one thousand Molotov cocktails."[37] The Saturday and Sunday confrontations between students and granaderos in the Nonoalco-Tlatelolco housing area were the most violent confrontations between students and government forces to date. Throughout the city, violence continued throughout the Federal District. Students burned buses and other vehicles, and riots and street battles erupted at UNAM, Poli, and around the National Museum of Anthropology.

Following the riots, reports circulated in the newspaper documenting the property damage. The newspapers reported that the damage to the Nonoalco-Tlatelolco areas was estimated to be in the millions of pesos.[38] United States Defense Intelligence Reports stated that there was an estimated business loss of thirty million pesos in Mexico City. Along with those damages, 803 buses, ten street cars, four ambulances, sixteen police motorcycles, and six radio controlled police cars had been destroyed or vandalized. Other damage included vandalism to street lights and signs.[39]

With the violence and chaos in the city, various professors and school directors sought to achieve some coherence in leadership. A group of professors and directors sent a letter asking the Governing Junta of UNAM to reject Barros Sierra's resignation in the hopes that he could negotiate some sort of truce with Secretary of Interior Echeverría. The governing board of UNAM then declined Barros Sierra's resignation, and he rescinded his resignation and continued as rector through the crisis. As hoped by university faculty and administrators, Barros Sierra demanded that the army leave the UNAM campus. With the rector remaining, the secretary of interior and the military now had the "legitimate authority" that they required before stopping the occupation of the campus. On September 30, 1968, 1,300 army soldiers withdrew from UNAM with the concession that the university return to its goals of education.

The return of UNAM to its "legitimate authority" did not defeat the students. Once UNAM was back in the hands of university personnel, the *Consejo Nacional de Huelga* (National Strike Council, CNH) held a press conference on October 1 in the *Facultad de Ciencias* (School of Sciences) to discuss the continuation of the protest and strike, while at the same time representatives from the CNH were in negotiations with the government in regards to public dialogue and their demands. During this press conference, members of the CNH fielded questions from international journalists. *El Día* reported that a North American asked if the students had enough power to force the government into dialogue or would further violence be necessary. *El Día* noted that the students simply responded by saying that they had the right to ask the government to listen to them.[40] Another journalist inquired if the students would hold demonstrations during the Olympics. The students were reported as having said, "If it is necessary to have a demonstration during it [the Olympic Games], then we will."[41]

At the end of the conference, the CNH called for a meeting the next day in the Plaza de las Tres Culturas to protest the violence that had taken place in Vocational 7 and in the Nonoalco-Tlatelolco complex. Demonstrators were to gather at the Plaza de las Tres Culturas in the Nonoalco-Tlatelolco housing complex for a public meeting, then march to IPN's Casco de Santo Tomás campus. This time, the government took seriously the students' veiled threat of protesting during the Olympics.

The Plaza de las Tres Culturas

The Plaza de las Tres Culturas lies within a multi-use high-rise apartment housing and business complex that is bordered by a major artery, Paseo de la Reforma. The name of the plaza refers to its proximity to the remains of an Aztec temple, the Spanish colonial Cathedral Santiago de Tlatelolco, and to the modern apartment and business buildings that comprise the Nonoalco-Tlatelolco complex that surround the plaza. Completed during the Economic Miracle of the 1960s, the Tlatelolco apartments housed the city's emerging middle class in its small two bedroom apartments. The subsidized complex contained apartments, businesses, stores, schools, parks, and government offices including the Secretary of Foreign Affairs. It is in some ways a small city in the heart of Mexico City. The Plaza de las Tres Culturas is located on the eastern side of the complex. Although accessible by foot and visible from the street, the apartments surrounding the plaza enclose it. The Aztec ruins in the plaza lie on a grassy yard that is crisscrossed with sidewalks that pass by the different structures. The Cathedral sits on the raised patio of the plaza. The patio and the ruins create an obstacle course.

The CNH called a meeting for 5:00 P.M., but people had begun to gather in the plaza by 4:00 P.M. Since the meeting was held in the large complex, there were bystanders and apartment dwellers in the plaza as well. The CNH arrived and installed itself on the third floor of the Chihuahua apartment building, close to the Cathedral and over-looking the Plaza.[42]

From that position, the council leaders could address the crowd. The meeting was not as large as previous ones; only an estimated ten to twenty thousand people gathered. Some of the demonstrators present actually lived in the complex and had been drawn to the movement by the invasion of local Vocational School 7. Other people in the plaza simply lived in the surrounding apartment buildings.

As reported in numerous newspapers at this time and later in personal accounts, the meeting began in a fairly predictable fashion with speakers addressing the issues of the movement. The army was present on the side streets, but the presence of tanks had become a common sight at the demonstrations across the city. Since the meeting was smaller and since the military was placed around the plaza, the student leaders decided to suspend the planned march to the Casco de Santo Tomás campus of IPN because the military had blockaded the area. Details are murky after 5:30 P.M. because of conflicting stories from the press and from eyewitnesses. But, it appears that at approximately 6:00 P.M., helicopters flying over the plaza illuminated it with Bengal lights, the same lights that were used in Vietnam. Shots then rang out from the sky, the rooftops, and around the plaza.[43] For the police and military, *Operación Galeana* had begun; for the civilians in the plaza, a massacre had begun.[44] Elivira B. de Concheiro, a mother who happened to be in the plaza recalled:

> When I realized that the helicopter had come down danger-
> ously low, circling right above the heads of the crowd in the
> Plaza de las Tres Culturas and firing on everybody—we
> could see the gray streaks of tracer bullets in the sky—I was
> so dumbfounded I said to myself, I can't believe it—it's like
> in a movie. I've never seen anything like this except in
> movies. Those just can't be real bullets. I wandered around
> in a daze, as though I'd gone out of my mind.[45]

Like Concheiro, the chaos that engulfed the plaza on October 2 remained fresh in the minds of many activists. Gilberto Guevara Niebla recalled that the speakers that day included CNH members David Vega, Florencio López Osuna, and Mirthokleia González Guardado, who served as the master of ceremonies, a representative from the railroad workers' union, and others. Guevara Niebla stated:

> We began to receive information from below that there were
> many *pelones* (literally bald men), people with short, mili-
> tary styled hair, at the same time, things began to happen. A
> so-called law student appeared: well-built, blond, that tried
> to break the ranks of students blocking access (to the CNH)
> and they had to violently remove him from the third floor.
> The incident surprised us because nothing like it had hap-
> pened before."[46]

At approximately the same time, Aída González arrived at the Chihuahua
building with her sister and two friends to deliver a message to Guevara
Niebla. González, like other women, occasionally served as messengers
for the CNH. González later remembered that CNH members were on
the third floor as well as the Italian journalist Oriana Fallaci. As she
reached the third floor, González encountered what she described as
"plainclothes police," who she said were provoking the CNH members.[47]
Perhaps this was one of the pelones that Guevara Niebla mentioned.

After delivering the message and observing a scuffle in the hall, she
exited the building. She remembered the Bengal lights on the circling
helicopters above as she entered to the plaza.[48] González's memory of the
event is vivid:

> The moment we arrived to the Plaza, we (saw) these two
> provokers (plainclothes police) putting a white glove on the
> left hand and taking their pistols from their vests. And, they
> started shooting all the people. We were very scared and we
> tried to go to the stairs (in the Chihuahua building). It (the
> stairwell) was full of students who were very much
> afraid... we stayed outside and saw groups of battalions of
> the army coming and shooting the people.... There were
> already three people dead in an area of five meters. In front
> of the door by the elevators, there was a guy who had his
> stomach out because he had been killed by an expansion
> bullet. He was bleeding all over; all his entrails were out. And
> then there was another young guy shot in the head, and a
> woman about forty-five years old who was also shot. She
> was lying on the (ground), and there were tanks coming in.

> The people were hit by the tanks, hit on the legs and the
> arms. . . . And then there was another battalion that brought
> people from the third floor, people that were in the tribune
> (CNH). There was a girl crying, she was very scared. One of
> the soldiers took the (butt) of his rifle and (smashed) her
> face saying "Callate vieja patetica" (Shut up pathetic
> woman). I thought they would kill her.[49]

Once she was able to get up after being thrown to the ground, González feared that she would be arrested because she was carrying student propaganda. She tore the papers and discarded them. She then tried to flee, but she and her friends were detained by the police. In the chaos, however, she and her friends along with two young men were able to link arms and run. They ran into a soldier who demanded to know if they were fleeing the plaza. Sniper shots from the rooftops interrupted the interrogation, and she was able to flee again. She and her companions flagged down a car on Reforma and finally escaped.

González was fortunate to be able to flee the housing complex. Other activists and bystanders were not so lucky. Mirthokleia González Guardado was also on the third floor, and she remembered the Bengal lights. González Guardado recalled. "When the red light shown, the shoot-out began. All of us who were there (on the third floor) began to run to the elevator, and you could imagine our surprise when the doors opened and we were received by the machine guns of the Olympic Battalion who were wearing one white glove. . . ."[50] She and many others were captured. González Guardado was detained and taken to the police station and interrogated about CNH members. She remained in custody until November when she escaped after being taken to a hospital.[51] She later fled Mexico.

Student leaders and activists detained in and around the Chihuahua building suffered humiliation and beatings. In December 2001, the weekly *Proceso* and the newspaper *La Jornada* released photos taken in the Plaza de las Tres Culturas on October 2, 1968.[52] In one, Florencio López Osuna, a CNH leader, was shown stripped to his underwear. His face showed signs of a beating. Interviews with activists detained that day confirmed this experience. They were often stripped, and many of the men were beaten. The photos were a grisly reminder of the past. Far worse than the images were the events that the photos triggered almost thirty-five years later. López Osuna, a sub-director of Vocational School 5 in 2001, was found dead in a hotel in the early hours of December 20, 2001. Officially, the death of the educator was ruled as heart failure triggered by alcoholism. *La Jornada* reported that the night before his death, López Osuna had met with other 1968 activists and proposed that a commission be created to demand that all the documents surrounding the movement be released and to investigate the disappearance of activists from the student movement.[53] In the days following the death, ex-activists demanded that the government investigate the death of the educator, and they restated López Osuna's demand that the government release the documents of the massacre.[54]

Some leaders were not in the Chihuahua building addressing the crowd. That day, Tita Avendaño and Ana Ignacia Rodríguez were in the plaza. In an interview, Avendaño expressed the shock of the governmental response:

> It never occurred to us that the government might attack us
> on October 2 because a few days before there had been a
> meeting at Tlatelolco and in the morning several members
> of the CNH . . . went to the Casa del Lago to talk with Caso
> and de la Vega [government negotiators], and we thought
> that a sort of tacit truce had been arranged, since it looked
> as though the government was about to reach an agreement
> with the students.[55]

Rodríguez explained how she and Tita, two of the leaders, escaped the plaza. She explained that when the shooting began, she and Tita followed the directions of the leaders to remain calm. Rodríguez was holding a banner when a comrade told her it was serving as a target. She tossed it and fled with Avendaño.

> At one point, we leaped over those pre-Hispanic walls
> there and fell into a sort of ditch. I lay there on the ground,
> and other people started falling on top of me. We heard
> shouts and groans and cries of pain, and I realized then
> that the gunfire was getting heavier and heavier. Tita and I

·crawled out of there and ran toward the Calle Manuel
González, and the soldiers yelled to us," Get the hell out as
fast as you can."[56]

Avendaño and Rodriguez made it out of the Plaza that day without
injury. Many people were injured and arrested in the mayhem that took
place in the Plaza de las Tres Culturas, but the actual number of dead
remains unknown. From eye-witness accounts, injuries and deaths
seemed to be far greater than what the government claimed in the aftermath.[57] Newspapers reported twenty-nine dead and eighty injured, but
the photos reveal a more horrific result. Shoes and clothing littered the
Plaza. Both foreign and Mexican journalists took photographs of hospital hallways lined with stretchers in mute denial of the government's
assertion that only twenty-nine died.[58] The official number of dead
fluctuated over the following days, eventually settling on forty-nine dead.

In the days following the massacre, expressions of public opinion
ranged from unconditional support for the government to deep, unyielding anger. By October 3, thirty delegates of the Mexican Senate supported
the decision of the Díaz Ordaz administration to intervene in the Plaza de
las Tres Culturas. Members of the Grand Commission denounced the
"participation [in the student protests] of foreign and national elements
that have pursued extremely dangerous anti-Mexican objectives."[59] The
following day, newspapers reported differing opinions of the events by
some political insiders who questioned the use of deadly force by the Díaz
Ordaz administration. Ex-president Miguel Alemán (1946–1952) denounced
the violence, but he did not specifically blame the government. Newspaper
journalists condemned the actions of the government as they reported on
those who were injured and those who died during the massacre, particularly those who were neither students nor protesters. The names and
affiliations of students who perished in the gun battle appeared in *El
Heraldo*. However, the newspaper provided more biographical information
regarding innocent bystanders who were killed. Among those, *El Heraldo*
reported on the deaths of Señora Gloria Valenica Larra de González who
was killed in her jewelry story in the Chihuahua building; unemployed
fifty-nine year old Jorge Ramirez González was killed in his apartment in
the 2 de Abril building; and José Igancio Caballero González who was shot
as he purchased bread in a bakery in the Chihuahua building.[60]

Many foreign journalists were in the Plaza de las Tres Culturas because of the approaching Olympics and the student protest. As a result, reports of the event reached the world. In these reports, Mexican and international journalists expressed their shock, dismay, and anger at the actions of the Mexican government. In the days following the massacre, foreign journalists who were in the Plaza countered statements made by the government. As activist Aída González recalled in an interview, Italian journalist Oriana Fallaci was in the Chihuahua building. Fallaci had gone to the Chihuahua building because she had been invited by the CNH. In her writings about October 2, Fallaci remembered that because of the military presence, the students had canceled a march that was to have followed the meeting. Fallaci reported that the CNH announced, "Compañeros, let's change the program. No one will go to the school because they are waiting to kill us. When the meeting ends, we will return to our houses."[61] She recalled that with the arrival of the helicopters and the lights, she had told the CNH that something bad was going to happen. Fallaci wrote that they replied "Come on, you are not in Vietnam."[62] Events were moving too fast and in less than ten seconds tanks and armed vehicles arrived and the shooting began. CNH representative Sócrates Campos Lemus, who was speaking as the violence broke out, yelled into the microphone." Compañeros...do not run...it is a provocation."[63] At the same time, plainclothes police entered the building. Fallaci was pulled by her hair, thrown to the ground, and beaten by the police. In Fallaci's descriptions of the event at Tlatelolco, she used references to what she witnessed in Vietnam, the explosions, the gunfire, the screaming, and the fear.

Another journalist Carolyn Pacheco was also in Tlatelolco. In 1968, Pacheco was a young correspondent for CBS's Mexican news desk who had started as a bilingual secretary later becoming a journalist. Throughout the summer of 1968, she had followed the student movement. On October 2, she and a film crew had gone to the Plaza de las Tres Culturas to document the demonstration. Pacheco's story is unique because she and her crew filmed the first few minutes of the massacre. With the tape in hand, Pacheco rushed to the airport booking the first flight from Mexico City to the United States. She feared that the police would be in the airport, but she was able to smuggle the tape out of Mexico. She flew to California where the film was aired.[64]

In the wake of the massacre, nearly all the surviving participants and supporters assumed that they would have broad political support to challenge the government. However, that did not happen. In the days that followed, many prominent Mexicans did denounce the government, but there was no mass uprising, no strikes, no revolution, no broad responses as in May 1968 in Paris, France. For many students the lack of solidarity demonstrated by the Mexican people contributed to feelings of failure and abandonment. How was the movement to survive?

Aftermath and Fallout

Many Mexican government officials, and foreign government officials as well, tried to understand the events and where to place the blame. General and ex-president Lázaro Cárdenas (1934–1940) condemned the violence but also denounced the involvement of foreigners and "anti-nationalists."[65] As Cárdenas implored the government to seek a solution to the continuing violence, he followed the official position that emphasized foreign influences in the movement. The claim that foreign agents were responsible for the violence led American government representatives to examine the role of U.S. citizens in the student protests as well as actions of citizens from other nations. United States State Department and Defense Department documents from the summer of 1968 assumed it was probable that U.S. citizens or other foreign citizens may have been involved. At the time of the October 2 massacre, however, the State Department acknowledged that this was a Mexican movement. One official telegram contained the following passage: "With respect to public statements about foreign conspiracy, important to note use of foreign scapegoat frequent in Mexico and in this instance designed to discredit student movement and perhaps to some degree to divert the attention from the deeper local roots of problem."[66]

Following the massacre, the government had gained control over the students, but it still needed parental assistance to ensure that no further demonstrations would take place. After Tlatelolco, UNAM, IPN, and Chapingo were placed under police watch as were the vocational and preparatory schools. Chief of Police Cueto de Ramírez insisted in the newspapers that parents rein in their children and prohibit them from

141

attending other protest meetings.[67] Thus, the Mexican government again demanded parents control their children. In the past, the chief of police had blamed Mexican parents for their failure to control their children's actions in earlier demonstrations. If parents simply took control of their children, the police asserted, the movement would end.

With the chief of police clamoring for more parental control to stop the demonstrations, the CNH defied the authorities by continuing to organize. It attempted to rally student supporters by holding public meetings and issuing statements criticizing the government's actions in the Plaza. Three days after the massacre, what remained of the CNH held a press conference at the Medical Center in University Center to denounce the government's violence and to affirm that the CNH and the student protesters were in no way responsible for the massacre. It disputed claims that demonstrators fired the first shots, thus provoking the full-scale offensive by the police and army. Instead, the CNH countered that there were groups that were armed with "guns like those used in Vietnam." The CNH tried to shift blame and responsibility from students to the government and to rally the movement in a climate of intense fear. However, few were prepared for the defection of one of its own, a defector who now jeopardized the movement and its advocates.

On October 5, 1968, detained CNH member Sócrates Campos Lemus read a public statement in Military Camp 1 to the press. He was accompanied by Salvador del Toro Robles, an agent of the Federal Public Ministry who was a representative of the office that advises the president on legal matters. Campos Lemus had been arrested on October 2, 1968 and had been held, with other activists, in Military Camp 1. One of the CNH members who had screamed for the people not to run on October 2 and the CNH representative who had proposed occupying the Zócalo during the August 27 demonstration, Campos Lemus' words electrified the government because it appeared to support and justify many of their theories. The statement, however, led to an utter denouncement by the CNH.

In his opening comments, Campos Lemus outlined how he became active in the movement. He initially joined the movement when he had been selected as a committee member to investigate the FNET. During the press conference, he explained how IPN students crafted their initial demands, and the later decision of UNAM students to join the strike. By explaining the evolution of the movement, Campos Lemus was not telling the press or the government anything that had not been widely reported. He described how the CNH was formed with two members being elected from each of the schools, and he estimated there were approximately seventy members. He then went on to name some members of the CNH and their institutional affiliations. At times, he claimed not to remember their full names, but he did mention twenty-four names that included students and faculty.

While listing names was damaging enough, Campos Lemus described factions that had appeared within the CNH.[68] He claimed that within the CNH, there were *tibios* (soft-liners) and *ultra-duras* (hard-liners). The tibios adopted a more reformist stance to promote democratic reform, while ultra-duras insisted on using the political brigades to mobilize workers and peasants. Like in France, he argued that some of the brigades' goals were to join workers to take over the factories. Other brigades would go "to the people" in the rural areas to form cooperatives. The purpose of all this, Campos Lemus stated, was to destroy the state in its present form and to build a new worker-student-peasant state, or Communist state.

While news that the students planned to construct a workers' state substantiated police and military suspicions of an objective other than demonstrations, Campos Lemus focused the blame for the strike on disenchanted politicians and intellectuals. He asserted that prominent Mexicans supported the students directly such as Elena Garro, a famous Mexican writer who he claimed acted as a go-between, carrying messages for student leaders. He also stated that Carlos A. Madrazo, ex-president of the Executive Committee of the PRI, worked closely with the Coalition leaders Heberto Castillo and Eli de Gortari. Humerto Romero, ex-Secretary of President López Mateos, allegedly contributed financially to the movement, and Víctor L. Urquidi, the director of El Colegio de México, provided the movement with the substantial sum of fifty thousand pesos. Finally, Braulio Maldonado, the ex-governor of Baja California, used student intermediaries to offer to help with money and arms.

After his disclosure of possible arms trafficking, Campos Lemus affirmed that there had been armed students in Tlatelolco. Students had been organizing armed columns headed by Guillermo and Jesús González Guardado, Sóstenes Torrecillas, Raúl Alvarez, and Florencio López Osuna, leaders of the movement. Campos Lemus alleged that arms had been purchased through a CNH member from the School of

Agriculture in Chihuahua, a state bordering the United States. The students had collected approximately twenty-five guns, and that the members of armed columns had been in and around the Plaza de las Tres Culturas. Consequently, it was possible that armed students may have set in motion events that led to the massacre.

Campos Lemus' testimony had a devastating effect on the movement, but his words also reveal the inherent complexity therein. In assessing his statement, he named CNH members and their alleged collaborators. For those activists who had not been arrested, the fear that one of their own was talking under duress or under his own accord had to have had horrible consequences on the organization and its ability to offer unified leadership. Moreover, Campos Lemus revealed that there were politically connected and important collaborators with the students.

After Campos Lemus's public disclosure, those disaffected politicians and intellectuals mentioned in his statement challenged the reliability of his denouncement. Madrazo declared that he had never had contact with striking students, and he deplored the violence. Maldonado insisted that he too was not involved with the students, nor did he know any member of the CNH. Urquidi, in turn, stated that neither he nor El Colegio de México had provided the students with funding. Garro, of course, was a different story. Her support for the students had been quite public since she had signed declarations that were published in the press. In an interview with the newspaper *Excélsior*, Garro, the ex-wife of Octavio Paz, did not deny her support for the students. She acknowledged that she had been active with the students because she accompanied her daughter, Elena, to meetings. However, she was quite indignant that Campos Lemus inferred that she had been working for the students. Instead, she challenged the limited vision of the students in dealing with the government and their relations with workers. She also recognized that many students viewed her as bourgeois. When asked why Campos Lemus had accused her, she replied, "Surely, he was pressured; someone paid him or they gave him an order."[69] Garro, however, did support aspects of Campos Lemus' statement, arguing that the students were pawns of intellectuals and professors of UNAM.

Campos Lemus' charges created an on-going and a confused debate that contained charges and counter-charges from both the students and the government. The army claimed that it had found an "arsenal" of weapons when they arrested students in the Plaza.[70] Thus, Madrazo, Maldonado, and Urquidi could have been held responsible for the violence from supplying funds and arms. Student attempts to tell their side of the story were not successful. To many people in Mexico, the students appeared to have been acquiring arms and committed to incite a revolution. In the next few weeks, the students were subjected to a cascade of blame that Campos Lemus seemed to have verified with his public statement.

In the days that followed, activists confronted staged and real opposition, and they tried to defend their movement and explain aspects of Campos Lemus' comments. Individuals masquerading as students made claims supporting the idea that the students were on the brink of inciting a revolt. These "students" were denounced by the CNH. Ayax Segura Garrido, an IPN professor who had been detained on October 3, stated in a rebuttal to Campos Lemus that he could not confirm external support for the students. Segura Garrido did, however, corroborate that there was dissent between a hard-line and those who wished to promote the Six Point Petition. The hard-liners embraced violence despite the fact that the Teacher's Coalition continued to encourage the students to seek a solution to the conflict.

The confusion in the days that immediately followed the massacre and the Campos Lemus statement may be seen in United States government documents. The United States State and Defense Departments and Central Intelligence Agency (CIA) attempted to provide viable intelligence, but the reports from the agencies reflected the confusion. CIA documents suggested that it was possible that students had received money from outside sources. However Walt Rostow wrote in a letter to U.S. President Lyndon B. Johnson that he did not think that the students were tied to Soviet or Cuban money.[71] United States Intelligence reports also recognized that there was indeed a hard-line, but U.S. officials were unsure of the exact political ideology that dominated the hard-line since there were many different ideologies at work in the movement.

CIA documents as well as activists' own testimony do confirm that there were students who advocated a more revolutionary stance.[72] In a 1993 television interview, Eduardo Valle mentioned that there was a hard-line within the movement, and that there was dissent even in the ranks of the ultra-duras. Marcelino Perelló also mentioned that there was dissent over the use of arming students and using violent means against the government.[73] Obviously, in a group as politically and ideologically diverse as the CNH, there was dissent in the ranks; however, few of its members were prepared for the comments of Campos Lemus.[74]

In the days that followed the massacre, the press, the Mexican government, and the U.S. State and Defense Departments and CIA reported that perhaps the students were responsible for the massacre. A Department of Defense document reported that Jorge Hernandez, in charge of the troops, arrived and told the students that they would not be permitted to march.[75] In the weeks that followed, U.S. officials tried to ascertain who was responsible and questioned some of the propaganda that came from the Mexican presidential palace. These documents confirm that the U.S. government was as confused by the events as were many international journalists.

The Collapse

The massacre on October 2 succeeded in what the government had been trying to do since early August: discredit the students and their proponents and undermine the movement. The government prevailed in its goals, but it also created an atmosphere of fear. It had successfully split the movement—students distrusted and denounced one another. Students' statements and counter-statements also reinforced people's fears that were, in turn, fed by the government that students were stockpiling arms and being assisted by politicians and intellectuals who through their actions contributed to the disturbances in the hopes of toppling the regime. In turn, intellectuals and politicians denounced the students.

With declarations, accusations, and counter-accusations being fired back and forth, fear spread among the students across the city. On October 2, 750 people were detained, and in the days following the massacre, more young people were arrested. Newspapers reported that citizens living in and around Tlatelolco were still being attacked by sniper fire from the rooftops after October 2. Editorial cartoons depicted the fear of those who lived in the areas surrounding Tlatelolco. In one published image, a man wearing armor passed by two men who comment, "It is González, he lives in Tlatelolco."[76]

Acknowledging the crisis in the movement and the precarious situation in which the students found themselves, the CNH attempted to regroup. Marcelino Perelló, one of the people chosen to negotiate with the government, exonerated Madrazo stating that he never had provided money to the movement.[77] Representing the student council, Perelló also avowed the continuation of the movement and of its demands. In a series of meetings held at Casa del Lago in Chapultec Park and in the homes of government representatives Jorge de la Vega and Andrés Corona, the student and government representatives engaged in a dialogue about the future of the movement. The student activists reported to their supporters that the representatives of the government had offered to stop detaining students, remove the police and military from schools, and assess minimum penalties for those students arrested and found guilty of crimes in exchange for a student guarantee to continue the movement in a legal manner.[78]

The meetings between the CNH and government representatives appeared to be moving toward some resolution. With the student strike continuing, with criticism being leveled at Mexico internally and internationally, David Franco Rodríguez, the attorney for Military Camp 1 announced to the press the release of 324 prisoners detained as a result of October 2. Officials released certain prisoners because they were found to be minimally or uninvolved in the movement, but the punishment of detained students and movement sympathizers continued. Those student leaders who had been arrested appeared before Judge Eduardo Ferrer MacGregor on October 9. The one hundred thirteen activists were charged with disturbing the peace, while fifteen activists were charged with federal crimes including inciting rebellion, sedition, property damage, attacks on communication lines, robbery, looting, arms stockpiling, and assault and murder of a federal agent. Included in those charged with federal offenses were Campos, Guevara Niebla, González de Alba and Segura Garrido. These charges were a harbinger of things to come elsewhere. In other parts of Mexico, an estimated ninety-six men and two women were charged with aiding and abetting the students in the Federal District.

On October 12, 1968, the Olympic Games opened in Mexico City. U.S. Defense Intelligence Reports commented on the heavy presence of the military on the streets of Mexico City and around Olympic venues.

The U.S. documents also noted that the appearance of the "Olympic Battalion" which the reports noted was not student led and organized, but rather was organized by the Mexican Army "to assist in security and other matters of conduct of the games."[79] The Olympic Battalion was not organized by the students to disrupt the Olympics. The student movement simply collided with the well-trained battalion because of timing. It has now been documented that the Olympic Battalion was in the Plaza de las Tres Culturas and may have infiltrated the movement.[80]

With the internal struggles and continued violence and arrests, student protests dwindled, prisoners remained imprisoned, and many students fled the country to avoid arrest and detention.[81] The CNH attempted to respond to the changing climate in the wake of these events, and it and other students spent weeks debating the return to classes or the continuation of the strike. After the closing of the Olympics on October 27, 1968, the CNH reiterated to the government its representation of the students. Furthermore, it issued a new set of demands. The council again requested that all students arrested since July 23 be released, that all repression cease, and that all police forces vacate all centers of education. The CNH went on to confront the charge that the arrested students had committed egregious federal crimes. The council defended their imprisoned comrades by stating, "On the contrary, we consider that these compañeros, far from delinquents, are distinguished defenders of democratic liberties in our country."[82] The CNH claimed that their movement's purpose went beyond demands for political prisoners. "Our movement is characterized by its decided push in favor of democracy. Therefore, it transcends the boundaries of the struggle for the liberation of political prisoners. With the present and certain repressive conditions, this struggle remains especially significant."[83]

Despite the violence of October 2 and the continued repression, many students continued to organize. In a 1993 interview, Martha Servin, a CNH representative from the National School of Biological Sciences at IPN captured the profound feelings of the students in the wake of October 2. She stated:

> In November, we entered the most difficult stage of the
> movement. I think it is much more difficult to discuss a
> moment that is less glorious when it is much easier to

discuss the ascent of the movement when all the glory is about you. Participating in a movement that had received a terrible blow as on October 2, struck fear in everyone. Nevertheless, it was impressive that after October 2 organizational elements were achieved and some public presentations were rapidly organized; This was unheard of in these absolutely repressive conditions that we endured, in which not only was the memory of October 2, but also the killings of *brigadistas* (brigade members) in the street.[84]

With the government firmly in control of the situation, students who continued to organize were attacked, detained, and imprisoned when caught organizing in public places as the brigades had done the entire summer. The continued violence greatly affected the activists. In the wake of the massacre, some students later recalled feeling depressed and angry. They had lost comrades, while others had betrayed them to the authorities. The violence of the government against the students led many young people to believe that revolution was indeed necessary in Mexico. As noted in U.S. intelligence reports, the mood in the city was quite somber. The document states:

> The immediate aftermath of the 2 October battle was to quiet and subdue the students. It is not known if this was due to the extent of the violence, or that the most militant of the student leaders were captured. It is generally believed that many of the militant leaders were arrested and their subsequent interrogation has resulted in the identification of others.[85]

Although Servin and others continued to engage in actions and discussions, the movement limped along after October. Student leaders advocated a continuation of dialogue. The CNH attempted to exert their influence by demanding that the military leave the Poli campuses, free the detained students, and cease all repression. Nevertheless, by late October, the CNH held meetings to ask students whether or not they wished to return to classes. Along with the CNH leadership, professors and Barros Sierra joined to organize committees to examine the movement and to agitate for improved conditions for student prisoners. By October 28, the strike council was publicly proclaiming its continued support for the strike; however, rumors circulated that the CNH no longer represented the interests of the majority of students because many students wished to return to classes. Thus, the movement was being undermined from all sides with divisions among students, continued violence, and stalled negotiations.

The events of October 2, the attacks on the students, further detainments, and the federal charges against students had a profound effect on activists within the movement. The youth of 1968 who were so sure they could initiate democracy and modernity in Mexico through non-violent methods were thwarted by a government committed to maintaining its power and claiming to represent modern Mexico. The government tolerated student protests up until ten days prior to the opening of the Games, but even before that, the government had been astute at containing the students and their movement.

In assessing the ability of students to hold their institutions, they may have enjoyed a level of freedom in their own domains—the university, the secondary schools, and some public spaces. However, the students' access to these spaces that they claimed as "theirs" was an illusion. As the patriarchs of the modern Mexican family, the government was not willing to permit its children to move beyond these social and political spaces that it deemed appropriate for them. UNAM, Poli, the vocational schools, prep schools, and the public plazas never completely belonged to the students; they were simply borrowing the space for a period of time that the government felt appropriate. As the movement grew to become an embarrassment in the wake of the UNAM and Poli invasions, the need for a quick response and conclusion was necessary. In turn, Díaz Ordaz and Echeverría demonstrated that they had never lost the upper hand throughout the summer months because the schools and other public spaces could easily, if not violently, be retaken.

The night of Tlatelolco lives in the minds of many Mexicans in ways akin to what Americans recall what they were doing when the World Trade Center was attacked on September 11, 2001. For Mexicans, whether they were students or not, they recognized that the massacre of October 2 was the requiem for the Mexican Revolution as was September 11 for the sense of security of Americans. What had been before would never be the same. Activist Francisco Delgado Sánchez recalled the valor and courage of the students as well as the injustice that followed. He stated:

> On October 2, 1968, the government and its army, defenders
> of the people, so full of glory, killed hundreds of stu-
> dents... [Mexico] the only place in the world, where one of
> the main assassins [Díaz Ordaz] rests in the Rotunda of
> Illustrious Men, and all the politicians have been awarded
> prime positions to try to erase the ignominy, but October 2
> is not forgotten.[86]

The massacre of October 2, 1968, crushed the movement, but the ideals and the questions that it provoked continued to simmer beneath the political and social surface of Mexico. Like Delgado Sanchez stated in an interview, the government could not erase what it had done or the questions the students had raised. Even the CIA recognized that the violence that had taken place in Tlatelolco would have damaging consequences for the Mexican government.[87] As CIA officials predicted, the demand for democracy played out in other arenas and would re-emerge in the following decades.

The attack on students in Tlatelolco ironically perhaps had helped create modern Mexico. Young people learned a tremendous lesson on the streets of the Federal District in the summer of 1968. They saw that they the so-called heirs of the Mexican Revolution, were simply pawns. Their nation, for all its debates on Article 34 and lowering the voting age, for all its modern trappings, and for its appearance as an economic and political international power broker was still mired in the past— a past that accommodated politics as usual through violence, co-option, and manipulation. The activists of 1968 found that they were little match for the power of the state, and their options were limited. Some would continue to be the political pawns of the traditional power brokers by serving in government posts in the decades that followed, while others adopted a path of resistance. Their movement may not have attained their political demands, but their cultural impact reverberated beyond that summer.

Chapter Five

APERTURA DEMOCRÁTICA:
Masculinity, Power, and Terror

With the brutal repression of the movement at Tlatelolco and the students' return to classes in December of 1968, the hegemony of President Gustavo Díaz Ordaz and PRI seemed triumphant, and the president's power and image in Mexico and internationally little damaged. The Olympics had opened and closed without incident. A movement of youth that had begun with such promise was being forced to fade into memory as a mere youthful folly. However, the demands and actions of the generation of '68 did not disappear from the political and social landscape of Mexico. The Six Point Petition, demands for civil liberties, mass mobilization of people within the Federal District and beyond, and the ensuing violence created an atmosphere of distrust among the people for the government.

After the massacre of 1968, a crisis of power emerged, and it had tremendous consequences that marred the political and economic successes of the Díaz Ordaz administration. Díaz Ordaz had governed Mexico during a time of economic growth and prosperity. When he left office in 1970, he left a balanced budget and had ensured the continued power of the executive position embodied in the president.[1] Yet, in the Plaza de las Tres Culturas, the power and prestige of this president had been tarnished. The Mexican people no longer viewed him as the benevolent father figure.[2] New President Luis Echeverría had to publicly reconceptualize his role as the caring but strong patriarch.

As Echeverría embarked on reforming the public view of the president, students began their own search for a new role in the post-Tlatelolco

153

Mexico. The struggles between youth and elders, men and women, and the powerful and the powerless that emerged in the summer of 1968 continued to mar the political, social, and cultural landscape of modern Mexico. This chapter examines how the ideals and outcomes of 1968 clashed with cultural constructions of political power and social control. Young men and women had sought to change Mexico from the grassroots level, and their attempts at reform were co-opted by the Echeverría administration. This chapter also considers the vehicles of resistance embraced by students following the movement that reflected shifting concepts of gender, power, and influence. In an attempt to regain control in the face of continued student organized resistance, those in positions of power interpreted the movement as something that had to be confronted to regain the confidence of the Mexican people in the president. At the same time, violence became a tool to ensure the continuation of the status quo and of the *Partido Revolucionario Institucional* (Party of the Institutional Revolution, PRI).

Hoping to mitigate the movement and end the violence, Echeverría initiated the *apertura democrática*, or the democratic opening, which embraced reforms that the students demanded such as the abolishment of Article 145 and the release of some of the political prisoners. The apertura democrática was in many ways an invitation for discontented youth to return to the Mexican revolutionary family. The Echeverría administration, on the one hand, reached out to students and the opposition. Echeverría even postured as a politician greatly affected by the 1968 movement, though he had been secretary of interior at the time of the repression. On the other hand, his administration engaged in what has now been recognized as a Dirty War in Mexico against those activists who did not accept his interpretation of the movement. The continued use of violence caused many students and other young people to reject the sanitized vision of progress in the democratic opening wholesaled to the revolutionary family. Students responded to the shift in presidential personality and authority in different ways depending on their gender, their ideology, and their goals. Those who resisted either by continuing to organize or by taking up arms experienced the abuse and violence of power. Ex-activists who accepted aspects of the democratic opening were shunned by their peers. Those who were brought back into the fold were rewarded by the

Echeverría administration. Young men were the primary targets of the reform since they had the most to gain from a re-entry into the power structures, but they had the most to lose by their resistance.

The Democratic Opening

From the beginning of his presidential term, Echeverría adopted a more populist stance, and he promoted and acquiesced to many student demands. However, he also manipulated and co-opted student leaders and politicians. For the elite and powerful, the legacy of 1968 played out in the struggle over responsibility for the violence and over the authority to name the culprits which created a strain on relationships between powerful men and the Mexican people. As the government sought to recapture its reputation and gain support, students had to contend with occupied campuses, arrests, and continued violence. Their movement was in a shamble due to the repression and the fear it triggered. Among the remnants of the movement that had survived Tlatelolco, students had to respond to shifts in presidential power and tone and to contend with their own demons from the movement. In the wake of the violence, students were shocked and outraged that a revolt did not follow the massacre.[3] Many students fled from the movement because they feared repression, arrests, incarceration, exile, or death. Consequently, the movement lost momentum once classes resumed.

In 1970, Echeverría became president of Mexico, and the nation's political pendulum swung to the left. Although Echeverría was a reformer, he was tainted by the events that took place in Tlatelolco. Even in 1968, it was acknowledged in Mexico that Echeverría played a key role in the violations of autonomy at the national university and the massacre. As secretary of interior, Echeverría held the power to issue orders to the army, the police, and the granaderos. As documented in the previous chapter as events led toward Tlatelolco, Díaz Ordaz continually referred the students to Echeverría because domestic issues were under his jurisdiction. Once president, Echeverría distanced himself from Díaz Ordaz and the events of the summer of 1968.

Echeverría was the first Mexican president who had moved up the political ranks through the complexities of the Mexican bureaucracy.

He had never held an elected position prior to being president. His bureaucratic career began when he married Guadalupe Zuno Hernández, the daughter of a Jalisco politician. He joined the PRI and held various bureaucratic positions in the party after his marriage. His move to national politics came when his mentor, General Rodolfo Sánchez Taboada, became secretary of the navy and Echeverría, Sánchez's protégé, received the position of director of accounts for the secretariat. From that position, he became chief of staff of the secretary of education. Later, he was undersecretary of interior and finally secretary of interior.[4]

His lack of elected political experience did not hinder his reformist attempts once president. Echeverría saw himself more as a *cardenista*, emulating the reforming government of Lázaro Cárdenas rather than that of his immediate predecessor. Once elected, Echeverría postured as a populist who, as reflected in his domestic policies, was influenced by the ideals of the student movement. His goal was to restore political legitimacy to the presidency and the party.[5] Thus, his administration attempted to address some of the demands of the students. At the same time, Echeverría tried to maintain his own grip on power and PRI hegemony in Mexico. These proved to be difficult tasks. His administration's quixotic and conflicting approaches made Echeverría and his policies appear contradictory.

In the end, Echeverría's administration reflected his own ambitious goals and the influence of the student movement in international policies and in domestic issues. In the international arena, Echeverría seemed influenced by the same people and events that Mexican youth celebrated. Echeverría sought greater power and respect within and outside the country. He visited Fidel Castro in Cuba and Salvador Allende in Chile.[6] He even sent intermediaries to attempt to reach a peace settlement in the Middle East. His activist style may have garnered support from some Mexican youth, but his international and domestic policies did not endear him to the Mexican elite, the business class, or foreign investors. However, many of his policies benefited the educated middle classes. In essence, he directed many of his policies at the generation of 1968.

Although the courting of controversial figures internationally caused a few political ripples, Echeverría's domestic policies triggered a wave of protests. Echeverría, like his intellectual mentor Cárdenas, was trapped between the demands of the people and the resistance of elites and the business class.[7] He hoped to bring forth social and political change in a peaceful context and set out to reform the government to attract those who felt marginalized from the political process. While many scholars and journalists believe that Echeverría was responsible for issuing the order for soldiers to fire on students on October 2, 1968, his administration also initiated contact with both students and the established left.[8] The 1970s reflected the impact of 1968—though the movement seemed crushed—for greater democracy and opposition participation, particularly with the political reforms that culminated in 1979 with the reform that permitted oppositional representation in the Mexican Congress.[9] After the international and national anger over the government's handling of the student movement, the self-proclaimed cardenista Echeverría announced the apertura democrática.[10]

Echeverría's democratic opening attempted to bring back into the PRI fold students, leftists, opposition party members, and women through educational, social, and political reforms. The opening presented some of the disgruntled children of the summer of 1968 a path to return to the revolutionary family through educational access and job opportunities. Echeverría offered educators and intellectuals a place in the Mexican government. Sociologist Pablo González Casanova was appointed rector of UNAM. In 1965, he had published *La democracia en México* which questioned progress and modernization.[11] A leftist intellectual, González's appointment was a nod to student influences in UNAM. Other intellectuals received positions in the president's cabinet such as the famous writer Carlos Fuentes.

To avoid continued greater student unrest, the government also proposed educational reforms. University administrators and politicians wished to avoid another 1968, so they supported the reforms. Echeverría included university faculty and administrators in his cabinet. The government removed obstacles to growth, centralized political and economic relations under local and federal governments, modernized educational administration, and imposed a system of negotiations to resolve conflicts in educational centers.[12] With university reform, Echeverría's administration also provided fellowships for the educated class to undertake postgraduate study abroad. *Consejo Nacional de Ciencias y Tecnología* (National Council of Science and Technology, CONACYT) offered students fellowships to study abroad with the idea that these educated scientists and technocrats would return to Mexico and help modernize and stabilize the country. Moreover, it provided financial support to study abroad or postgraduate studies to the middle class.

Along with educational reforms, public spending increased and new programs were put into place. Ex-activists received positions in the public sector that resulted from increased public spending. Students found opportunities in *Compañía Nacional de Cámaras Industriales* (National Staple Products Corporation, CONASUPO), *Banco Nacional de Crédito Rural* (National Bank of Rural Credit, BANRURAL), *Instituto Mexicano de Protección a la Infancia* (Mexican Institute for Infant Protection, IMPI), and *Instituto Nacional del Fondo para la Vivienda de los Trabajadores* (National Institute of Workers' Housing Fund, INFONAVIT).[13]

University reform led to the establishment of a new university, *Universidad Autónoma Metropolitana* (Metropolitan Autonomous University, UAM), constructed in the 1970s to meet the challenge of the nation's population boom that became another focus of the Echeverría administration. Like UNAM, UAM had high enrollment standards, and it too was autonomous. Some activists from 1968 were hired as faculty members at UAM, including *Consejo Nacional de Huelga* (National Strike Council, CNH) leader Roberto Escudero among many others.[14]

Although Echeverría initiated many reforms, his election laid bare the growing schisms between the political class and the middle class. Voter absenteeism reached an all time high of 58 percent in the 1970 election. However, he won with 85 percent of the vote. Echeverría took office in a time where there was evidence of a rapidly declining economy.[15] His attempts to reach the students and incorporate their demands and issues in his own policies did not result in their entrance or return to the revolutionary family. In fact, many of Echeverría's costly policies did not lead to the return of the prodigal son or daughter, but rather a continued struggle between the contenders of 1968 who continued to interpret, criticize, debate, and challenge one another.

Political Prisoners

Due to low voter turnout, Echeverría lacked the clear political "mandate" of his predecessors. He also faced festering problems in the Federal District due to the student movement, internal migration into the city, and the economic problems. To address the nation's and the city's social, economic, and political issues, Echeverría adopted policies that reflected his acknowledgement of the influence of modernity and the demands of 1968. Immediately after taking office, he addressed students' concerns, particularly their demand for the release of political prisoners. The continued imprisonment of students and other political prisoners from the protests served as a reminder for the continued need to mobilize Mexico City youth.

The existence and plight of political prisoners really emerged in 1969 and 1970 through the use of film. Film documented the lives of prisoners becoming a vehicle to criticize the government and its policies. The film, *2 de octubre*, offered a shocking condemnation of Mexican politics and society.[16] The wife of José Tayde smuggled the small cameras into Lecumberri prison. Tayde had been a representative to the CNH from the Chapingo National Agricultural School. With the cameras, he and other prisoners shot the footage. The documentary served as an example of students' continued resistance to the government and its attempts to bring them back into the revolutionary family. Shot in 1969 with audio and other film footage added later, the film described the international pressure that led to Echeverría releasing some political prisoners.[17] The film reveals the quixotic nature of Echeverría's offer of amnesty and the democratic opening. While recruiting ex-activists into the universities and government, the film claimed that the same administration forced many other students to agree to a gag order in exchange for their freedom.

With the Super 8 cameras, prisoners documented their daily lives, but also their historical struggle. Rather than focusing exclusively on the 1968 movement, the film explored the historical evolution of the student protest by showing clips of peasant uprisings, rail workers' strikes, and earlier student protests. Using images of peasants being executed—perhaps referring to the death of Rubén Jaramillo—the film opened with the following message:[18]

> This film presents images of the social movements that
> occurred from 1958 to 1970. The large anonymous mass of
> workers, peasants, and students are the ones who have
> written the true history of our country.[19]

The film offered startling political images, but an element of the actual student uprising was missing. It referred to struggles of the people, but it excluded women. Women from the student demonstrations were imprisoned in the Women's Prison. They did not appear in the film, and they went unmentioned. They were part of the masses in the real world, but from the images in the film, those that paid for their political activism were men. Instead of being activists, women were portrayed in their traditional roles of mothers and wives. The film did however depict the disruption to family lives. An image of Eli de Gortari carrying his children in his arms during visiting hours behind prison walls reflected the difficulties endured by the families of prisoners. In *2 de octubre*, these images of reunited families mingled with the solitary shots of prisoners gazing out of the window hatches in cell doors.

2 de octubre offered evidence that contradicted the official position that Mexico had no political prisoners. Furthermore, the film revealed the continuing struggle of students. Family and friends of prisoners, those who remained on the outside of the prison, organized to offer their solidarity and support so that the prisoners would not feel forgotten. To guardia activist Carmen Landa, in the wake of October 2, 1968, her visits to prisoners were a vehicle to continue her struggle for the ideals of the movement.[20] Contradicting the visual images of women in traditional roles as depicted in the film, Landa saw her visits as revolutionary.

With images of political prisoners in front of the public and continued denunciations filtering through the various media, President Echeverría set out to address student demands and defuse the potential for continued conflict. In 1969, activists imprisoned in Lecumberri had initiated a hunger strike to draw attention to their continued detainment. In 1970, the student organizers at the national university and the polytechnic university held demonstrations demanding the release of political prisoners during the summer of 1970 perhaps hoping to force President Díaz Ordaz to release the prisoners prior to the elections.[21] Student activists, however, were not successful. On November 12, 1970, Judge Eduardo Ferrer MacGregor handed down harsh sentences to student leaders just a few short weeks before Echeverría took power.[22] The sentences ranged from three to seventeen years. Sócrates Campos Lemus, Gilberto Guevara, Luis González de Alba, José Revueltas, Fausto Trejo, and others—twenty-three activists in total—received sentences of sixteen years. Among the women, CNH members Roberta Avendaño Martínez and Ana Ignacia Rodríguez Márquez were sentenced to sixteen years. Adela Salazar de Castellejos, director of the *Comité de Padres de Familia en Apoyo al Movimiento* (Committee of Parents in Support of the Movement) received a sentence of ten years.[23] *Juventud Comunista Mexicana* (Mexican Communist Youth, JCM) members Arturo Zama Escalante, Felix Coded Andreu, and Rubén Valdespino García received sentences of ten years, while PCM members also got ten years each. Deported foreign activist Mika Seeger, daughter of American folk singer Pete Seeger, was sentenced to three years in absentia.[24]

Along with the four women who received sentences in November of 1970, sixty-five men were sentenced and imprisoned. The condemned included twenty members of the CNH, six from the Comité de luchas, four leaders of the Teacher's Coalition, two leaders of the *Comité de Padres* (Committee of Parents), one from the Assembly of Intellectuals, Artists, and Writers, and fourteen members of the Communist Youth and the Communist Party.[25] What is interesting about the detention and incarceration of PCM and JCM members was that even the CIA recognized that the PCM was not responsible for the violence. A CIA document from October 5, 1968, states, "The PCM has gone on record as endorsing the student demands, but party leaders have privately stated that none of their principal functionaries should become directly involved in the violence."[26]

Shortly after being elected, Echeverría began to free political prisoners thus addressing a key student demand, but also creating an ideological schism between himself and Díaz Ordaz. He freed railroad workers strike leaders Demetrio Vallejo and Valentin Campa from Lecumberri prison. Besides freeing the activists from the railroad workers' strike, Secretary of Interior Mario Moya Palencia and activists began to develop policies to free other prisoners. The possibility of leaving prison created a schism among some of the prisoners. Raúl Alvarez Garín, CNH leader from IPN, explained how students attempted to negotiate with Moya Palencia.

> During March and April, there were a series of meetings with
> Secretary of Interior Moya Palencia to analyze the possibility
> of (some student activists) leaving the country immediately.

> From the prison, we studied the possibility of this option
> and accepted it. . . . We selected a relatively small group of
> compañeros, the ones who had the charges of the greatest
> responsibility and the longest sentences with the idea that if
> this group left the prison and the country they could create
> an untenable situation for the rest of the detained.[27]

Alvarez Garín, Gilberto Guevara Niebla, and Luis Tomás Cervantes Cabeza de Vaca accepted self-exile. These activists had been found guilty of numerous crimes and sentenced to sixteen years in prison in 1969. After their release, Alvarez Garín and the others first went to Peru where the government had authorized visas. The group was eventually expelled from that country to Chile after being under Peruvian police surveillance. They spent the rest of their time in Chile, welcomed by President Salvador Allende; however, the activists encountered other difficulties. They were criticized in Mexico by José Revueltas who published a virulent condemnation of those who chose self-exile. Adding to their troubles, Moya Palencia published a declaration in *Excélsior* that claimed that the activists who fled the country had not been forced to flee. Instead, they had wanted to leave.[28]

The struggle between young men who accepted exile and Revueltas and Moya Palencia reflected class, ideology, and gender constructions of the time. Those students who were imprisoned carefully studied, contemplated, and argued about the offer of exile thinking that from abroad they could draw attention to political prisoners and bring pressure for their release.[29] As a group, they chose the activists that would go into exile. Unfortunately, they had again misread the government's ability to rally the press and public sentiment in its favor. The student exiles also felt betrayed by one of their mentors in the left: Revueltas had attacked them as traitors to the cause and to the new left. However, once the exiled activists returned to Mexico, they arrived just in time for a new student uprising.[30]

Usually donning his *guayabera*, Echeverría postured to be more leftist than his predecessors in his foreign and domestic policies; however, his administration still encountered opposition from students outside the prison walls. In 1971, students in Mexico City organized another movement. By this time, some fifty ex-activists had been released from prison. An event that occurred in the northern Mexico, however, was what provided ex-activists an opportunity to re-group and try to re-assert the ideals of 1968.

Los Halcones:
The Corpus Christi Massacre of 1971

When the exiles, Salvador Martínez della Roca, Cervantes Cabeza de Vaca, Alvarez Garín, Federico Emey, and Guevara Niebla, returned to Mexico, the educational system was rapidly changing because of the reforms introduced by the Echeverría administration. On June 4, activists and students gathered in the Che Guevara auditorium at UNAM to welcome the returning exiles. They were greeted by three standing ovations. However, in the state of Nuevo León, an event offered the ex-activists the occasion they sought to mobilize the students. The re-emergence of the movement tested the Echeverría administration's rhetoric of *cardenismo* and shifts in state power.

In March of 1971, the governor of Nuevo León, Eduardo Elizondo found himself immersed in a university struggle at the University of Nuevo León located in the industrial city of Monterrey. There, in the center of the nation's conservative business community, the university had been a center of contention among educators, state officials, and the business community. Internally, rightist and leftist students were vying for control of the institution leading to the resignation of the rector.[31] Although a new rector was elected, Governor Elizondo intervened changing the administrating body from one similar to UNAM, containing representation from various sectors of the university population, to a popular assembly that included workers, peasants, and business people. Thus, people from outside of the university had greater control. Elizondo was governor and a PRI member, and he maintained his privilege to appoint the new university governing assembly.[32] Although the popular representation may have seemed positive to some activists, the university community disavowed the plan because Elizondo appointed PRI party members and conservatives to positions. To the university community, Elizondo was in violation of the university's autonomy. Elizondo's hopes of gaining further control of the institution set into motion a series of political machinations of intra-elite power struggles between national PRIistas and those from Nuevo León. The result was casualties within the PRI as well as among youth.[33]

Provoked by these events in Monterrey, students in Mexico City involved in the *Coordinador de Comités de Lucha* (Coordinator of the Committees of Struggle, Coco)—comprised of 1968 left-leaning activists—decided to stage a demonstration against PRI involvement in university life, whether in Nuevo León or in Mexico City.[34] The students demanded that the government must not intervene in any autonomous university, whether it received state or national revenues. As students were in their planning stage, Echeverría had sent one of his men to Nuevo León to ensure that Elizondo did not institute his plan for hand-picked university leadership because he feared another student rebellion. Echeverría was successful in crushing Elizondo's plan and Elizondo resigned on June 4. On June 5, Luis M. Farias, a federal senator from Nuevo León, became the governor.[35] Farias recognized a new rector and university autonomy. According to the U.S. Consul in Monterrey, conservatives who thought they had been victorious in gaining some control at the university were shocked by the granting of autonomy. It was widely believed in the city that the new rector, Trevino Garza was forced to resign. Moreover, the Consul contended that future problems could emerge in the city.[36]

In Mexico City, students held the march anyway. They wanted to express solidarity with textile workers on strike by advocating union democracy and demanding a halt to charrismo. They also showed their continued support for university autonomy. Lastly, they demanded freedom for political prisoners.[37] With the return of exiled activists, June 10, 1971 was a perfect time to resurrect the student movement. Activists and scholars alike have recognized the decision to hold the march was a tactical error because Echeverría had already solved the problem with the support of UNAM Rector González Casanova. Furthermore, the students did not have the type of encompassing agenda that they did in 1968 that could garner further support from people outside the university in the Federal District.[38]

As students marched from Instituto Politechnico Nacional (National Polytechnic Institute) Casco de Santo Tomás campus in Mexico City around 5:00 P.M. on June 10, young men armed with clubs attacked demonstrators and onlookers on the streets of San Cosme. The police did

Figure 14: Clash between halcones and students on June 10, 1971. Colección Universidad Sección: Movimientos Estudiantiles, AHUNAM-CESU, Folio 4634.1.

not intervene, and the *halcones* (falcons) continued to beat the demonstrators in the streets and in surrounding buildings (See Figure 14). The halcones were a paramilitary group trained in martial arts in the *Escuela de Policía* (Police Academy) under the direction of the government of the Federal District. The 1,500 cadets were paid during their training.[39] As halcones' statements reveal, they were recruited and trained in Japanese martial arts for the purpose of quelling riots.[40] Halcones, led by martial arts expert Candelario Madera Paz, arrived at the demonstration in bulletproof school buses and then clashed with students. Street fighting continued for hours on June 10, and tanks were sent to clear the Zócalo and city center. *Excélsior* reported that students were assaulted as they marched singing the National Anthem.[41]

While students were beaten, reporters covering the clash reported that the military blocked the Green Cross (emergency medical assistance) from entering the area to help the injured. Echeverría later claimed he had absolutely no contact with the halcones, and the Regent of the Federal District Alfonso Martínez Domínguez vehemently denied that any such group—"*halcones, charros, or gorillas*"—was employed by the police.[42] In the news reports that followed, journalists criticized the

Mexican government because reporters were beaten during the attack.[43] Many people suspected that—despite his denials—Echeverría was tied to the halcones because of his role in 1968. One theory alleged that a more conservative faction of the PRI wished to humiliate the cardenista Echeverría and his social programs by using the halcones. Recent documents show, however, that the former proposed theory was true. The halcones had existed before the 1970s. In a document addressed to Echeverría dated September 25, 1969, he was informed of the number of halcones who received payment during their "studies" at the police academy.[44]

At a press conference following the violence, a journalist for *Excélsior* asked Mayor Martínez Domínguez, "Don't you think, Regent, that this situation is very similar to that of 1968?" Martínez Domínguez shunned the question and instead focused on how the city should continue to operate and how it could guarantee rights for everyone. Martínez Domínguez blamed students for the violence, saying that student groups existed to "provoke disorder, provoke the authority, and to provoke one another to alter the public peace."[45] As in 1968, students were held responsible for the violence and for the government's response.

The use of the halcones on June 10 was both a success and fiasco for Echeverría. In the end, Martínez Domínguez, the attorney general, and the police chief all resigned under pressure, something that had not happened in 1968. As with the 1968 student movement and Díaz Ordaz, Echeverría effectively distanced himself from the violence and from those who were held responsible. Exercising executive power, he forced others to accept blame for June 10 so that he could still appear to be the champion of the students. Mexican political analyst Samuel Schmidt argued that Echeverría used the June 10 incident to rid himself of political competition from Martínez Domínguez. The halcones incident offered Echeverría an excellent vehicle to enhance his authority and power. By expunging himself of all blame, perhaps the president thought he could wash away the blood and his complicity in 1968. Echeverría also used the incident as a political maneuver. He and he alone, he seemed to say, was saving Mexico from fascist and militarist forces evidenced by the actions of Elizondo, Martínez, and the halcones. However, his ability to ensure a veil of silence failed.

Eight years after the halcones incident, ex-Mexico City Mayor Martínez Domínguez gave Heberto Castillo an interview that rocked

Mexico. Castillo seemed to be an unlikely choice for Martínez Domínguez, as an informant, to choose to publicize his story. Castillo had led the Teacher's Coalition during the 1968 student movement, and he had been an anti-PRI activist for many years. In the 1979 interview, Martínez Domínguez asserted that he had been forced to resign by Echeverría, and after 1971, the Nuevo León native saw his political star decline. In 1979, Martinez Domínguez returned to politics and ran for governor of the state of Nuevo León, thus he offered an interview with Castillo for the news magazine *Proceso*. In turn, he created a fervor for the truth.[46]

In 1971, Martínez Domínguez was called to a meeting at Los Pinos (Mexican presidential home) to discuss the approaching demonstration. At this gathering, he told Castillo that he argued for restraint, but Echeverría saw the march as an opportunity to centralize his authority and control. Martínez Domínguez and other high-level politicians were at Los Pinos when the riots took place. He stated that Echeverría took phone calls during the meetings, and the president stated in one, "Burn the bodies so that nothing remains. Don't permit photos." Martínez Domínguez described Echeverría's response as "blood chilling."[47]

In response to Castillo's questions about his resignation, Martínez Domínguez stated that Echeverría forced him to speak to the press and to create an illusion of popular support. Echeverría briefed him on his responses to the press, which included denials of the existence of the halcones and an announcement of an investigation into the violence. Following the press conferences, Martínez Domínguez had to organize a demonstration that supported Echeverría's position since he was a PRI party leader as well as the directors of the *Confederación Nacional de Organizaciones Populares* (National Confederation of Popular Organizations, CNOP). The march took place, and Echverría assured 500,000 demonstrators that "the right to dissent is the essence of democracy."[48] Meanwhile Echeverría continued to argue publicly that the groups responsible for the violence were foreign-influenced. The Mexico Attorney General's office issued bulletins insisting that students were fighting among themselves.[49] The same day as the pro-government demonstration, Martínez Domínguez resigned, stating that he did not want to be an obstacle to the investigation, but many believed he had resigned because he was responsible for the violence.

What was striking about the Martínez Domínguez interview and the subsequent fallout was the schizophrenic political machinations of Echeverría. Echeverría used the same old accusations about foreign interlopers and instigators among student activists, but he needed a show of support when he proclaimed that dissent was part of the beauty of democracy. Echeverría manipulated and betrayed members of his own party, whether the governor of Monterrey or the PRI president who had supported his presidential candidacy. He intervened in Monterrey on the side of the students, but turned around a few days later and gave the orders to the halcones to attack students in the Federal District. A U.S. State Department report at the time refers to Echeverría as an egomaniac who was dismayed by the fact that the students continued to defy him despite his efforts to appease them. The report states: "Possibly out of anger over the fact that the students insisted on demonstrating even after he had gone to great lengths to meet their aspirations, Echverría may well have given his blessing to the use of the group against the IPN demonstrators."[50] On the one hand, Echeverría argued that the suppression of the demonstration was necessary to restore legitimacy to the president and popular forces as well as to progress the democratic opening. On the other hand, he used the march to clean house of potential political competitors such as Martínez Domínguez.[51]

Harkening back to 1968, Echeverría used the power of his position and status as president in a brutal fashion when dealing with Mexican youth. On June 10, 1971, Echeverría manipulated both students and halcones. During his administration, he had addressed many of the student demands. He had developed programs that offered ex-activists positions. He had appointed university officials to government posts and had placed administrators in UNAM that were more acceptable to students. He also held meetings with student leaders. His actions on June 10, however, showed that he also viewed students as politically expendable if a crisis of power emerged. The students were masses placated or manipulated when politically necessary.[52]

The summer of the halcones reflects another form of the manipulation of masculinity and power. As in 1968, young men were controlled by highly placed authorities to attack other young men and women who dared to criticize the regime. As some 1968 male activists had been co-opted into the Echeverría democratic opening, others found that they were still a threat to the president. The halcones too found that they could not rely on the benevolence of the president. After doing the bidding of the government on June 10, the halcones discovered the extent of their usefulness to Echeverría. The halcones were never adequately rewarded for their attempts to maintain the revolutionary family's control over Mexico though they were recruited from PRI supporters.[53] Like the granaderos during 1968, young men who supported the government were disposable once they had served their usefulness. The halcones were disbanded by January 1972. Each member was provided an indemnity of five thousand pesos. After their separation from service, some could not find employment, so they resorted to crime such as bank robbery, during the same period that guerrillas in the north were kidnapping and ransoming business people.[54] Thus, the alleged activities of ex-halcones may have been conflated in news stories with those of the guerrillas. At the same time, halcones who had turned to a life of crime to support themselves may have used the activities of the guerrilla movements as a cover. Additionally, the crimes of the halcones in the cities supported the government's claims about rural and urban attempts to stifle the progress of the revolution.

The 1971 movement was an attempt to recapture the ideals of 1968. Specifically, focused on university politics, demonstrators demanded that university autonomy be respected. Students also continued to demand their rights guaranteed under the Mexican Constitution. The attack on students on June 10, 1971, exemplified the government's continued willingness to use force to maintain a political monopoly. Echeverría may have been reaching out to students and allowing greater democratic freedom at some level, but the culpability of his administration in the June 10 incident revealed that the president and certain sectors of the PRI demanded the right to arbitrate which civil liberties would be respected and which voices would be heard. The Corpus Christi Massacre of June 10, 1971, displayed the internal strife within the PRI that emerged in the wake of the 1968 Mexican student movement. As powerful men battled one another over the government's response to students and their demands, young people sought ways to perpetuate the ideals of 1968. Some sought continuity through social protests, but others adopted a more direct approach, an eye for an eye.

Going to the People and the Dirty War

After 1968, the student protests dwindled, prisoners remained in prison, and other students fled the country to avoid arrest and incarceration.[55] The response to the repression on October 2, 1968, was not rage, but silence. The silence that immediately followed the movement also seemed to permeate the politics of Mexico. A revolution did not begin on October 3, 1968. Instead, political machinations and discussions took place behind closed doors. There was no public dialogue, only a steely silence. In his analysis of the silence of the revolutionary family, the PRI, and government officials in the wake of the massacre, 1968 activist Arturo Warman suggested, "The explanation for the silence in the family, one has to know the nature of the beast: the confirmation of the political system and its traditions."[56] Silence eventually became acceptance. Nevertheless, some students found it impossible to accept the silence of the powerful and set out to undermine it or, in the most extreme cases, destroy it.

As previously discussed in Chapter Four, there existed a "hard-line" and a "soft-line" in the student movement. The hard-line advocated direct action and, in some cases, armed response. In the wake of October 2, some members of the hard-line, particularly those students affiliated with the Communist Youth and other leftist groups embraced armed struggle. Hardliners had unsuccessfully demanded that the students escalate the conflict to urban warfare prior to and after October 2, 1968, but certain students followed this line of thought and joined guerrilla movements in the north and in the urban centers of Mexico after 1968.[57] To avoid imprisonment, some activists went to the mountains in northern Mexico; others "to the people," where they worked as union organizers or rural teachers; while others simply fled Mexico to wonder what happened. After the June 10, 1971, incident, a new wave of activists decided guerrilla movements were an appropriate response to state-sponsored violence.

Revolutionary activity was not new to Mexico. The modern Mexican government sprang from the social revolution that began in 1910. Indeed, the government continued to celebrate revolutionary figures. Those revolutionary figures, particularly Emiliano Zapata and Pancho Villa, may have been enshrined in the official nationalistic rhetoric of the nation and in public monuments, but their ideals and the areas where they struggled became hot points again in the 1970s. After 1968, urban and rural guerrilla warfare emerged. Both forms attracted and drew ex-activists from 1968. Educated children of the bourgeoisie abandoned their comfortable lives to head to the mountains, following the examples of Fidel Castro and Che Guevara, or to go underground in urban centers. President Echeverría's attempts to mitigate student concerns and to co-opt them into the government did not succeed with all ex-activists. During his administration, youth still rebelled against his role as revolutionary patriarch. This time, however, the attacks became more violent, and for Echeverría, more personal.

Since the 1960s, various rural guerilla groups had been operated in Mexico. One that became influential existed in the northern state of Chihuahua. Rural professor Arturo Gamíz and medical doctor Pablo Gómez were influenced by the Cuban Revolution as a model to fight corruption and challenge government policies. Gamíz had been a student activist at the IPN in the 1950s, and he had been forcibly removed from Poli on September 23, 1956.[58] In the 1960s, Gamíz and Gómez had worked with rural organizations for self-defense in land issues.[59] They were further concerned by the closing of rural schools and the reduction of student scholarships.[60] On September 23, 1965, they issued a statement directly confronting the constant corruption in the Chihuahuan state government. The following day, a group led by Gamíz and Gómez assaulted the Madera military compound; both of these leaders as well as six soldiers perished in the resulting battle. It was a suicide assault like Castro's July 26, 1953, attack on the Moncada barracks; however, a guerrilla group that emerged in the late 1960s and early 1970s would embrace Gamíz and Gómez's ideology.

Other militant groups were also active. In 1965, Victor Rico Galán did a story on Gamíz and Goméz. He was greatly influenced by the story he covered in Chihuahua. In 1967, Rico Galán, journalist for *Sucesos* and later *Siempre*, was accused of organizing an urban guerrilla school. Subsequently, he was arrested and imprisoned for that alleged crime. By April 1968, the Mexican government had recognized four guerrilla groups that it identified as "Pro-Chinese."[61] One of the most recognized groups was that associated with Genaro Vázquez Rojas, which operated in the state of Guerrero. According to the Mexican government, this organization used methods of kidnapping to make public their political demands. Vázquez Rojas explicitly stated their demands:

1. The abolishment of the capitalist oligarchy and pro-
   imperialist government;
2. The establishment of a coalition government composed of workers; peasants, students, intellectuals,
   and teachers;
3. Achievement of a plan of political and economic independence for Mexico;
4. The institution of a new social order of life that benefits
   the majority of workers in the country.[62]

Vázquez Rojas was the leader of *Comité Cívico Guerrerense* (Civic Committee of the People of Guerrero) that combated government corruption, poverty, and violence in the state of Guerrero. During the 1960s, the state of Guerrero was a hotbed of activity with groups led by Vázquez Rojas and Lucio Cabañas of the *Partido de los Pobres* (Party of the Poor).[63] These groups were led by educators, and students joined in rural struggle. Vázquez Rojas and Cabañas served as intellectual mentors to disenchanted youth from 1968 who knew about the struggle in the mountains of Guerrero.[64]

With rural revolts in Guerrero and Chihuahua, emerging urban guerrilla groups had learned lessons from their Mexican as well as international peers. Various groups emerged throughout Mexico. Some had ties to the student left and student movement in Mexico City, others emerged from young people in the north who became radicalized by working with the poor. In Monterrey, Ignacio Salas Obregón, a student from *Instituto Tecnológico de Monterrey* (Technological Institute of Monterrey) and activist in the Professional Student Movement, a lay Catholic organization, came into contact with communists while working with urban poor. Salas Obregón would lead a number of activists into armed struggle.

Other groups such as *Frente Revolucionario Estudiantil* (Revolutionary Student Front, FER) drew students and ex-activists from urban cores in Guadalajara. The FER and *Frente Revolucionario de Acción Popular* (Popular Action Revolutionary Front, FRAP) embarrassed and humiliated Echeverría by kidnapping the American consul in Guadalajara Terrance

George Leonhardy. This led to criticism of Echeverría from the U.S. government.[65] Far worse, FRAP dealt a brutal personal blow to Echeverría by kidnapping his father-in-law José Guadalupe Zuno. In turn, the FER and ERAP became targets of the Mexican government, and Mexico began its own Dirty War characterized by secret military and police campaigns against these guerrilla organizations. To combat the guerrillas, the Mexican government permitted the use of torture and murder.

In 1973, various guerrilla groups formed the *Liga Comunista de 23 de septiembre* (Communist League of September 23, LC-23), led by Salas Obregón.[66] LC-23 took its name from the 1965 guerrilla assault on the military compound in Chihuahua that was led by Gamíz and Gómez. By the early 1970s, LC-23, as well as other guerrilla groups, were kidnapping and holding business leaders hostage for money to finance their actions.[67] The LC-23's kidnapping and murder of Eugenio Garza Sada, a prominent Monterrey businessman, did not help the Echeverría administration's reputation among business elites of northern Mexico.[68] Documents reveal that the government had infiltrated what became LC-23, knowing that it had ties not only to communist youth but to Christian Democrats. Later, the government linked the LC-23 with ex-activists from 1968.[69]

The guerrillas targeted politicians, business people, and even Echeverría's family. Some guerrilla groups also attacked politically and physically student activists who embraced non-violent approaches. Thus, the armed guerrillas created further factions among ex-activists through certain acts of violence and vengeance. In an interview eight years after Tlatelolco, Raúl Alvarez argued that FER and FRAP, and "*Los Enfermos de Sinaloa*" ("The Sick Ones of Sinaloa"), drew greater support from the moral and political demoralization that took place in 1970s Mexico. Furthermore, FER, FRAP, and Los Enfermos saw reformist activists that worked to promote democratic actions as ineffectual because of the continued violence against students when they engage in formal political dissent.

This ideology led to the murder of leftist activists. Gilberto Guevara Niebla recalled in an interview the murder of a professor who was affiliated with the Communist Party. Guevara Niebla stated: "A professor of the Communist Party, Rojas, who had been a student leader in Monterrey, was looking at a book in the library where he worked; the guerrillas came in and killed him. He was a very respected man in the university." Another professor, Peralta, was murdered in northern Mexico while giving classes. He, too, had been a leftist activist, but his death was celebrated by guerillas as "one less pig."[70] Guevara Niebla and other activists had much to fear from the guerrilla groups themselves. In particular, Los Enfermos were a militant group that targeted leftists, who in their view, had been co-opted.[71] The existence of these groups and their attack on activists revealed a growing ideological schism within the generation of 1968.

The rise of LC-23 and other guerrilla groups and their ability to strike close to the president led to Mexico's Dirty War. On the one hand, students and ex-activists with fellowships, bureaucratic positions, and educational appointments were enticed to join to support the government. At the same time, the government brutally dealt with those who did not willingly return to the revolutionary family. Under Echeverría, disappearances and state-sponsored torture became tools of control to ensure the democratic opening resulting in the murder of at least 275 people, if not 1,500, including the intellectual architects of LC-23.[72] The government considered youth suspect and dangerous, as it did in 1968. Although the government viewed youth as a threat, ex-activists were their own enemies within the movement. As in the United States, France, Italy, and Germany, student armed fronts de-legitimized the demands of other students for reforms. Activists who wanted democratic reform found themselves not only seen as enemies of the state, but also as enemies of their ex-comrades in the armed left.

With the initiation of various guerrilla movements and a growing fear of insurrection, Mexico reacted similarly to other Latin American nations. Fear of the left and of guerilla insurrection, whether real or imaginary, provided the background to the military coups in Brazil, Chile, and Argentina. The Mexican government waged a low-intensity war against guerrillas, particularly in northern Mexico.[73] Arrests of known activists of 1968 continued throughout the late 1960s and early 1970s. The government also continued to monitor university campuses, ensuring that students did not organize.[74] Thus, a Mexican Dirty War emerged in which ex-activists of 1968 still engaged in politicized work found themselves targets of attack.[75] With the kidnappings and growth of guerrilla groups, the government became suspicious of civilians involved in protests leading to growing human rights violations.[76]

Because of the violence, Echeverría dealt harshly with even peaceful critics of his policies. Thus, when peasants and workers demonstrated, they were attacked by government forces. The democratic opening actually closed to some.

In summary, the 1968 student movement and the guerrilla movements of the 1960s and 1970s exposed the fragility of the power of the ruling party and also the president. Although the student movement was demoralized by the events of October 2, students continued to question the authority of presidents Díaz Ordaz and Luis Echeverría. Echeverría's attempts to co-opt students may have been successful with some ex-activists, but the violence that broke out in the late 1960s and 1970s shows that the patriarchs still could not control all of the children of the revolution. In 1975, when Echeverría went to give a talk at UNAM, he was attacked by the students and forced to flee.[77] All of his attempts to bring youth back into the revolutionary fold and to the PRI had failed to quiet the protests. The experience of young people on the streets of Mexico City during the summer months of 1968 contributed to an ideological shift in how politics and the political functioned in Mexico. The massacre on October 2, 1968, that was supposed to be a show of force and power by the government, instead ensured that politicized Mexican students continued to agitate for changes at the university, in politics, and in society.

Chapter Six

LA NUEVA OLA:
Gender Rebels

If some ex-activists selected the path of the guerrilla, other activists adopted a different approach that proved no less revolutionary in its impact on Mexico in the decade following the 1968 student movement. Many young educated women who participated in the 1968 movement had been politicized by their experiences. Women who mobilized in 1968 were politically and socially transformed. In the guardias, lightning brigades, meetings, and demonstrations, women and their male comrades considered various political ideas whether it was democracy, Marxism, revolution, or freedom. Women activists considered political and social ideas in the movement, but these ideas did not stay confined to the movement. In the early 1970s, ideas of liberation seeped into personal relations.

A new wave of feminism had erupted in Europe and the United States. In the early 1970s, this new wave of Mexican feminism grew from the cultural shifts that had occurred during the 1960s and 1970s. Young women were influenced by the rise of youth culture and their involvement in the student protests that politicized their views of Mexico. Like the 1968 Mexican student movement itself, Mexican feminism was also influenced by events that took place beyond the nation's borders but also within the country itself. Women of the generation of 1968 questioned gender and power and applied theories of democracy and liberation that they learned on the streets in 1968 and 1971 to their own lives.

On the surface, Mexican gender relations seemed very rigid, circumscribed by concepts of masculine dominance and feminine submissiveness. Although Mexican society, as all societies, was structured by concepts of traditional gender, Mexico has had a long history of gender rebels. In the early twentieth century, women participated in the resistance against Mexican dictator Porfirio Díaz (1876–80, 1884–1911), they founded political journals for women, and they fought in the Mexican Revolution.[1] In the midst of the Mexican Revolution, women gathered for the first feminist conference in the Yucatan in 1915 where they debated concepts of gender equality and access to work.[2] Although women did not gain the vote in the wake of the revolution, women continued to organize until they were successful in 1953.

The history of Mexican feminism combined with nascent ideas and images of contemporary international feminism in the 1960s and 1970s. These new ideas reached women in Mexico through the publications of intellectuals and journalists. In 1968, the media had portrayed the internationalism of the student protests throughout the world. In the 1970s, the international feminist movement also received heavy media exposure. In 1970 two influential Mexican writers opened a new topic for discussion: feminism. Rosario Castellanos in the newspaper *Excélsior* and Marta Acevedo in the cultural magazine *Siempre* reported on the emergence of a new wave of feminism in the United States.

Castellanos wrote an influential editorial piece for *Excélsior* on September 5, 1970, that covered a domestic workers' strike in the United States in which feminists joined strikers in solidarity.[3] This strike focused on labor issues, but Castellanos used the strike to question concepts of Mexican femininity. Castellanos juxtaposed her support of the strike with a discussion of the position of women—all of whom she viewed as domestic workers. As "professional" domestic work was unprotected, so too, was the work of a housewife and/or mother. Through a discussion of one American incident, Castellanos opened the door to more feminist discussion that rapidly followed.

A well-known Mexican writer, Castellanos saw the strike and the rise of the feminist movement in the United States as a contextually rich incident that could apply to Mexico. Using the theories of Mexican cultural critic Samuel Ramos, who argued that Mexicans were excellent at mimicking other countries' political, economic, and social institutions, Castellanos asked, "If we imitate all other things, why do we not imitate this movement? Is it that there are no women among us?"[4] Using the model of the domestic servant to represent all women, Castellanos went on to criticize the lack of mimicry in this respect with the question, "Is it because of the appearance of the Virgin of Guadalupe that we have nothing in common with other nations? Here [in Mexico], feminine nature is so natural that it has attained...all its necessities and goals?"[5] Castellanos questioned whether women were content with the way in which Mexican society was organized. She urged Mexican women to awaken to the contradictions that existed between women and men and that ultimately extended into the workplace.[6] She ended her discussion with a call for women's equal participation in society.

Later in September 1970, the cultural newspaper *Siempre's* weekly insert, *La cultura en México*, published a report by Marta Acevedo on a demonstration held in San Francisco, California, that commemorated the fiftieth anniversary of women's suffrage.[7] While Castellanos wrote about women organizing in solidarity with domestic workers, Acevedo went a step beyond to explicitly outline the need for Mexican women to develop feminist consciousness. From this consciousness, she argued, women could promote changes in their lives through feminist organization. Like Castellanos' piece, *Fem* magazine reported in a history of Mexican feminism that Acevedo's article created, "enthusiasm, curiosity...desire to organize a movement in Mexico."[8]

By covering the demonstration, Acevedo incorporated aspects of U.S. feminist thought and its criticism of contemporary society, and she applied these to Mexican society. Acevedo opened her piece with Judith Brady's "I want a wife," which sarcastically discussed how wonderful it would be to have a wife. A wife remains monogamous, does not nag, does not engage in intellectual pursuits, and never asks questions. Acevedo quoted Brady's conclusion, "*Dios mío, quién no quiere una esposa!*" (My God, who wouldn't want a wife!).[9] Besides taking on the myth of the wife, Acevedo revealed the diversity of the feminist movement in the United States. She reported on the appearances in San Francisco of Carmen Alegría, who spoke for Chicanas, and Julia Hare, who represented "Gay Women," as well as women who represented groups like the National Organization for Women.[10] She also noted the participation and presence of men in the demonstration. Some had attended with their wives or girlfriends, while others worked in neighboring offices.

Departing from her discussion about the U.S. feminist movement, Acevedo spoke about the general experience of women. Embracing the theories of Ernst Mandel, Friedrich Engels, and other Marxist theorists, she, like Castellanos, criticized women's place within the workforce. Acevedo also examined the construction of a "wife" in a section titled "The Perfect Woman." Here she described a housewife as an "educator, laundress, cook, administrator, public relations officer, and sexual being."[11] She placed her analysis on sexual relations between men and women in a Marxist paradigm. She claimed that the purpose of monogamy was to ensure male supremacy and that neither partner ever contracts a marriage exclusively for love.[12] Acevedo concluded her article with a call to organize. She stated that the liberation of women in Latin America must come from an analysis of their situations, and that women must develop radical language and action to criticize the system that has been in place. She stated: "The decision to change is slow until every woman develops a consciousness of her potential and is ready to collectively resolve her problems and demonstrate her creative capacity, not only in maternity, but in all acts of life."[13]

With the work of Castellanos and Acevedo—two pieces of early feminist criticism in the national press—other voices soon joined the emerging feminist discourse. A group called Unión de Mujeres (Union of Women) formed among Acevedo and her friends in the Federal District. By March of 1971, these women planned their first action, a demonstration on Mother's Day to counter myths of motherhood. Following Acevedo's lead, these women hoped to publicly criticize how the veneration of the biological function of women is used to cover up oppression.[14] By April, this group had a new name: *Mujeres en Acción Solidaria* (Women in Solidarity Action, MAS).

The name MAS was adapted more out of accident than ideology when member Magdalena Zapian, a member of Unión de Mujeres, inquired about a permit for a demonstration. A bureaucrat from the Federal District who processed the paper asked Zapian who was hosting the demonstration and the purpose of the meeting. Zapian informed the bureaucrat that it was a festival of music and theater. When asked the name of the organization sponsoring the event, she gave the name MAS. For some reason, the bureaucrat assumed that this was not a feminist action. Somehow, rumors spread that this "action" was a "celebration of mothers." When the demonstration began, miniskirt-clad Las Señoritas de México and representatives from Channel 2 attended to televise the celebration of mothers.[15] That type of demonstration was not exactly what MAS had envisioned.

MAS members who went to the meeting and women who saw the coverage found the presence of Las Señoritas frustrating because they were there celebrating mothers while flaunting feminine wiles for the cameras. Attention was diverted from MAS members to these young women who were paid models, whose presence mocked the purpose of the event. The Mother's Day demonstration was not a mass action. Only fifteen MAS members actually attended, while another 150 people were spectators.[16] Many women who did not attend situated the beginning of the feminist movement in Mexico at the Mother's Day protest. Perhaps the reason for this was that the event was covered in the press and on television, thus women who did not attend saw the coverage on television or read about it in the newspaper. The demonstration sparked other feminist actions.[17] Though the La Señoritas women were present, the televised coverage allowed certain feminist statements to be circulated. In the televised coverage, there was an interview with a woman who stated that, "Behind every Mexican macho, there is a sacrificing mother" (*Detrás de cada macho mexicano hay una madrecita abnegada*).[18]

The statement reflected a small change in consciousness among some women present at the demonstration and among those women who recalled hearing this statement that contained a number of meanings.[19] A macho is the public face of masculinity, the opposite of the self-sacrificing and private woman. The macho is violent, demanding, and self-serving; however, he is also the protector of family honor. The anonymous woman's statement, as well as the demonstration on Mother's Day, became part of the collective memory of the new wave of feminism in Mexico. As recent historical works show, the use of events—whether one was a participant or not—constructs the memory of the past.[20] In the twentieth anniversary issue of the feminist magazine *fem*, the editors discussed the Mother's Day statement on machos thus positioning its centrality in the history of Mexican feminism. Activists of 1968 Aída González, Carmen Landa, and Lilian Liebermann recalled this statement as significant in marking the evolving consciousness of Mexican women. An example of how the event and the comment entered the social memory came up in interviews where women recalled the incident. Liebermann, who later joined MAS, recalled the statement "a macho is not born, he is created" showed that the macho's mother, father, and other family members were responsible for creating women's oppressors.[21] Many women saw in this statement that men enjoyed an elevated position in the family simply because they were men, and both women and men contributed to this arrangement.[22] Thus, according to this perspective, at times women conspired against themselves and their daughters by elevating their husbands and sons.

The acknowledgment and recognition that women contributed to the creation of machos and therefore to their own oppression led some to address the need to change. The macho represents more than just the man in the household. As in the works of Samuel Ramos, Octavio Paz, and Oscar Lewis, machismo, in its social construction, served to structure Mexican society in a traditional manner in which the man is public, outspoken, boisterous, and controlling.[23] The woman, as a compliant complement to the macho, is supposed to be private, self-deprecating, and self-sacrificing. These constructions of masculine and feminine roles permeated Mexican society and formally dictated relations between men and women. With the writings of Castellanos and Acevedo and the demonstration on Mother's Day, the consciousness of many women grew, leading to the organization of feminist groups and resulting in individual and societal change. Like the student riots of July 26 that sparked the student movement of 1968, the MAS demonstration ignited the modern feminist movement.

While MAS gained some publicity, the emerging feminist movement needed another event to coalesce. That event came in November 1971 and brought many ex-activists from 1968 and 1971 to the new social movement. The *Facultad de Ciencias Políticas y Sociales* (School of Political and Social Sciences) at UNAM organized a conference and invited feminist writer and cultural critic Susan Sontag to speak.[24] Many women attended the event.[25] As described by attendees, Sontag spoke about how the personal is political, building upon women's emerging consciousness regarding the power relations between the sexes.[26] While Sontag spoke, a young woman passed around a notebook with a statement signed by MAS: "If you want to attend a feminist meeting, write your name and phone number."[27]

The meeting with Sontag and the creation of a sign-up list were very important in the emergence of the new wave of feminism in Mexico.

Women who attended noted that this was the first time they had heard a woman speak specifically about politics as something more than class struggle. As one woman explained, "political was also the sexual relations with men, the relations with your parents, the childhood of your children, the relation between women, etc; political was all those relations, concrete and ordinary, that signified power."[28] Most important for the future, the lecture provided MAS a large organizing event that brought young women into the organization.

In her speech, Sontag discussed the changing boundaries of the political; a theme many young Mexican activists had come to know first hand. During the 1968 student movement, many young women had been mobilized. Most continued to perform many of the same chores that women had always performed in social and political movements. They prepared coffee, provided secretarial skills, and listened to male speakers in the assembly.[29] Nevertheless, after the massacre at Tlatelolco, women of the generation of 1968 in Mexico City wondered if there was more to the ideas that influenced the movement. They questioned how democracy and liberation translated into everyday life. Their increasing desire to discuss feminism and the changing notions of what was political grew and became transformative.

After the Sontag meeting, women who had attended her presentation and signed the MAS sheet formed two feminist discussion groups, one in the north of the city and one in the south. Each group had approximately seventy-five members. In these groups, women discussed the problems of daily life and women's oppression in the home and under capitalism. The two groups served as a vehicle for raising consciousness and for discussing feminist issues. Acevedo was active in the southern group, close to UNAM; consequently, it became more radical than the northern one.[30] The southern group, due to its proximity to UNAM, had close ties to the organized left since the university was still a hotbed of leftist activity. These two feminist groups jointly organized meetings outside the Federal District to include other women in the discussions and to raise the consciousness of other women. This led to women in other parts of Mexico holding conferences and assemblies to discuss feminism in the early part of 1972.[31] While the Federal District saw the most activity, the idea of feminism was spreading to the provinces in the form of conferences and meetings between women.

Throughout 1972 and 1973, MAS was very active, holding conferences in the states of Zacatecas, San Luis Potosí, Morelia, Guanajuato, Jalapa, and Chihuahua. Members also supported worker's strikes and became active in independent unions. In 1972, MAS produced *Ser or no ser*, its own feminist bulletin. As suggested by Acevedo's earlier writing, MAS would remain Marxist in its approach. In August 1972, the group published "La situación de la mujer en México (The Situation of the Mexican Woman)" in *Punto Crítico*, a journal founded by ex-1968 activist and CNH member Raúl Alvarez Garín.[32] The article applied Marxist analysis to examine the economic and social position of women in Mexico.[33]

In the months that followed, MAS addressed many issues that were concerns of women; however, rifts developed over political ideology. Although MAS held conferences on "The Condition of Women," "Abortion and Sexuality," and "Feminism and Politics" at the Faculty of Sciences at UNAM and published other articles in *Punto Crítico*, divisions in the group emerged over whether a socialist revolution or the organized left could bring about gender equality.[34] Examples of women's liberation in the left or revolutionary struggle did not exist to the satisfaction of some women in MAS.[35] The debates over the role of the left and its ability to offer a path to women's liberation led to conflict. In 1974, a group broke from MAS over ideological differences.

This new group took the name *Movimiento de Liberación de la Mujer* (Women's Liberation Movement, MLM) and consciously identified with the international women's movement.[36] Ex-1968 activist Marta Lamas emerged as MLM's leader. As Lamas stated in an interview, the MLM saw itself as an independent women's organization separate from and independent of the organized left.[37] The objectives of MLM included an analysis of women's relation to the capitalist system, the establishment of an autonomous women's movement, and the examination of the international struggle of the women's movement.[38] Although MLM clearly stated its solidarity with the international women's movement, it was ironic that the group was excluded from an international women's meeting that was held in their own backyard, the International Year of the Woman meeting in Mexico City.

With the emergence of feminism as a worldwide phenomenon, the United Nations announced that 1975 would be the International Year of the Woman. President Luis Echeverría and Mexico hosted the conference in Mexico City located, ironically, close to the Plaza de las Tres Culturas where the October 2 massacre had occurred. The conference logo was a symbol of a woman enclosed in the image of a dove; coincidentally, the dove was also the image used for the 1968 Olympics.[39] The meeting was attended by over 5,000 representatives from 133 nations, officials of various United Nations offices and programs, specialized agencies, and intergovernmental organizations. Observers came from three smaller nations and national liberation movements recognized by the United Nations.[40] This platform provided Echeverría an excellent area for demonstrating his progressive policies and modern nation and, as he hoped, to take his place as an impressive leader in the international arena.

At the opening ceremonies, Echeverría, the populist leader, welcomed the international community to Mexico. He relied on the well-worn argument that the situation of women would improve with the improvement of the lives of all Mexicans. He stated that, "The essential problem of our times is no longer the achievement of equal rights, imperative and indispensable though this is. The hope of the modern age is the liberation of all people from institutions and patterns of conduct imposed in the interests of the great majority."[41] He went on to propose an amendment to incorporate women into all aspects of political, economic, and social life. He argued that for women to attain full societal participation, there must be efforts from all sectors of the society.[42]

Echeverría's opening statements and his later encouragement of women from the developed countries to "use their moral force to support the poor nations of the world," as well as his discussion of greater inclusion of all people into the political, economic, and social exemplified hypocrisy.[43] Echeverría had been in a position of power during one of Mexico's largest demonstrations demanding greater democracy and inclusion in the political system. Moreover, his claims to promote the inclusion of women in political and social life had not extended to those young women active in organized feminism in Mexico. As in other countries, the government of Mexico selected organizations and individuals who would represent their countries. For Echeverría, the international meeting offered an opportunity to promote himself as a populist reformer on the world stage. In fact, the organizations that had grown from the experience of the student movement of 1968 were actually marginalized at the conference. Female activists from 1968 found themselves on the fringes of a movement that they had helped mobilize and organize.

Although officially slighted by the Echeverría administration, the women veterans of 1968 became central to the new wave of feminism, the founding of women's journals, and to challenging traditional gender roles. Ex-activist of 1968 Carmen Landa exemplified the changes that had occurred and how the feminist movement could change a life. She was active in 1968 in a guardias, and she recalled that she rarely spoke in public in 1968. However, with the emergence of feminism, she found her voice. She embraced personal changes in her life, leaving her first husband and becoming a single mother. In the early 1970s, she became an organizer in the professors' unions. Her participation in 1968 led her to feminism which in turn contributed to her union activities at UNAM in the 1970s.[44]

Although many women ex-activists found a place in feminism, other women of "la generación de '68" saw feminism as contradictory to their ideals.[45] A common argument in Latin America was that feminism was too bourgeois, too individualistic. For them, many people in Mexico—men and women—were oppressed, thus there had to be a general uprising to overcome their status.[46] These ideas were not new, particularly among women who grew up in families of the left and continued to work within the left in Mexico. Consequently, feminism for them contributed to a splintering among leftist groups as some privileged women might support feminist objectives rather than class struggle. Some women resisted participation because they claimed they found feminist organizations too similar to leftist organizations, dominated by one faction or another and closed to other participants and perspectives.

Though criticizing "organized feminism," many women who were active in 1968 invoked the ideals of the movement in their daily lives and through their actions. Their experiences show that women embraced the legacy of 1968 in various fashions. Mercedes Perelló, Alejandra Herrera, and Vida Valero Borrás all demonstrate how 1968—the movement and its ideals—became a part of their lives leading them to continue to question the government and status quo. Perelló remained active through union ties, and Herrera and Valero through teaching.

After the decision was made to return to classes in 1968, Perelló abandoned her university studies. Building on their ties to the Spartacus league and influenced by Maoist thought, she and her husband went to the people. They lived among workers, and organized in working class neighborhoods.[47] She found organized feminism too narrow and felt it was dominated by middle class women who did not wish to change Mexico's power structures.[48] Perelló's ties to the ideals that stemmed from her activism in 1968 transcended her organizing efforts among workers. She stated that as her husband advanced through the union hierarchy, he insisted that they move out of their home in a working class neighborhood into a middle-class area. Perelló found her compañero's decision to move into a middle-class neighborhood offensive, and the two went their separate ways as a result of this issue.[49]

Alejandra Herrera and Vida Valero Borrás, professors at UAM-Azcapotzalco in the north of Mexico City were both activists in 1968. Herrera became active through her *prepa* (college preparatory high school) in 1968 when it was invaded by soldiers, and she later attended marches and demonstrations. Her compañero was also arrested and imprisoned. Valero was in a lightning brigade. Their teaching at UAM offers an interesting legacy to 1968. With the emergence of UAM and its ties to the left and particularly *la generación de 1968* (the generation of 1968) due to its faculty composition, women found a place where they were recruited and offered positions. Activists of 1968 like Valero Borrás and Herrera considered themselves Marxists.[50] In 1997, organized feminism did not interest either of them because of its shortcomings.[51] Similar to Perelló, Herrera and Valero saw feminism as too bourgeois.

The movement that gave birth to the second wave of Mexican feminism was also middle class and bourgeois: the 1968 student movement. Although there were certain sectors within the student movement that wanted to transform Mexican society to a much greater degree, the moderate view prevailed. By their demand of dialogue, students hoped to have their demands heard by their leaders. Similarly, feminists wanted to have a platform to voice their demands, and like the students, the Echeverría administration denied young feminists that platform.

Despite the fairly moderate demands of the students, they, like the feminists, transformed contemporary Mexico in ways that activists may not have originally planned. These were not huge shifts, but incremental changes that grew over time. Whether ex-activists considered themselves feminists or not, they all agreed that 1968 contributed to social change in Mexico. Herrera and Valero recalled that a tremendous shift in gender relations took place in the 1970s due to the role of young women in the student movement. After 1968, both remembered that students at UNAM took a far greater role in their studies by questioning what books were assigned, using the informal *tú* (you) rather than the formal *usted* (you) to refer to professors, and in demanding greater student participation in the decision-making process.[52] Thus, the student uprising of 1968 dramatically altered how students interacted with professors and with the university administration since students had gained greater power. Herrera also noted that after 1968, young women began to live alone rather than with their parents or husbands. This change in living arrangements also contributed to women's attitudes toward sexual relationships. [53] Although this is difficult to document, women active in 1968 later challenged traditional gender roles by divorcing, taking lovers, and/or living alone at levels never seen before. As in other countries, the sexual revolution came to Mexico in the late 1960s, but it was more evident in Mexico after 1968 with the emergence of the feminist movement that built upon those cultural and societal shifts that came in the wake of the student movement.

Conclusion

The 1968 Mexican student movement was a window into the future of Mexico, and it continues to be a watershed event. The events of 1968 initiated a new age in Mexico; an age of turmoil, challenge, and hardship, but also one of creativity, reflection, and progress. The 1968 Mexican student movement transcended its linear historical boundary of 120 days of "action." The students never achieved their ultimate goals, but their successes far exceeded the imagination of Gustavo Díaz Ordaz, Luis Echeverría, the CNH, and the nation. The gendered construction of power was changed, and the cultural shifts that took place in Mexico were never fully reversed through social or political policies or violence. The power and image of the president was forever flawed. He was no longer the paternal father figure of the nation. After 1968, the de-legitimized position of president became the target of fervent, and at times irreverent, criticism. In 1968, students taunted President Díaz Ordaz, but they wanted his attention, hoping he would address and meet their demands. In 1975, however, President Luis Echeverría fled the national university as students threw rocks at him.[1] During the summer of 1968 and in its aftermath, Mexican youth slowly chipped away at the power of the ruling party.

In the summer of 1968, young, politicized, educated men became the objects of gendered character assassination. In the press, their demands and mobilization were tarnished by being portrayed as anti-Mexican, foreign-led dupes. In the end, however, they emerged as the polished voices of a new generation of national leaders. These activists became the consciousness and heirs of a changing Mexico. Through their continued attempts to organize, their writings, their newspapers and journals, their teaching, their opposition parties, and their continued resistance to the government, young men and women demonstrated a legacy of revolution and resistance that remain a part of Mexico's recent past and future.

Conclusion

What took place on the streets of Mexico City in the summer of 1968 profoundly affected relations between men and women, powerful and powerless, elders and youth. Although young, middle class, men, and women were the key beneficiaries of PRI politics in the 1960s and 1970s, these young people asserted a new vision of power, nation, and culture. Young women who took to the streets found a space to become political actors voicing their ideas, their ideologies, and their criticisms. Through their uprising, men and women were thrown into their own power struggles. In the guardias, brigades, Comités de lucha, and CNH, they negotiated new social, cultural, and political terrain. It was not a simple journey. They clashed over gender roles, over leadership, and organizational methods.

In their struggles with one another, age old questions emerged: who does what and who does what for whom? Young women engaged in a two-front gender battle. They subverted gender roles and social and political constructs of their elders by becoming public, but they also struggled with their male comrades in the movement who continued to view their female peers through a traditional lens. No longer content with making coffee or copies, some young women mobilized and demanded to be part of the movement. They challenged their government, parents, and peers but also themselves. Those physical and intellectual conflicts led, in part, to the second wave of feminism in Mexico.

In the years following the movement, the students' challenge to their elders could not be ignored or silenced. Echeverría promoted some of the ideas that emerged on the streets in 1968 with his apertura demócratica (Democratic Opening). His policies even benefited many ex-activists in the wake of the movement. Prisoners were released, while exiled activists were permitted to return to Mexico. In some cases, young leaders, whether free, imprisoned, or exiled after 1968, found themselves recruited into the government, bureaucracy, or universities by the same government that had attacked them. Although some accepted their new-found respect and entry in bourgeoisie life or a life of service to the government, maybe hoping to reform it from within, some ex-activists took a different path, going to the people whether in rural or urban solidarity or in armed struggle. Those young people who chose the path of resistance experienced the wrath of a government still not willing to share power or endure a threat. The inability of the government to enter into a public dialogue with youth and its violent response continues to mark Mexico.

Even in 2003, reports emerged that snipers fired from an apartment in Tlatelolco that has been traced back to a person related to Luis Echeverría.[2] The following year, Mexico's Special Prosecutor for Social and Political Movement of the Past Ignacio Carrillo Prieto, appointed by President Vicente Fox in 2001, sought an arrest warrant for Luis Echeverría for genocide.[3] Carrillo argued that he used the term genocide to sidestep statutes of limitations.[4] The following day, a judge threw out the arrest warrant as more photos of the Corpus Christi Massacre were published in Mexico City newspapers.[5] In response, the *New York Times* published an editorial that questioned the sincerity of Vicente Fox to investigate the crimes of the past and the existence of Mexican democracy.[6] The editorial in the *New York Times* led to a rapid response by Carrillo Prieto and Mexican intellectual Enrique Krauze.[7] Carrillo Prieto, who will appeal the decision, insisted that it was under Mexico's new system that action has finally been taken, arguing that one of Fox's main objectives was to fight against impunity of previous Mexican leaders. Moreover, Krauze, who recognized that the old ruling party still exists and yields tremendous power, argued that the transparency of the judiciary process and ability of the press to report on the case reflects a very recent, and more democratic, shift in Mexico. These on-going inquiries and investigations into 1968 and 1971 show that since the student movement, Mexicans, as well as the international community, are still seeking to understand what happened, who was responsible, and who should be punished almost forty years later.

The years directly following the 1968 student uprising reveals a kaleidoscope of interpretations about the challenges to authority and the means by which the demand for democracy transcended and survived the repression of October 2, 1968. Ex-activists and those people influenced by the events voiced their continued struggle in film, music, and literature. Others formed associations, joined the opposition, or fled to armed struggle. Mexico's 120 days in the summer of 1968 echoed across the political and social landscape of the 1970s into the present. As Roger Bartra proposed, the 1968 Mexican student movement shattered the romantic image of a content revolutionary family idyllically strolling arm-in-arm toward the future.[8] Even in 2004, a brutally destroyed social movement and its remnants continue to haunt the political, social, intellectual, and cultural landscape of Mexico.

Notes

Introduction

1. Marcelino Perelló, interview with the author, June 6, 1997, México, D.F.
2. Mercedes Perelló, interview with author, June 10, 1997, México, D.F.
3. Marcelino Perelló, interview.
4. Gilbert Josephs, Anne Rubenstein, and Eric Zolov, *Fragments of a Golden Age: The Politics of Culture in Mexico Since 1940*, (Durham, N.C.: Duke University Press, 2001); Alan Knight, "Cardenismo: Juggernaut or Jalopy," in Gilbert M. Josephs and Daniel Nugent, eds., *Everyday Forms of State Formation: Revolution and the Negotiation of Rule in Modern Mexico* (Durham, N.C.: Duke University Press, 1994); Jeffrey Rubin, "Decentering the Regime: Culture and Regional Politics in Mexico," *Latin American Research Review* 31 (3): 85–125 (1997), and Mary Kay Vaughn, *Cultural Politics in Revolution: Teachers, Peasants, and Schools in Mexico, 1930–1940* (Tucson: University of Arizona Press, 1997).
5. José Agustín, *La contracultura en México: La historia y el significado de los rebeldes sin causa, los jipitecas, los punks, y las bandas* (México, D.F.: Editorial Grijalbo, 1996); Carlos Monsiváis, *Días de guardar* (México, D.F.: Biblioteca Era, 1970); David Maciel and Joanne Hershfield, *Mexico's Cinema: A Century of Film and Filmmakers* (Wilmington, Delaware: Scholarly Resources Press, 1999); Anne Rubenstein, *Bad Language, Naked Ladies, & Other Threats to the Nation: A Political History of Comic Books in Mexico* (Durham, N.C.: Duke University Press, 1998); Eric Zolov, *Refried Elvis: The Rise of the Mexican Counterculture* (Berkeley: University of California Press, 1999).
6. For a discussion of the continued struggle against the Mexican state, see Sergio Aguayo Quezada, *1968: Los archivos de la violencia* (México, D.F.: Grijaldo, 1998). Aguayo's exhaustive study exposes the sophisticated, if not repressive, security apparatus of Mexico.
7. Roger Bartra, "Culture and Political Power in Mexico," *Latin American Perspectives* 16, no. 2 (Spring 1989): 69.
8. The historiography of the 1968 student movement continues to grow with new insights and analysis, particularly on the role of the government and its

security forces. See Aguayo's *1968: Los archivos de la violencia*; and Raúl Jardón, *El espionaje contra el movimiento estudiantil: Los documentos de la Dirrección Federal de Seguridad y las agencies de inteligencia estadounidenses en 1968*, (México: Ithaca, 2003).

9. Sandra McGee-Deutsch, "Gender and Sociopolitical Change in Twentieth Century Latin America," *Hispanic American Historical Review* 71 (1991): 259–306; Marcela Lagarde, *Género y feminismo: Desarrollo humano y democrácia* (Madrid: Horas, 1997); Marta Lamas, "Introducción," in *El género: La construcción cultural de la diferencia sexual*, edited by Marta Lamas (México, D.F.: Grupo Editorial Miguel Angel Porrda, 1996); Joan W. Scott, "Gender: A Useful Category of Historical Analysis," *American Historical Review* 91 (December 1986): 1053–75.

10. See Ana María Alonso, *Thread of Blood: Colonialism, Revolution, and Gender on Mexico's Northern Frontier* (Tucson: University of Arizona Press, 1995), 74–90. See also Marit Melhuus and Kristi Anne Stølen, "Introduction" in *Machos, Mistresses, and Madonnas: Contesting the Power of Latin American Gender Imagery* (New York: Verso Press, 1996), 1–33; Karin Aljeandra Rosenblatt, *Gendered Compromises: Political Culture and the State in Chile, 1920–1950* (Chapel Hill: University of North Carolina Press, 2000).

11. For a discussion on masculinity, see Peter M. Beattie, "The House, the Street, and the Barrack: Reform and Honorable Masculine Space in Brazil 1864 to 1945," *Hispanic American Historical Review* 76, no. 3 (August 1996): 439–73; Gail Bederman, *Manliness and Civilization: A Cultural History of Gender and Race in the United States* (Chicago: University of Chicago Press, 1995); Matthew Gutmann, *The Meanings of Macho: Being a Man in Mexico City* (Berkeley: University of California Press, 1996); Michael Kimmel, *Masculinity in America: A Cultural History* (New York: The Free Press, 1996); and George Mosse, *The Image of Man: The Creation of Modern Masculinity* (New York: Oxford University Press, 1996).

12. Judith Butler, *Gender Trouble: Feminism and the Subversion of Identity* (New York: Routledge, 1990), 140.

13. The mobilization of the students and the brutal repression of the movement has continued to fuel a great deal of analysis and interpretation since the beginning of the movement, and the historiography continues to grow every year with ever more sophisticated approaches. Elena Poniatowska's classic work, *Massacre in Mexico*, Helen Lane, trans. (Columbia: University of Missouri Press, 1992), originally published in Spanish 1971, is a compilation of interviews, student protests and chants, and statements by the main actors that is still a useful tool on 1968. Activists in the movement also contributed to the study of 1968 including Raúl Alvarez Garín, Gilberto Guevara Niebla, Hermann Bellinghausen, Hugo Hiria,

Editors. *Pensar el 68*. (México, D.F.: Cal y Arena, 1988); Heberto Castillo, *Si te agarran te van a matar* (México, D.F.: Ediciones Oceano, 1973); Luis González de Alba, *Los días y los años* (México, D.F.: Ediciones Era, 1971); José Revueltas, *México 68: Juventud y Revolución* (México: México, D.F.: Ediciones Era, 1978); and Eduardo Valle, *Escritos sobre el movimiento del 68* (México: Universidad Autónoma de Sinaloa, 1984). Along with activists who wrote or collected testimonies and interviews, other authors sought to analyze the movement as a sociological phenomena, such as Sergio Zermeño, *México: Una democracia utópica: El movimiento estudiantil del 1968* (México: Siglo Veinturno Editores, 1978) and César Gilbert, *El habito de la utopía: Análisis del imaginario sociopolítico del movimiento estudiantil de Mexico, 1968* (México, D.F.: Instituto Moro: Miguel Angel Porrua, 1993). Numerous documentary collections offer insights on what the activists and their supporters said about themselves and the propaganda that they produced, see Leopoldo Ayala, ed., *Nuestro Verdad: Memorial popular del movimiento estudiantil popular y el dos de octubre* (México, D.F.: Joaquín Porrda, 1989); and Ramon Ramírez, *El movimiento estudiantil de México: Julio/diciembre de 1968, Análisis/Cronología* and *El movimiento estudiantil de México: Julio/diciembre, Documentos* (México, D.F.: Ediciones Era, 1969). More recent collections examine the documents that have recently been released by the *Dirección Federal de Seguridad* (Directorate of Federal Security, DFS) in a search to understand what happened during the movement and who is culpable for the massacre of October 2, 1968, see Julio Scherer García and Carlos Monsiváis, *Parte de guerra, Tlatelolco 1968: Documentos del general Marcelino García Barragán : los hechos y la historia* (México, D.F.: Nuevo Siglo, 1999). Both Sergio Aguayo Quezada, *1968: Los archivos de la violencia*, and Raúl Jardón, *El espinaje contra el movimiento estudianil*, analyze the reports of the DFS as well as other documents of the Secretary of Interior, the Secretary of Defense, and the Office of the President. Available on the internet, the work of Kate Doyle and the archivists at the National Security Archive and Mexico's *Proceso* magazine have linked Mexican as well as U.S. intelligence reports on 1968, see http://www.gwu.edu/~nsarchiv/.

14.   Paul Berman, *A Tale of Two Utopias: The Political Journeys of the Generation of 1968* (New York: W.W. Norton & Company, 1996). Berman contemplates how students questioned all aspects of their society. Of course, depending on their national origin, the students had different challenges and demands.

15.   Guardias were comprised of students who occupied school and university campuses. They guarded the building from invasion by soldiers or police.

Chapter One

1.   Enrique Krauze, *Mexico, Biography of Power: A History of Modern Mexico*,

1810–1996, trans. by Hank Heifetz (New York: Harper Perennial, 1997), 680–81.

2.   Paco Ignacio Taibo, *Guevara, Also Known as Che* (New York: St. Martin's Press, 1997), 67–70.

3.   Paco Ignacio Taibo, "Viva Che," presentation at the Socialist Scholars Conference, March 1998, videocassette. I want to thank Jim Cockcroft for loaning me this video.

4.   For example, in the United States, *Ramparts* published portions of Che's diary. See "The Diary of Che Guevara," *Ramparts* vol. 71 (27 July 1968).

5.   For a complete biography of Guevara, see Jorge Castañeda, *Compañero: The Life and Death of Che Guevara* (New York: Alfred A. Knopf, 1997), and Taibo's *Guevara*. Both authors have argued that the bond between Che Guevara and his mother was forged during his childhood when she cared for and educated him at home because of his asthma.

6.   Ernesto Che Guevara, *The Motorcycle Diaries: A Journey Around South America*, trans. Ann Wright (London: Verso Books, 2003).

7.   Jacobo Arbenz Guzmán was elected president of Guatemala in March 1951. Once president, he embarked on social and economic reforms. His agrarian reforms called for the expropriation of fallow land for redistribution. In turn, the Guatemalan government expropriated land held by the United Fruit Company (UFCO). The UFCO had powerful friends in the United States government. Thus, the United States government immediately launched a harassment campaign that ultimately ended with the overthrow of Arbenz from the U.S. backed and CIA financed army under Carlos Castillo Armas. The overthrow of Arbenz plunged Guatemala into a vicious civil war that lasted over forty years. See Stephen Schlesinger and Stephen Kinzer, *Bitter Fruit* (New York: Doubleday Press, 1982), and Piero Gleijeses, *The United States and the Guatemalan Revolution* (Princeton, N.J.: Princeton University Press, 1989).

8.   Sócrates Campos Lemus, interview, "1968: El fuego de la esperanza," by Raúl Jardón, unpublished manuscript, 1996. For this study, I worked from Jardón's unpublished manuscript. The interviews were from a program commemorating the twenty-fifth anniversary of the 1968 student movement that was on Radio Educación from July to December 1993. For the published version, see Raúl Jardón. *1968: El fuego de la esperanza* (México, D.F.: Siglo Veintiuno Editores, 1998).

9.   For discussions of Che and his army, see Taibo's *Guevara: Also Known as Che*.

10.   An example of this attitude is found in Alonso Martinez Zúñiga, *Los 68: Drama político-social en catorce cuadros* (México D.F.: Editorial Manuscrito 68, 1994).

11.   Octavio Paz, *The Labyrinth of Solitude: The Other Mexico, Return to the Labyrinth of Solitude, Mexico and the United States, The Philanthropic Ogre*

(New York: Grove Press, 1985).

12. Ibid., 37.

13. Paz, *The Labyrinth of Solitude*, 18.

14. See discussion of Paz and the presidency in Ana Maria Alonso, *Thread of Blood: Colonialism, Revolution, and Gender on Mexico's Northern Frontier* (Tucson: University of Arizona Press, 1995), 82–84.

15. Mariano Azuela, *The Underdogs* (Pittsburgh: University of Pittsburgh Press, 1992).

16. Carlos Fuentes, *The Death of Artemio Cruz*, trans. Alfred Mac Adam (New York: Farrar, Straus, and Giroux, 1991), first issued in 1962. Like Paz, Fuentes also explored Mexican character in *Where the Air is Clear*, trans. Sam Hileman (New York: Ivan Oboliensky, 1960), first published in 1958.

17. Wendy B. Faris, *Carlos Fuentes* (New York: Frederick Ungar Publishing Company, 1983), 55.

18. George Mosse, *The Image of Man: The Creation of Modern Masculinity* (New York: Oxford University Press, 1996), 56–106. Mosse notes how certain men were feminized and consequently marginalized by society.

19. Dale Story, "Policy Cycles in Mexican Presidential Politics," *Latin American Research Review* 20, no. 3 (1985): 139–61.

20. Alan Knight, "Cardenismo: Juggernaut or Jalopy," *Journal of Latin American Studies* 26, no. 1 (1994): 73–107. See also Adrian A. Bantijes, *As If Jesus Walked on Earth: Cardenismo, Sonora, and the Mexican Revolution* (Wilmington: Scholarly Resources Press, 1998).

21. While Calles was president from 1924 to 1928, he controlled the executive office until Cárdenas' administration.

22. Fernando Benítez, *Lázaro Cárdenas y la revolución mexicana*, vol. 3, *El Cardenismo* (México, D.F.: El Colegio de México, 1978); Luis González, *Los artífices del Cardenismo* (México, D.F.: 1979), *Los días del residente Cárdenas* (México, D.F.: 1979); Enrique Krauze, *General misionero: Lázaro Cárdenas* (México, D.F.: 1987).

23. For a discussion of Cárdenas' power base, see Enrique Krauze, *Mexico, Biography of Power: A History of Modern Mexico, 1810–1996* (New York: Harper Perennial, 1997), 438–80. His government also contributed to the organization of the *Confederación Nacional Campesina* (National Peasant Confederation, CNC) and the *Confederación de Trabajadores Mexicanos* (Confederation of Mexican Workers, CTM). The incorporation of peasants and workers into the state was a decisive move on Cárdenas' part because it brought the government and the official party support from these long-excluded sectors of society.

24. The official party, now known as the *Partido Revolucionario Institucional*

(Institutional Revolutionary Party, PRI) has its roots in the *Partido Nacional Revolucionario* (National Revolutionary Party, PNR) established by Calles in 1929. Cárdenas changed its structure and name to the *Partido Revolucionario Mexicano* (Party of the Mexican Revolution, PRM). In 1946, under Manuel Ávila Camacho (1940–1946), the PRI became the official party. For a discussion of agrarian reform, see David A. Brading, ed., *Caudillo and Peasant in the Mexican Revolution* (Cambridge: University of Cambridge Press, 1980); and Ann L. Craig, *The First Agraristas: An Oral History of a Mexican Agrarian Reform Movement* (Berkeley: University of California Press, 1983).

25.   Héctor Aguilar Camín and Lorenzo Meyer, *In the Shadow of the Mexican Revolution: Contemporary Mexican History, 1910–1989* (Austin: University of Texas Press, 1993), 167.

26.   Peter Smith, "Mexico Since 1946," in *Mexico Since Independence*, ed. by Leslie Bethell (New York: Cambridge University Press, 1991), 324.

27.   Stephen Niblo, *Mexico in the 1940s: Modernity, Politics, and Corruption* (Wilmington: Scholarly Resources Press, 1999), 75–141; Raúl Trejo Delarde, "The Mexican Labor Movement: 1917–1975," trans. by Aníbal Yáñez, *Latin American Perspectives* 3, no. 1 (Winter 1976): 144–47.

28.   John Sherman, "The Mexican Miracle and Its Collapse," in *The Oxford History of Mexico*, edited by Michael Meyer and William Beezley (New York: Oxford University Press, 2000), 575–76. See also Stephen Niblo, *Mexico in the 1940s*, 183–244.

29.   Héctor Aguilar Camín and Lorenzo Meyer, *In the Shadow of the Mexican Revolution*, 164. See also Cynthia Hewitt de Alcántara, "Ensayo sobre la satisfacción de necesidades básicas del pueblo mexicano entres 1940 y 1970," *Cuadernos del CES* 21 (1977).

30.   See Banco de México, S.A., *Información económica. Producto interno bruto y gasto, Cuaderno, 1960–1977* (México, D.F.: Banco de México, 1978). Data from 1939–1977 reprinted in Aguilar Camín and Meyer, *In the Shadow of the Mexican Revolution*, 172–73.

31.   Aguilar Camín and Meyer, *In the Shadow of the Mexican Revolution*, 168.

32.   "200 milliones va a destinar el Depto. del Districto Federal, este ano, a obras públicas," *Excélsior*, February 5, 1958, 1.

33.   Michael C. Meyer and William L Sherman, *The Course of Mexican History* (New York: Oxford University Press, 1995), 647.

34.   Sherman, "The Mexican Miracle," 588–89.

35.   For a discussion on women's suffrage see, Anna Macías, *Against all Odds: The Feminist Movement in Mexico to 1940* (Westport, Ct.: Greenwood Press, 1982). Despite Cárdenas attempts to gain women's suffrage, Mexican suffrage came after Brazil (1932), Cuba (1934), El Salvador (1939), Dominican Republic

(1942), Argentina (1946), and Chile (1949).

36. For a discussion about attitudes toward women's voting, see William Blough, "Political Attitudes of Mexican Women: Support for the Political System Among a Newly Enfranchised Group," *Journal of Interamerican Studies and World Affairs* 14, no. 2 (May 1972): 201–24.

37. Macias, *Against all Odds*, 152–53.

38. "UN Aid Sought in Mexican Vote," El Paso *Herald Post*, December 27, 1957, reprinted in *Excélsior*, February 10, 1958. Besides targeting the female vote, Alvarez undertook other options hoping to promote the PAN and offset the PRI's election domination. He pursued a new avenue of political criticism that had not been used in Mexico. In December 1957, the El Paso *Herald Post* printed an article stating that Alvarez was collecting 1,000,000 signatures to petition the United Nations to observe the 1958 elections. Alvarez's pursuit of international monitoring of the election confirmed the widespread supposition that the official party perhaps was not winning by a democratic majority. Plus, Alvarez's move was a slap at nationalism because it invited outsiders in to observe a national political process.

39. Enrique Krauze, *La presidencia imperial: Ascenso y caído del sistema político mexicano* (1940–1996), 218.

40. López Mateos's distribution of land is well known. See Enrique Krauze's discussion of López Mateos in *Mexico, Biography of Power: A History of Modern Mexico, 1810–1996*, 625–64.

41. For a photographic report of López Mateos' social and economic programs, see Banco Nacional de México, *Adolfo López Mateos: Un pueblo unido con esfuerzo* (México, D.F.: Banamex, 1985.)

42. Article 145 of the Federal Penal Code was added under Manuel Ávila Camacho to use against citizens or foreigners who criticized the regime. It violated freedom of speech as guaranteed in the Mexican Constitution. David Alfaro Siqueiros was imprisoned by López Mateos in 1962, but López Mateos released him in 1964. See "El Presidente de la República, Mediante la libertad a David Alfaro Sigueiros el 11 de julio de 1964," in *Diario Official*, June 11, 1964, republished in a collection of López Mateos' presidential documents, *Historia de la acción pública: Adolfo López Mateos, 1958–1964*, vol. 1, *Sus Ideas*, Lourdes Celis, et al., eds. (México, D.F.: Fondo para la Historia de las Ideas Revolucionarias en México, Partido Revolucionario Institucional, 1978).

43. Aguilar Camín and Meyer, *In the Shadow of the Mexican Revolution*, 164.

44. "Paro nacional de telegrafistas desde ayer a las 2 de la tarde," *Excélsior*, February 7, 1958, 1.

45. Ibid., 1.

46. "El paro tiene incomunicado al país hace más de cuarenta horas," *Excélsior*,

February 8, 1958, 1.

47. Editorial, *Excélsior*, February 11, 1958.

48. See photo from the Día de Telegrafista *Excélsior*, February 15, 1958, 15.

49. "Los electristas irán a la huelga 16 de marzo, si no logran lo que pide," *Excélsior*, February 15, 1958.

50. Enrique Ávila Carrillo and Humberto Martínez Brizuela, *Historia del movimiento magisterial (1910–1989): Democracia y salario* (México, D.F.: Ediciones Quinto Sol, 1990), 31.

51. *Excélsior*, May 26 and 28, 1958.

52. Kevin Middlebrook, "State-Labor Relations in Mexico: The Changing Economic and Political Context," in *Unions, Workers and the State in Mexico*, ed. by Kevin J. Middlebrook (San Diego: Center for U.S.-Mexican Studies, University of California, 1991), n. 6, 7.

53. For more information, see Elba Esther Gordillo, *La construcción de un proyecto sindical: Mi testimonio* (México, D.F.: Aguilar, Altea, Taurus, 1995).

54. Valetín Campa, "Movimiento ferrocarrilero," in *50 años de oposición en México*, Javier Rosas, ed. (México: Universidad Autónoma de México, 1979), 216; For more information, see Barry Carr, "Labor and the Left," in *Unions, Workers and the State in Mexico*.

55. Campa, "Movimiento ferrocarrilero," 216.

56. Lázaro Cárdenas nationalized Líneas Nacionales on June 23, 1937, effective on January 1, 1938. Many of the Mexican rail lines had been nationalized during the Cárdenas years.

57. Valetín Campa, *Mi testimonio: Experiencias de un comunista Mexicano* (México, D.F.: Ediciones de Cultura Popular, 1978).

58. "Vallejo: Simbolo, Grito, Resistencia de la Lucha Sindical Independiente," *Proceso* (March 7, 1983), 6–7.

59. Carlos Fuentes, *Tiempo mexicano* (México, D.F.: Joaquín Mortiz, 1973), 118. Fuentes interviewed Jaramillo while he was in hiding. For more on Jaramillo, see Rubén Jaramillo and Froylán López Manjarrez, *Rubén Jaramillo, Autobiografía y Asesinato* (México, D.F.: Editorial Nuestro Tiempo, 1967) and Renato Revelo, *Los jaramillistas* (México, D.F.: Editorial Nuestro Tiempo, 1978).

60. Samuel Brunk, "Zapata and the City Boys: In Search of a Piece of the Revolution," *Hispanic American Historical Review*, 73, no. 1 (1993): 33–65.

61. Various images of Vallejo can be found. For example, see Colección de Impresos Esther Montero, no. 991/0043, Archivo Historico de Universidad Nacional Autónoma de México Centro de Estudios Sobre la Universidad, Biblioteca Nacional, México, D.F. (hereafter, AHUNAM-CESU) This image was reproduced and circulated. Also published in Grupo Mira, *La gráfica del `68: Homenaje al movimiento estudiantil* (México, D.F.: Ediciones Zurda, 1993).

62. *2 de octubre*. 1969, video-cassette, 60 minutes. I want to thank David Maciel for sharing this film with me.

63. Gilberto Guevara Niebla, interview, Jardón, "1968: El fuego de la esperanza," 153.

64. Ignacio Chávez was replaced by Javier Barros Sierra on May 5, 1966. Chávez had attempted to reform various aspects of UNAM. His administration was controversial due to his attempts to raise attendance and matriculation rates. A riot led to students storming the rectory and holding Chávez and others captive. He and other professors resigned. For a discussion about Chávez and his administration, see Donald Mabry, *The Mexican University and the State: Student Conflicts, 1910–1971* (College Station: Texas A&M Press, 1982).

65. Roberto Escudero, interview, Jardón, "1968: El fuego de la esperanza," 136.

66. José Revueltas, *México 68: Juventud y revolución* (México, D.F.: Ediciones Era, 1978). Revueltas, a Marxist, was a faculty member in Philosophy and Letters (Liberal Arts) in 1968.

67. "A los estudiantes que integran la Facultad de Ciencias Políticas de la UNAM," statement from Demetrio Vallejo, August 7, 1968, document 1023, box 10; and "Boletín de presa," statement by Demetrio Vallejo, August 26, 1968, document 1025, box 10, Impresos Sueltos del Movimiento Estudiantil Mexicano, Fondo Reservado, Biblioteca Nacional, México, D.F. (hereafter CME). Also see, Demetrio Vallejo, *Yo Acuso* (México, D.F.: Editorial Hombre Nuevo, 1973), 16. Vallejo, while imprisoned, wrote *Yo acuso* as the statement he would read to Judge Eduardo Langle Martínez at his sentencing. Vallejo listed those who were detained with him.

68. Aída González, interview with author, November 21, 1996, San Mateo Tlaltenango, México.

69. Raúl Jardón, interview with author, March 6, 1997, Mexico City.

70. Edmundo Jardón Arzate, *De la Ciudadela a Tlatelolco* (México, D.F.: Fondo de Cultura Popular, 1969).

71. "Compañero Obrero," republished in Jardón, "1968, El fuego de la esperanza," 218.

72. Many of the activists in the independent unions had been purged from the CTM in the 1940s. Communists were expelled from the union.

73. Gilberto Guevara Niebla, "Antecedentes y desarrollo del movimiento de 1968," *Cuadernos Políticos* (July-September 1978), 12. See Gerardo Unzueta, "Crisis en el partido, crisis en el movimiento," in *Historia del Comunismo en México*, edited by Arnoldo Martínez Verdugo (México, D.F.: Grijalbo, 1985), 189–238. Khrushchev initially denounced Stalin in a closed door session at the XX Congress of the Communist Party in the secret speech. He criticized Stalin's cult of personality and his persecution of Communists. See William

Taubman, *Khrushchev: The Man and His Era* (New York: W.W. Norton & Company, 2003).

74. Raúl Alvarez Garín, "Los años de gran tentación," in *Pensar el 68*, ed. by Raúl Alvarez Garín, et al. (México, D.F.: Cal y Arena, 1993).

75. Guevara, "Antecedentes y desarrollo del movimiento de 1968," 12.

76. Porros were young men who terrorized other students, at times with the support of the government or municipal body. Up until 1968, porros were firmly in control of university student politics. See Alfredo Ramirez, *Yo, porro: retrato hablado* (México, D.F.: Editorial Posada, 1984).

77. Jardón, "1968: El fuego de la esperanza," 6–7.

Chapter Two

1. There were student movements in Czechoslovakia, France, Germany, Italy, Japan, Spain, and the United States.

2. Report about the agitation for lowering the voting age by Frente Estudantil Progresista, July 16, 1968, Box 521, Investigación Politicas y Sociales, Secretaría de Gobernación (hereafter IPS), Archivo General de la Nación (hereafter AGN), México, D.F. The reports contained in the IPS documents are government surveillance reports.

3. In Mexico, IPN and UNAM, as well as state and private institutions, host college preparatory secondary schools. These schools prepare students to enter university level study.

4. See Daniel Cazés, *Crónica 1968* (México, D.F.: Plaza y Valdés, 1993); Raúl Jardón, "1968: El fuego de la esperanza," unpublished manuscript, in possession of author, 1996. Elena Poniatowska, *Massacre in Mexico*, trans. by Helen Lane (Columbia: University of Missouri Press, 1991).

5. Under Ávila Camacho, Mexico declared war on the Axis powers during World War II. See Enrique Krauze, "Manuel Ávila Camacho: The Gentleman President," in *Mexico, Biography of Power: A History of Modern Mexico, 1810–1896*, trans. by Hank Heifetz (New York: Harper Perennial, 1997), 491–525.

6. See González de Alba, *Los días y los años*; and Poniatowska, *Massacre in Mexico*. Also see Hiber Conteris, "Marcha," Año XXX, No. 1418 (September 27, 1968) republished as "New Outbreak of the Student Rebellion," *NACLA* (November 1, 1968), 6.

7. "Plan de acción de CNED," July 22, 1968 box 521, IPS, AGN. The attack on the Moncada barracks marked the beginning of the Cuban Revolution.

8. "Violentos choques entre estudiantes y la Policía," *El Día*, July 27, 1968.

9. Ibid.; "La policía exculpa a los estudiantes de los alborotos," *El Sol*, July 27, 1968; and "El foco de la agitación," *El Universal*, July 27, 1968.

10. For a map of the streets that were barricaded, see *Novedades*, August 16, 1968.

11. González de Alba, *Los días y los años*, 26–28. Elena Poniatowska, who incorporated part of González's prison diary, wondered how rocks got into the garbage bins. Poniatowska, *Massacre in Mexico*, 326.

12. Aída González, interview with author, San Mateo de Tlatenango, México, November 30, 1996.

13. Mario Ortega Olivares, interview, transcript in "1968, El fuego de la esperanza," Raúl Jardón, 104–5.

14. Prior to his death, it was known that Che Guevara's policies and anti-Soviet stance had been repudiated by Fidel Castro. See Central Intelligence Agency, Directorate of Intelligence, "Intelligence Memorandum: The Fall of Che Guevara and the Changing Face of the Cuban Revolution" 18 October 1965, no. 2333/65. National Security Archive, http://www.gwu.edu/~nsarchiv/.

15. "76 Agitadores Rojos que Instigaron los Disturbios Estudiantiles Están Detenidos," *Novedades*, July 28, 1968.

16. Jardón, "1968: El fuego de la esperanza," 17. Raúl Jardón, interview with author, March 6, 1997.

17. "Declaración del presidium del Comité Central del Partido Comunista Mexicano," July 30, 1968, document 993, box 9, Impresos Sueltos del Movimiento Estudiantil Mexicano, 1968, Fondo Reservado, Biblioteca Nacional, México, D.F. (hereafter, CME).

18. Edmundo Jardón Arzate, *De la Ciudadela a Tlatelolco* (México, D.F.: Fondo de Cultura Popular, 1969).

19. *El Universal*, July 28, 1968.

20. Ibid.

21. "76 Agitadores Rojos que instigaron los disturbios estudiantiles están detenidos," *Novedades*, July 28, 1968.

22. Manifesto del PCM, July 1968, Partido Comunista de México, Box 65, Document 10, Centro de Estudios Sobre Movimientos de Obreros y Socialistas, Mexico City (hereafter CEMOS).

23. Ibid.

24. "Una Demonstración de Barbarie," *El Sol*, July 29, 1968.

25. Ibid.

26. *El Universal*, July 29, 1968

27. *Excélsior*, July 31, 1968.

28. The Mexican government's response to activists was not dramatically different than how young men were perceived in the other nations. See George Katsiaficas, *The Imagination of the New Left: A Global Analysis of 1968* (Boston: South End Press, 1987); and Robert V. Daniels, *Year of the Heroic Guerrilla: World Revolution and Counterrevolution in 1968* (New York: Basic books, 1989).

29. Telegrama de protesta por la repression a Comunista en el estado de Guerrero, April 17, 1968, PCM, box 64, document 7; Proyecto de declaración del C.C. del PCM con motivo de la repression en Guerrero, January 24, 1968, box 64, document 10, CEMOS.

30. Enrique Semo, personal communication, Summer 1997.

31. See Enrique Garza, León Tomas Ejea, and Luis Fernandez Macías, *El movimiento estudiantil* (México, D.F.: Editorial Extemporaneos, 1986), 3.

32. One of the few documents reflecting the earliest meetings between Poli and UNAM is a statement issued at the end of July discussing police and government violence. "A la opinión pública," July 1968, box 5, document 492, CME.

33. For a discussion of Mexican student politics at UNAM, see Donald Mabry's *The Mexican University and the State: Student Conflicts, 1910–1971* (College Station: Texas A&M Press, 1982).

34. UNAM has had a long and confrontational history with government. In 1945, UNAM was reorganized returning to the status of an agency of the federal government. For a discussion of the relation between UNAM and the republic, see Mabry's, *The Mexican University and the State*, 188–94.

35. Orden de operaciones num. Uno, Campo Militar Uno, July 29, 1968, reprinted in *Parte de guerra Tlatelolco 1968: Documentos del general Marcelino García Barragán: los hechos y la historia*, edited by Julio Scherer García and Carlos Monsiváis (México, D.F.: Nuevo Siglo, 1999), 60.

36. Informa las actividades realizadoas con motivo de la Misón ancomendada a esta unidad, July 30, 1968, Secretaria de la Defensa Nacional, México, D.F. reprinted in Scherer García and Monsiváis, *Parte de guerra Tlatelolco 1968*.

37. San Ildefonso is a historic building from colonial times. Currently, it houses a gallery.

38. Informa las actividades realizados con motivo de la Misón ancomendada a esta unidad.

39. Comité Nacional de lucha, August 14, 1968, box 4, document 482, CME. This document lists the names of fifty-six students who had been killed, disappeared, or incarcerated.

40. See Orden de Operaciones no. Uno, August 1, 1968, reprinted in Scherer García and Monsiváis.

41. Comité de lucha estudiantil, A la opinión pública, July 31, 1968, box 4, document 357, CME.

42. Lucy Castillo, interview, transcript in Jardón, "1968, El fuego de la esperanza."

43. Landa, interview with author.

44. Ibid.

45. Julia Túñon Pablos, discussion with author, May 11, 2001, New Haven, Connecticut.

46. Anne Rubenstein, *Bad Language, Naked Ladies, & Other Threats to the Nation* (Durham N.C.: Duke University Press, 1998).

47. Deborah Cohen and Lessie Jo Frazier, "No sólo cocinábamos...' Historia inédita de la otra mitad del 68," in *La transición interrumpida, México, 1968–1988*, ed. by Ilan Semo (México, D.F.: Editorial Patria, 1993), 75–105.

48. The demands were published in several newspapers. See *El Universal*, July 30, 1968, and *El Día*, July 30, 1968.

49. To activists, FNET's actions seemed suspicious. Working primarily in schools and universities under the Secretary of Education, FNET was seen by radical and activist students as a tool of the government. Students distrusted FNET leaders who they felt received favors or personal gain from the government for their activities.

50. "La Policía Exculpa a los Estudiantes de los Alborotos," *El Sol* (July 27, 1968). A subtitle to this article was: "Las fuerzas de orden intervinieron en auxilio y a petición de la FNET."

51. "1968: Una cronología," *Nexos*, 249 (September 1998).

52. "Violentos Choques Entre Estudiantes y la Policía," *El Día* (July 27, 1968).

53. *El Día*, August 4, 1968. Also see Ramon Ramírez, *El movimiento estudiantil de México: Análisis-Cronología*, vol. 1 (México, D.F.: Ediciones Era, 1969), 184.

54. Gastón García Cantú, *Javier Barros Sierra: 1968* (México, D.F.: Siglo Veinturno Editores, 1993). This work contains interviews conducted by García Cantú with Barros Sierra.

55. María Luisa Mendoza, "La O or el Redondo," *El Día*, August 2, 1968.

56. "Un ordenada manifestación," *El Universal*, August 2, 1968.

57. For the photos, see *El Universal*, August 2, 1968. Also see *Novedades*, August 2, 1968, *El Día*, August 2, 1968, and *Excélsior*, August 2, 1968.

58. "1968: Universidad y Cultura," directed by Rolando Cordera, *Nexos* TV, August 15, 1993, videocassette.

59. Ibid.

60. Fidel Velázquez took control of the CTM in 1941. It was under his tenure (which lasted until his death in 1997) in the 1940s, that Velázquez moved away from Cárdenas's populist policies and purged the leftists. In the years that followed, the CTM continually supported the government.

61. Quoted in Daniel Cazés, *Crónica 1968* (México, D.F.: Plaza y Valdés, 1993), 25; See also "1968: Una cronología" *Nexos*, 249 (September 1998), 83.

62. Ibid. See also Gerardo Medina Valdez, *El 68, Tlatelolco, y el PAN* (México, D.F.: 1990).

63. *Excélsior*, August 2, 1968; also reprinted in Ramírez, *El movimiento estudiantil de México*, vol. 2: 33.

64. Raúl Jardón, interview with author, March 6, 1997. Jardón's mother had been

a member of the Union and demonstrated in 1968. Also see Cohen and Frazier, "`No sólo concinábamos . . . ," 89.

65. Ibid.

66. For a complete transcript of the speech, see *Excélsior* and *El Día*, August 2, 1968. Translation in Poniatowska, *Massacre in Mexico*, 328.

67. "Hay una mano tendida, la de un hombre que ha demostrado que sabe ser leal: Díaz Ordaz," *El Día*, August 2, 1968.

68. Díaz Ordaz referred to the so-called outstretched hand in his annual address to the nation on September 1, 1968. For a discussion and partial transcriptions of the speech, see *El Heraldo de México*, *Novedades*, and *El Universal*, September 2, 1968.

69. Herbert Braun, "Protests of Engagement: Dignity, False Love, and Self-Love in Mexico during 1968," *Comparative Studies in Society and History* 39 (July 1997): 511–49.

70. Profesores de la Escuela Nacional de Ciencias Biológicas, open telegram to the President of the United States of Mexico, July 31, 1968, *El Día*, reprinted in Ramírez, *El movimiento estudiantil*, vol. 2: 19.

71. Profesores de la Escuela Nacional de Economía, "A la opinión pública," July 30, 1968, *El Día*, reprinted in Ramírez, *El movimiento estudiantil*, vol. 2: 9–20.

72. Estudiantes, profesores, e investigadores de El Colegio de México, *El Día*, July 31, 1968, reprinted in Ramírez, *El movimiento estudiantil*, vol. 2: 21–22.

73. Profesores de la Facultad de Ciencias Poíticas y Sociales, "A la opinión pública," July 31, 1968, *El Día* reprinted Ramírez, *El movimiento estudiantil*, vol. 2: 22–23.

74. Ibid.

75. "En perfecto orden se llevó a cabo la manifestación de estudiantes y maestros," *El Día*, August 6, 1968.

76. Ibid.

77. Ibid.

78. "Embestida contra prensa y gobierno," *El Sol*, August 6, 1968.

79. Integrantes del Consejo Nacional de Huelga, Consejo Nacional de Huelga, document reprinted in Jardón, "1968: El fuego de la esperanza," Jardón and Corona identified 128 CNH members, but estimated that there were more.

80. Adriana Corona, interview, Jardón, "1968: El fuego de la esperanza," 179. Corona was a CNH representative from Preparatory School 6 of UNAM. She argues that at times, the active participants in the CNH numbered over 500, but she claims the official and elected representatives numbered around 230.

81. Jardón, "Integrantes del Consejo Nacional de Huelga en 1968," in "1968: El fuego de la esperanza," 207.

82. Aída González, interview. González, a teacher in an UNAM preparatory

school, was not a member of the CNH; however, she worked closely with members because of her ties to education and to the left. In interviews that I conducted, many activists referred to a female CNH member who was never on the CNH. I later found that this particular woman was the lover of one of the prominent male activists. Other women simply assumed she was an elected CNH member due to her close affiliation.

83. Mabry, *The Mexican University and the State*, 254–55.

84. Judith Hellman, *Mexico in Crisis* (New York: Holmes & Meier Publishers, 1979). Hellman argues that the number on the CNH was necessary for its survival.

85. Jardón, "Integrantes del Consejo Nacional de Huelga en 1968." Jardón and Corona documented the various leftists affiliations: JCM, PCM, *Liga Comunista Espartaco* (Spartacus Communist League, LCE), *Alianza Revolucionario Espartaco* (Revolutionary Spartacus Alliance, ARE), *Movimiento Maxista Leninista Mexicano* (Mexican Marxist-Leninist Movement, MMLM), *Partido Obereo Revolutionario* (troskista) (Revolutionary Workers Party, Trotskites, POR(t)), or *Liga Obrero Marxista* (Marxist Workers League, LOM).

86. In 1968, the school of gynecology and obstetrics was part of the school of nursing at UNAM. Medicine was, and to some degree, continues to be dominated by men.

87. Roberta Avendaño, interview, *Nexos*, 121 (January 1988), 80, reprinted in Elviria Hernández Carballido, "La Tita, la Nacha, y...las demas," *Doble Jornada* (September 7, 1988), 4.

88. Mirthokleia González Guardado, interview, Jardón, "1968, El fuego de la esperanza," 172–74.

89. María Alvarez, interview, Jardón, "1968, El fuego de la esperanza," 112.

90. José López Rodríguez, interview, Jardón, "1968: El fuego de la esperanza," 110.

91. "Integrants del Consejo Nacional de Huelga en 1968"; Marcia Gutiérrez, interview, Jardón, "1968 El fuego de la esperanza," 169–71. For a discussion of the LCE, see Paulina Fernández Christlieb, *El espartaquismo en México* (México, D.F.: Ediciones El Caballito, 1978).

92. "Exhortó el Dr. Massieu a los estudiantes a actuar dentro de las lineas legales," *El Universal*, August 6, 1968.

93. "Coalición de Maestros de Enseñanza Media y Superior Pro-Libertades Democráticas," *El Día*, August 8, 1968.

94. Ibid.

95. "Maestros, Empleados, Administrativos y Manuales de la Secundaria," No. 59, *El Día*, August 8, 1968 reprinted in Ramirez, *El movimiento estudiantil*, vol. 2: 62.

96. Quote in Daniel Cazés, *Crónica 1968* (México, D.F.: Plaza y Valdés, 1993), 43.

97. Grupo de Profesores, Intectuales, y Artistas, "Los estudiantes defienden los derechos de todo el pueblo," August 9, 1968 reprinted in Ramírez, *El movimiento estudiantil*, vol. 2: 69–77.

98. Ibid., 73–75.

99. The regent of Mexico City was similar to a mayor, but he was appointed by the president. Thus, the regent came from the PRI party. The position of regent of Mexico City was an important post in the party and political structure because it was and is the most important and largest city in Mexico.

100. "Carta de Corona del Rosal a Massieu," *El Día*, August 9, 1968. The key figures included Luis Cueto Ramírez, Raúl Mendiolea Cueto, and Alfonso Frías.

101. "Llamado a la Concordia, en bien de México, formuló Corona," *Excélsior*, August 9, 1968.

102. "A la opinión pública," *El Día*, August 10, 1968.

103. "A la opinón pública," *El Día*, August 10, 1968.

104. *Gaceta: Boletín Informativo del Comité Corrdinadoor de Huelga de UNAM*, no. 1, August 13, 1968. box 7, no. 787, CME.

105. Images and speeches from the march can be found in Leobardo López Arteche and CUEC, *El grito*, 1968, 120 min., videocassette. I would like to thank Dr. David Maciel for originally sharing this film with me.

106. *Gaceta*, No. 1, August 13, 1968.

107. "A la opinión pública," *El Día*, August 12, 1968, reprinted in Ramírez, *El movimineto estudiantil de México: Documentos*, vol. 2: 84–86.

108. Ibid.

109. See for example, Frente Universitario Mexicano, Ahora o nunca, " Sr. President," August 1, 1968, box 9, document 901, CME. In this public letter, right-wing student group FUM blames the PCM as the creators of the conflicts. Also Movimiento Universitario de Renovadora Orientación, "Viva México: Muera el comunismo," August 25, 1968, box 9 document 903, CME. MURO, like FUM, blames the PCM for the disturbances.

110. See *El Día*, August 12, 1968. There is a published call to join that march for 13 August 1968.

111. "Se anuncia para hoy una marchas de estudiantes del Politécnico," *El Sol*, August 13, 1968.

112. Victor Rico Galán was a journalist for *Sucesos*. He would remain in prison until he was pardoned by Luis Echeverría.

113. "Carta de Victor Rico Galán a los estudantes," *Gaceta*, no. 2, August 15, 1968, box 7, document 787, CME. Also reprinted in Ramírez, *El movimiento estudiantil de México*, vol. 2: 88–90.

114. Ibid.

115. Colección de impresos Esther Montero, AHUNAM-CESU.

116. Photo of young men in *El Heraldo de México*, August 14, 1968, also in Leobardo López Arteche and Centro Universitario de Estudios Cinematográficos, *El grito* 120 mins., 1969.

117. Posters can be seen in López, *El grito.*

118. Quoted in Daniel Cazés, *Crónica 1968*, 53.

119. Ibid.

120. Ibid.

121. Quoted in *Gaceta*, No. 2, *Boletín Informativo del Comité Coordinador de Huelga de la Universidad*, August 15, 1968, CME.

122. *El Heraldo de México*, August 14, 1968.

123. "Insultos al ejército y las autoridades," *El Heraldo*, August 14, 1968.

124. Ibid.

125. For a hagiography of García Barragán, see Hector Francisco Castañeda Jiménez, *Marcelino García Barragán: Una vida al servicio* (Guadalajara: Gobierno de Jalisco, 1987).

126. Dibujos de Carreño, "Familiaridad," *Novedades*, August 15, 1968.

127. "El Mundo Hoy," *El Universal*, August 4, 1968.

128. *Le Monde*, August 14, 1968, reprinted in *El movimiento estudiantil mexicano en la prensa francesa*, edited by Carlos Arriola (México, D.F.: El Colegio de México, 1979), 34–35.

129. *Excélsior*, August 14, 1968.

Chapter Three

1. Judith Butler, *Gender Trouble: Feminism and the Subversion of Identity* (New York: Routledge Press, 1990), 140–41.

2. Herbert Braun, "Protests of Engagement: Dignity, False Love, and Self-Love in Mexico During 1968," *Comparative Studies in Society and History* 39 (July 1997): 511–49.

3. *El Día*, August 14, 1968.

4. Facultad de Química, "Tareas frente a la actual situación." September 1968, box 4, document 353, Impresos Sueltos del Movimiento Estudiantil Mexicano, Fundo Reservado, Biblioteca Nacional, México, D.F. (hereafter CME).

5. See Comité de lucha, Facultad de Ciencias Politicas y Sociales, "La formación y funcionamiento de brigadas politicas estudiantiles de secundaria, preparatoria, UNAM, e IPN," August 26, 1998, box 3 document 213, CME. Also republished in Leopoldo Ayala, *Nuestra Verdad: Memorial popular del movimiento estudiantil popular y el dos de octubre de 1968* (México, D.F.: Joaquín Porrúa, 1989), 106. Also Comité de lucha, "Organigrama," September 1968, document 14, box 1, CME; "Brigadia lleva la verdad al pueblo, aprender la prática, venceremos! Brigadias, hace la clase obrera!, Compañeros

brigadieres," September 1968, document 350, box 4, CME.

6. Edgard Sánchez, interview, Raúl Jardón, "1968: El fuego de la esperañza" (unpublished manuscript in possession of author), 109.

7. Anonymous interview, Jackie Skiles Quayle, translator, "Student Interviews," *North American Congress on Latin America* (NACLA), November 1 1968, 21. NACLA devoted a two-part issue to Mexico. The first report, "Repression," profiled the student movement, the second part, "Domination," examined the Mexican economy.

8. For example, see Comité de lucha estudiantil, "A todo el pueblo de México," August 30, 1968, document 384, CME. This document refutes the official reports of what happened on August 27–29.

9. See film-footage, *1968: El movimiento y el CNH*, Nexos TV, August 22, 1993, videocassette in possession of author.

10. Margarita Isabel, interview excerpt in *Massacre in Mexico*, Elena Poniatowska, trans. by Helen Lane (Columbia: University of Missouri Press, 1991), 20–22.

11. Ibid.

12. Ibid.

13. Vida Valero Borrás, interview with author, April 3 and 10, 1997.

14. See for instance studies on women in the Mexican Revolution, Elizabeth Salas, *Soldaderas in the Mexican Military: Myth and History* (Austin: University of Texas Press, 1990).

15. Judith Butler, *Gender Trouble*, 140.

16. Anonymous interview with author, 1997.

17. Marta Lamas, interview with author, June 5, 1997, Mexico City. Lamas is a leader of the contemporary Mexican feminist movement.

18. Raúl Jardón, interview with author, March 6, 1997, Mexico City.

19. Isabel Huerta, interview, Jardón, "1968: El fuego de la esperañza," 113.

20. Eduardo Valle, excerpt of interview, *Massacre in Mexico*, 90. See also Valle's own work on his role in 1968, *Escritos sobre el movimiento del 68* (México: Universidad Autónoma de Sinaloa, 1984).

21. Mercedes Perelló, interview with author, June 6, 1997, Mexico City, Mexico.

22. See for example, Elizabeth Kuznesof and Robert Oppenheimer, "The Family and Society in Nineteenth Century Latin America: An Historiographical Introduction," *Journal of Family History* 10, no. 3 (1985): 215–34; Donna Guy, "Introduction," in *White Slavery and Mothers Alive and Dead: The Troubled Meetings of Sex, Gender, Public Health, and Progress in Latin America* (Lincoln: University of Nebraska Press, 2000); and Asunción Lavrin, *Women, Feminism, and Social Change in Argentina, Chile, and Uruguay, 1890–1940* (Lincoln: University of Nebraska Press, 1995).

23. Frank Ralph Brandenburg, *The Making of Modern Mexico* (New York: Prentice Hall, 1944); Arthur Schmidt, "Making it Real Compared to What? Reconceptualizing Mexican History Since 1940," in *Fragments of a Golden Age: The Politics of Culture in Mexico Since 1940*, edited by Gilbert Joseph, Anne Rubenstein, and Eric Zolov (Durham N.C.: Duke University Press, 2002), 23–68; Eric Zolov, *Refried Elvis: The Rise of the Mexican Counterculture* (Berkeley: University of California Press, 1999); Anne Rubenstein, *Bad Language, Naked Ladies, & Other Threats to the Nation: A Political History of Comic Books in Mexico* (Durham N.C.: Duke University Press, 1998); and Arturo Warman, "Secreto de familia," in *Pensar el 68*, ed. by Raúl Alvarez Garín, et. al (México, D.F.: Cal y Arena, 1988), 131–34.

24. Escuela Nacional Preparatoria Plantel No. 8, "A todos los padres," August 1968, document 118, box 1, CME.

25. "Facultad de Derecho, A Todos Los Padres," August 27, 1968, document 253, box 2, CME; Facultad de Medicina, Comité de Prensa, Unión Cívica de Padres de Familia, "Sres. Padres de familia," August 23, 1968, document 322, box 3, CME.

26. Colección de impresos Esther Montero Archivo Histórico de Universidad Autónoma de México-Centro de Estudios Sobre La Universidad, AHUNAM-CESU, Biblioteca Nacional, Mexico City.

27. Carmen Landa, interview with author; Carmen Ramos Escandon, discussion with author, May 11, 2001, New Haven, CT. Ramos recalled that her mother made copies of student propaganda for her and her friends.

28. Quotes in *El Día*, August 21, 1968, also in Ramirez, *El movimiento estudiantil de México*, vol. 1: 237.

29. "Carta Abierta al Sr. Presidente de la República Lic. Gustavo Díaz Ordaz," *Gaceta* 6 (September 7, 1968), document 787, box 7, CME. Also issued to *El Día*, September 7, 1968. This is a common practice in Mexico. Associations publish their demands, solidarity, or forthcoming actions in various newspapers in the Federal District.

30. The Mexican government stated that it would open the 1968 archives in the latter half of 1998. While many documents have been released, many others have not.

31. "Habla una madre: A todas mas mujeres mexicana," document 853, box 8, CME. This is an unsigned piece of propaganda.

32. "Madre Mexicana," document 411, box 4, CME.

33. For a dramatization of parent's fear, See Jorge Fons, *Rojo amanecer*, (1988), 90 minutes, Videocassette.

34. Uniones y sociedades de padres de familia, "Padres de familia," September 11, 1968, document 917, box 9, CME. This document calls on parents to forbid

their children from attending the Great Silent March which occurred on September 13, 1968.

35. Corona, interview, Jardón, "1968: El fuego de la esperanza," 179.

36. Ibid.

37. See Oscar Lewis, *Five Families* (New York: Mentor Books, 1959). Introducing the Mexican family to United States academic circles, Lewis embraced the dichotomous relationship between Mexican men and women. When he perceived a strong or economically independent woman, he questioned the sexuality of the husband. For application in women's history see Evelyn Stevens, "Marianismo: The Other Face of Machismo in Latin America," in *Female and Male in Latin America: Essays*, Ann Pescatello, ed. (Pittsburgh Pennsylvania: University of Pittsburgh Press, 1973). The double standard within Mexican society has been discussed in literature since the seventeenth century. Recent research on the dichotomous constructions of gender and the double standard have begun to assert that with the changes in the economic situation, where more women work outside the home, women are gaining greater independence. See Elizabeth Dore, ed. *Gender Politics in Latin America: Debates in Theory and Practice* (New York: Monthly Review Press, 1997). Moreover, recent studies focusing on sexuality reveal that gender constructs are much more fluid than those earlier discussed by Lewis and Stevens. See for example, Daniel Balderston and Donna J. Guy, eds., *Sex and Sexuality in Latin America* (New York: New York University Press, 1997).

38. Corona, interview, Jardón, "1968: El fuego de la esperanza," 179.

39. Mercedes Perelló, interview with author, June 10, 1997, Mexico City.

40. Marcelino Perelló, interview, and Mercedes Perelló, interview.

41. Marcelino Perelló, interview.

42. Lilia Granillo, interview with author, April 6, 1997, Mexico City.

43. Ibid.

44. Consejo Nacional de Huelga, "Al pueblo de México, a los estudiantes, maestros, y padres, de familia," *El Día*, August 16, 1968, also published in Ramirez, *El movimiento estudiantil*, vol. 2: 95.

45. See Mabry, *The Mexican University and the State*, 252; and Poniatowska, *Massacre in Mexico*, 53. The FNET issued demands on July 26 that called for the firing of police chiefs and indemnification. After the August 1 march, students from Poli and UNAM demanded the abolition of Article 145 and granaderos, release of student prisoners, and respect for democratic liberties, as well as indemnification, and firing of police chiefs. The release of all activists arrested was expanded to include all political prisoners.

46. Marcelino Perelló, interview, Jardón, "1968: El fuego de la esperanza," 1490.

47. Rufino Perdomo, interview, Jardón, "1968: El fuego de la esperanza," 164.

48. Conteris, "New Outbreak of the Student Rebellion," 9.

49. Under Ávila Camacho, Mexico declared war on the Axis powers during World War II. This was also a period of growth for United States investment. See Enrique Krauze, "Manuel Ávila Camacho," *Mexico Biography of Power: A History of Modern Mexico, 1810–1996* (New York: Harper Perennial, 1997), 491–525.

50. Marcelino Perelló, interview with author, June 6, 1997, Mexico City.

51. Eduardo Valle, interview, *1968: El movimiento y el CNH*, Nexos Television, August 22, 1993, videocassette; Coalición de Maestros de Ensenanza Media y Superior Pro Libertades Democráticas, "A los CC Diputados y senadores del Districto Federal," *El Día*, August 21, 1968.

52. Coalición de Profesores de Enseñanza Media y Superior Pro-libertades Democráticas, "A la opinión pública," *El Día* August 25, 1968; Consejo Nacional de Huelga, "Al pueblos de México," August 25, 1968, reprinted in Ramírez, *El movimiento estudiantil*, vol. 2: 153–54.

53. "Ondeó la Bandera Rojinegra en el Asta Monumental," *El Heraldo de México*, August 28, 1968.

54. Jardón, "1968: El fuego de la esperanza," 36–37.

55. Demetrio Vallejo Martínez, *Boletín de prensa*, August 26, 1968, document 1025, box 10, CME. Also reprinted in Ramírez, *El movimiento estudiantil*, vol. 2: 155–56.

56. Victor Rico Galán, Segunda carta de Rico Galán a los estudantes, August 26, 1968, document 1024, box 10. Also reprinted in Ramírez, *El movimiento estudiantil*, vol. 2,: 156–58.

57. Jardón, "1968: El fuego de la esperañza," 37.

58. "Fueron desalojados," *El Universal*, August 28, 1968.

59. F. Carmona Neclares, "Queremos la Palabra del Señor Presidente," *Excélsior*, August 29, 1968. The journalist encouraged the government to begin the dialogue for the sake of the nation.

60. Marcelino Perelló, interview, Jardón, "1968: El fuego de la esperañza," 148.

61. Gilberto Guevara Niebla, interview, Jardón, "1968: El fuego de la esperañza," 154.

62. See "Ceremonia de Desagravio a la Ensena Nacional en el Zócalo," *Novedades*, August 29, 1968; and coverage in *Excélsior*, August 29–30, 1968.

63. Aida González, interview with author; Marcelino Perelló, interview, Jardón, "1968: El fuego de la esperanza," 148.

64. *El Día*, September 21, 1968, republished in Ramírez, *El movimiento estudiantil*, vol. 2: 320–21.

65. *El Día*, September 9, 1968; and "Manifestación Anticomunista en la Plaza México," *El Heraldo*, September 9, 1968.

66. "Mujeres de Acción Católica Mexicana," August 1968, document 911, box 9, CME.

67. "Al Pueblo Mexicano," *El Día*, September 11, 1968, 3, and *Gaceta*, no. 7, September 13, 1968, document 787, box 7, CME. Also reprinted in Ramírez, *El movimiento estudiantil*, vol. 2: 263–64.

68. "Heberto Castillo habla a El Universal: Diálogo Público, no Función de Ciro," *El Universal*, August 30, 1968. See also, Oscar Menéndez, director, *Los años difíciles* 28 mins., 1997, videocassette.

69. *El Heraldo de México*, August 28, 1968.

70. "Comisión Organizadora de Telefonistas," *Gaceta*, no. 3 (August 20, 1968), document 787, box 7, CME; Consejo Nacional Ferrocarrilero, "Solidaridad con los Estudiantes" *La Voz de México*, 1949, August 27, 1968, reprinted in Ramírez, *El movimiento estudiantil*, vol. 2: 126–28; Organisamos del Partido Comunista en la UNAM y IPN, "Declaración de los organismos del partido comunista mexicano en la Universidad Nacional Autónoma y el Instituto Politécnico Nacional," *Historia y Sociedad*, 12 (April–July 1968), reprinted in Ramírez, *El movimiento estudiantil*, vol. 2: 139–41.

71. "A la Opinón Pública," *El Día*, August 31, 1968.

72. "Defenderé a Méxcio y Arrostro las Consecuencias," *El Heraldo de México*, September 2, 1968; "Haremos Nuestros Deber; Llegamos Hasta Donde se nos Obligue: G.D.O," *Novedades*, September 2, 1968; and "Toda la Energía si es Necessario," *El Universal*, September 2, 1968.

73. Ibid.

74. Marcelino Perelló and the CNH to President Díaz Ordaz, September 10, 1968, reprinted in *El Día*, September 18, 1968.

75. Perelló, interview, Jardón, "1968: El fuego de la esperanza."

76. Ibid. Escuincles are small almost hairless dogs native to Mexico; the term is colloquially used in reference to children.

77. Consejo Nacional de Huelga, "Invitación al pueblo de México," September 13, 1968, reprinted in Jardón, "1968: El fuego de la esperañza," 230.

78. Jardón, "1968: El fuego de la esperanza," 48.

79. Mabry, *The Mexican University and the State*, 261; Evelyn Stevens, *Protest and Response in Mexico* (Cambridge: Massachusetts Institute of Technology Press, 1974), 213.

80. CNH, "Pueblo de Mexico," reprinted in "1968: El fuego de la esperañza," 231

81. Ibid.

82. "Colonia Olivar del Conde," August 1967, document 982, box 9, CME; Colonias Nueva Atzacoalco y Martín Carrera, August 1968, document 984, box 9, CME; Barrio de Tepito, August 1968, document 985, box 9, CME. Neighborhoods complained about police and granaderos fining and arresting people, but they also made demands for better social services.

83. See news coverage in *El Universal*, *El Día*, *Excélsior*, September 14, 1968.

84. Eduardo Valle, Jardón, "1968: El fuego de la esperañza."

85. Luis González de Alba, *Los días y los años* (Mexico, D.F.: Biblioteca Era, 1971), 118–19.

86. Manuel Moreno Rodríguez, interview, transcript reprinted in "1968: El fuego de la esperañza," 110.

87. González de Alba, *Los días y los años*, 119.

88. Ibid.

89. Moreno Rodríguez, interview.

90. José López Rodríguez, interview, Jardón, "1968: El fuego de la esperañza."

91. Photo, *El Universal*, September 14, 1968.

92. Luis González de Alba, *Los días y los anos*, 121.

Chapter Four

1. See Eric Zolov, *Refried Elvis: The Rise of the Mexican Counterculture* (Berkeley: University of California Press, 1999). Zolov contemplates the government's manipulation of rock music.

2. "A la opinión pública," August 1968, document 163, box 2, Impreso sueltos Movimiento Estudiantil Mexicano, 1968 (CME), Fondo Reservado, Biblioteca Nacional, Mexico City. This document counters the argument set forth by the government that the student unrest would lead to an international boycott of the games. The students replied that the government held the solution to end the protests.

3. "Habla Uno de los Lideres de Movimiento Estudiantil," *Excélsior*, September 18, 1968, reprinted in Ramírez, *El movimiento estudiantil* II, 293–96. In an interview, Perelló mentioned that he was also portrayed as a "foreigner" during the movement because his parents were from Spain. Marcelino Perelló, interview with author, June 6, 1997, México, D.F.

4. "Perecen Cuatro Empleados Poblanos, Linchados en San Miguel de Canoa," *Excélsior*, September 15, 1968.

5. Despite the fact that that the Mexican government did not have a concordat with the Holy See in 1968, the ringing of the cathedral bells during the August 27 student march galvanized the faithful. Although a Catholic country, Mexico has had a long history of anti-Catholicism from the presidency of Benito Juárez (1867–1872) to the Cristero Revolt of the 1920s. Under Juárez, two laws were instituted that angered the Catholic Church. Ley Juárez abolished special dispensations that exempted clerics from having to stand trial in civic courts. Ley Lerdo prohibited the Church from holding and administering property that was not used for Church business. The Constitution of 1917 also attempted to control the Catholic Church leading to tensions between the Church and the state that resulted in a three year strike by the Church. A band of Catholic

guerrillas, the Cristeros attacked government institutions and its representatives. In response, the military attacked the Cristeros leading to an escalation of violence that contributed to the assassination of ex-president and victorious presidential candidate Alvaro Obregón (1920–1924) on July 17, 1928.

6.   Felipe Cazas, director, *Canoa*, 120 mins., videocassette. The melodrama *Canoa* is about the events in Puebla.

7.   Jorge Azala Blanco, *La condición del cine mexicano (1973–1985)* (México, D.F.: Editorial Posada, 1986), 303. See also Leonardo Garcia Tsao, *Felipe Cazals habla de su cine* (Guadalajara: Universidad de Guadalajara, 1994).

8.   "Los confundieron con Comunistas y los mataron a machetazos," *El Heraldo*, September 18, 1968.

9.   Carlos Monsiváis, "Los lichermientos de Canoa," *Excélsior*, March 20, 1976; Guillermina Meany, *Canoa: El crimen impune* (México, D.F.: Editorial Posada, 1977). For a modern discussion of a lynching for alleged crimes in Mexico, see Sam Quinones, *True Tales from Another Mexico: The Lynch Mob, the Popsicle Kings, Chalino, and the Bronx* (Albuquerque: University of New Mexico Press, 2001), 31–52.

10. See *El Día*, *El Heraldo*, and *El Universal*, September 19, 1968.

11. Raúl Jardón, "1968: El fuego de la esperanza" (unpublised manuscript, 1996), 51.

12. *El Día*, September 19, 1968.

13. Esteban Bravo, interview, in Jardón, in "1968: El fuego de la esperanza," 110–11.

14. "El Ejército Ocupó la Ciudad Universitaria," *El Día*, September 19, 1968; Bravo, interview with Jardón; and "Eyewitness Report," September 24, 1968, *NACLA* (November 1968), 12.

15. "El Ejército Ocupó la Ciudad Universitaria," *El Día*, September 19, 1968; "Ocupación Militar de C.U.," *El Universal*, September 19, 1968; "El Ejército Ocupó Ciudad Universitario," *El Heraldo de México*, September 19, 1968; "Declaración Oficial del Gobierno Federal," *Excélsior*, September 19, 1968; and Mabry, *The Mexican University and the State*, 261–62.

16. For a history of the relations between the university and the state, see Mabry, *The Mexican University*; and Gilberto Guevara Niebla, *La rosa de los cambios: Breve historia de la UNAM* (México, D.F.: Cal y Arena, 1990).

17. Jardón, "1968: El fuego de la esperanza," 51.

18. "El Ejército ocupó la Ciudad Universitaria," *El Día*, September 19, 1968.

19. Ibid.

20. Ibid.

21. "El Ejército no desea conservar por tiempo indefinido los planteles," *El Día*, September 20, 1968.

22. See for example, Gilberto Keith, "Un hecho Triste: La Fuerza Otra Vez,"

Excélsior, September 19, 1968.

23. "El rector delpora lo cocurrido y llama a la razón y la serenidad," *El Día*, September 19, 1968.

24. Ibid.

25. "Declaraciones en torno a la Ocupación de CU," *El Día*, September 20, 1968, and Gerardo Medina Valdez, *El 68, Tlatelolco, y el PAN* (México, D.F.: Partido Acción Nacional, 1990). The PAN, as well as the left, has demanded that the government papers on 1968 be opened. The PAN has also published a collection of their documents that demonstrate the PAN opposition to the Díaz Ordaz administration during the 1968 student movement.

26. "Al C. Presidente de la República," *El Día*, September 20, 1968.

27. Unión Nacional de Mujeres Mexicanas, *Historia y Sociedad*, no. 13–14, julio-diciembre 1968, appendix, lvii–lviii reprinted in Ramírez, *El movimiento estudiantil*, vol. 2: 312–13.

28. "Grupo de Profesionistas, public letter to President of the Republic," *El Día*, September 21, 1968. Also reprinted in Ramírez, *El movimiento estudiantil*, vol. 2: 320–21.

29. "Partido Revolucionario Institucional, Al Pueblo de México," *El Día*, September 20, 1968. Also reprinted in Ramírez, *El movimiento estudaintil*, vol. 2: 307–9.

30. "Heberto Castillo, Marcué, y Eli de Gortari Detenidos," *El Heraldo de México*, September 20, 1968.

31. "Refriega entre estudiantes y granaderos en Zacatenco," *El Universal*, September 21, 1968.

32. "El ejército no desea conserver por tiempo indefinido los planteles," *El Día*, September 20, 1968.

33. "Impedirán mítines estudiantiles en Oaxaca; paros in Monterrey, Mérida, y otros lugares," *Excélsior*, September 23, 1968.

34. Letter to Junta de Gobierno de la Universidad Nacional Autónoma de México from Javier Barros Sierra, text reprinted in *El Heraldo*, September 23, 1968.

35. "Violentos disturbios en Nonoalco-Tlatelolco," *El Día*, September 22, 1968.

36. "Por 6 horas grupos de jóvenes hacen frente a la fuerza pública; un granderos muerto," *Novedades*, September 22, 1968.

37. Department of Defense Intelligence report, "Army Participation in Student Situation, Mexico City," document 88, October 18, 1968, *The Tlatelolco Massacre: U.S. Documents on Mexico and the Events of 1968*, National Security archive, Washington, D.C., http://www.gwu.edu/~nsarchive.

38. "Cuantiosos Daños en Tlatelolco," *El Heraldo*, September 23, 1968.

39. Department of Defense Intelligence report, "Army Participation in Student Situation, Mexico City."

40. "La situación estudiantil," *El Día*, October 1, 1968.

41. "Salen las tropes de la universidad," *Novedades*, October 1, 1968.

42. All of the buildings in the Tlatelolco complex are named after cities and states in Mexico or important dates in Mexican history. It is a huge complex with lawns in the interior. It spreads over numerous city blocks.

43. "Files Point to Official Use of Snipers in '68 Mexico Massacre," *New York Times*, October 2, 2003.

44. Jorge Alejandro Medellín, "De la Barreda debe comparecer hoy," *El Universal* (August 4, 2004). Ex-Capitan of the Federal Security Directorate Luis de la Barreda Moreno confirmed that the October 2, 1968 operation was called "Operación Galeana."

45. Elena Poniatowska, *Massacre in Mexico*, 212.

46. Interview with Gilberto Guevara Niebla, "El dos de octubre," in *Pensar el '68*, edited by Gilberto Guevara, et al. (México, D.F.: Cal y Arena, 1993), 117.

47. González, interview with author.

48. The sound of the helicopters and the Bengal lights has been recalled in numerous works. See Poniatowska, *Massacre in Mexico*, and the melodramatic film, Jorge Fons, *Rojo amanecer*, videocassette, 95 mins.

49. González, interview with author. Upon exiting the building, González had been thrown to the ground by one of the soldiers. He laid on top of her, while he was shooting. She watched what she recalled from under the soldier, hearing his gunfire next to her.

50. Mirthokleia González Guardado, interview, in "1968: El fuego de la esperanza," 173–74. The white gloves of young men served to identify the government forces from the students and other activists.

51. Ibid.

52. See *Proceso*, December 9, 2001 and *La Jornada*, December 16, 2001.

53. "López Osuna murió debido a 'congestión visceral generalizada': primeros datas de la autopsia," *La Jornada*, December 22, 2001.

54. "Denuncian sesgo manipulador en el caso López Osuna," *La Jornada*, December 23, 2001.

55. Poniatowska, *Massacre in Mexico*, 218.

56. Ibid., 216.

57. "Reprueba Alemán la Violencia y Pide Laborar por México," *El Heraldo*, October 4, 1968. See also coverage in the other major newspapers *El Dia*, *Excélsior*, *El Universal*, and *El Sol*, October 3–4, 1968.

58. For example, see Poniatowska, *Massacre in Mexico*.

59. Ramon Morones, "El ejército actuó con apego a la Constitución," *Excélsior*, October 3, 1968.

60. Rodolfo Anaya, "Subió a trienta el número de la muerto de antier," *El*

Heraldo, October 4, 1968.

61. For a personal recollection of the event, see Oriana Fallaci's statement published in *La Voz de México*, no. 1958, (December 1, 1968) reprinted in Ramírez, *El movimiento estudiantil*, vol. 2: 451–55. Also see Oriana Fallaci, "The Shooting of Oriana Fallaci," *Look*, November 12, 1968, 20–21.

62. Ibid., 452.

63. This warning by Sócrates Campos Lemus is well remembered. Many recalled the statement in interviews and it became part of the collective memory of the movement in films such as Fons, *Rojo amanecer*.

64. Caroline Pacheco, interview with author, February 6, 1997. Pacheco continues to work and live in Mexico.

65. "El Géneral Cárdenas Condena a los Agitadores," *El Heraldo*, October 6, 1968.

66. Telegram to Secretary of State from U.S. Embassy in Mexico, document October 1968, Tlatelolco Massacre: Declassified U.S. Documents on Mexico and Events of 1968, National Security Archive, http://www.gwu.edu/~nsarchiv/.

67. "Reitera Cueto: Energía Para Evitar Motines," *El Sol*, October 4, 1968.

68. "Revelaciones sobre el movimiento," *Excélsior*, October 6, 1968. Campos Lemus was wrong in his estimates of CNH. Nonetheless, his testimonial told the government that the CNH involved more than simply the people they had previously identified.

69. "Neigan cargos los cinco señaldos," *Excélsior*, October 7, 1968.

70. "Los alborotadores tenían un arsenal en Tlatelolco," *El Sol*, October 7, 1968.

71. Walt Rostow, Memorandum to the President, "Mexican Riots Extent of Communism," October 5, 1968, Lyndon B. Johnson Library, CO-Mexico, vol. IV, Box 60, "Mexico, memos & misc., 1/68–10/68," document 102, Tlatelolco Massacre: Declassified U.S. Documents on Mexico and Events of 1968, National Security Archive. http://www.gwu.edu/~nsarchiv/.

72. For the documents revealing the confusion, see Tlatelolco Massacre: Declassified U.S. Documents on Mexico and Events of 1968, National Security Archive, http://www.gwu.edu/~nsarchiv/.

73. Eduardo Valle, interview, *1968: El movimiento y el CNH*, Nexos Television, (August 22, 1993), videocassette; Perelló, interview with author.

74. CIA Station in Mexico, confidential intelligence information cable, "Mexico City Sitrep," October 8, 1968, Tlatelolco Massacre: Declassified U.S. Documents on Mexico and Events of 1968. National Security Archive, http://www.gwu.edu/~nsarchiv/. In this document, the CIA asserts that many students felt that Sócrates Campos Lemus was a government informer.

75. Department of Defense Intelligence Information Report, "Army Participation in Student Situation," October 18, 1968, document 23; CIA

Intelligence Information Report, Status of Brig.-General José Hernandez, October 23, 1968, Tlatelolco Massacre: Declassified U.S. Documents on Mexico and Events of 1968, National Security Archive, http://www.gwu.edu/~nsarchiv/.

76. "Precaución," *El Universal*, October 5, 1968.

77. "El ejército no disparó primero; repelió la agresión," *El Sol*, October 8, 1968, and Ramírez, *El movimiento estudiantil*, vol. 2: 417.

78. See Department of Defense Intelligence Report, "Army Participation in Student Situation, Mexico City." Tlatelolco Massacre: Declassified U.S. Documents on Mexico and Events of 1968.

79. Ibid. The Olympic Brigade and Olympic Battalion are the same.

80. *La battalion Olympica*, Canal 22, 35 mins., 1998, videocassette.

81. For a discussion of the life of a political prisoner, see Luis González de Alba, *Los días y los años* (México, D.F.: Biblioteca Era, 1971); Heberto Castillo, *1968: El principio del poder* (México, D.F.: Proceso, 1980) and Castillo, *Si te agarran, te van a matar* (México, D.F.: Ediciones Oceano, 1973); and Oscar Menéndez, *Los años difíciles*, video-cassette, 28 mins., 1997. Menéndez's film is a documentary about Heberto Castillo and his incarceration as a political prisoner.

82. Quoted in Daniel Cazés, *Crónica 1968*, (Mexico, D.F.: Plaza y Valdés, 1993), 268.

83. Ibid.

84. Martha Servin, interview, in "1968: El fuego de la esperanza," 177.

85. Department of Defense Intelligence Report, "Army Participation in Student Situation, Mexico City," October 18, 1968.

86. Francisco Delgado Sánchez, interview, transcript in "1968, El fuego de la esperanza," 125.

87. CIA Weekly Special Report, "Challenges to Mexico's Single Party Rule," January 17, 1969, Tlatelolco Massacre: Declassified U.S. Documents on Mexico and Events of 1968, National Security Archive, http://www.gwu.edu/~nsarchiv/.

Chapter Five

1. Enrique Krauze, *Mexico Biography of Power: A History of Modern Mexico, 1810–1996*, trans. Hank Heifetz (New York: Harper Perennial, 1997). Krauze writes that the Díaz Ordaz, as well as Adolfo López Mateos (1958–1964) had the same Finance Minister Antonio Ortiz Mena.

2. Ignacio Rodríguez Reyna and Jacinto R. Munguía, "El hijo del expresidente Díaz Ordaz rasga el silence," *Milenio*, 57, September 28, 1998, 30–35.

3. Many former activists expressed feelings of betrayal in interviews with the author. Carmen Landa, interview with author, October 21, 1997, Mexico City; Aída González, interview with author, November 30, 1997, San Mateo

Tlatenango, Mexico; Lilian Liebermann, interview with author, April 4, 1997, Mexico City; and Marcelino Perelló, interview with author, June 6, 1997, Mexico City.

4. For a biography of Echeverría, see Krauze, *Mexico: Biography of Power*; Samuel Schmidt, *The Deterioration of the Mexican Presidency: The Years Luis Echeverría*, trans. Dan A. Cothran (Tucson: University of Arizona Press, 1991), 5.

5. Sergio Tamayo, "The 20 Mexican Octobers: A Study of Citizenship and Social Movements" (PhD diss., University of Texas at Austin, 1994), 187.

6. Salvador Allende was president of Chile from 1970 to 1973. Allende was a socialist victim of the Cold War. He was overthrown by a military coup that received assistance from the United States' Central Intelligence Agency and the Nixon administration.

7. Dan Cothran, "Editor's Introduction: Pacification through Repression and Distribution: The Echeverría Years in Mexico," in Schmidt's, *The Deterioration of the Mexican Presidency*, xxi; The idea of the cardenista being part of the tradition of the Mexican left is derived from Adolfo Gilly, *México, la larga travesía* (México, D.F.: Nueva Imagen, 1985), 175–79. Also see Arturo Anguiano, *Entre el pasado y el futuro: La izquierda en México, 1969–1995* (México, D.F.: Universidad Autónoma Metropolitana, 1997), 46.

8. See Heberto Castillo, "Alfonso Martínez Domínguez: 'La matanza fue preparado por Luis Echeverría,'" *Proceso* (June 4, 1979), 6–13; Antonio Jáquez, "La verdad no sirve para vengarse sino para hacer injusticia," *Proceso* (February 8, 1998), 15–20; Carlos Monsiváis, "Tlatelolco entre cortinas de humo" *Proceso* (February 8 1998), 16–17.

9. Enrique Semo, discussion with author, March 1998.

10. Mexican intellectuals like as Octavio Paz expressed outrage over 1968 in various ways. Paz relinquished his ambassadorship to India. Rosario Castellanos expressed her rage through her poetry. The international community and Mexican intellectuals expressed shock and disbelief when Díaz Ordaz was given the ambassadorship to Spain under Echeverría. In response, Carlos Fuentes renounced his ambassadorship to France.

11. Pablo González Casanova, *Democracy in Mexico* (New York: Oxford University Press, 1970). González Casanova was rector of UNAM from 1970 to 1972.

12. Olac Fuentes Molinar, "Las épocas de la universidad mexicana," *Cuadernos Politicos* 33 (April–June 1988), 50. For general discussions about the contemporary history of UNAM and educational reform see Cuauhtémoc Ochoa, "La reforma educativa en la UNAM (1970–74)," *Cuadernos Politicos* 9 (July–September 1976), 67–82; Olac Fuentes Molinar, "Universidad y democracia: La mirada hacia la izquierda," *Cuadernos Politicos* 53 (January–April 1988), 4–18.

13. Schmidt, *The Deterioration of the Mexican Presidency*, 88. For a broader study on CONASUPO, see Kenneth Mitchell, *State-Society Relations in Mexico: Clientelism, Neoliberal State Reform, and the Case of CONASUPO* (London: Ashgate Publishing, 2001). CONASUPO provided more subsidized consumption goods. BANRURAL and INFONAVIT restructured credit practices to make credit for land or housing more accessible to the peasant and working classes. Recently, the programs have been extended to the Mexican professional and middle classes. I would like to thank Arq. Javier Alvarez-Isasi and Arq. Bertha Belem Alvarez Isasi for explaining to me how INFON-AVIT functions.

14. This is common knowledge in Mexico City among the educated classes, see cultural critic Ilan Stavans, "Unmasking of Marcos" in *The Riddle of Cantinflas: Essays on Hispanic Popular Culture* (Albuquerque: University of New Mexico Press, 1998), 13–24. Stavans discusses the importance of UAM-Xochimilco and its ties to Subcommandante Marcos rumored to be Rafael Sebastián Guillén Vicente, an ex-professor at UAM-Xochimilco.

15. Schmidt, *The Deterioration of the Mexican Presidency*, 32; and Daniel Cosío Villegas, *La sucesión: Desenlace y perspectivas* (México, D.F.: Cuadernos de Joaquín Mortiz, 1976). For a discussion about the declining economy see Jorge Martínez Rios, *El perfil de México en 1980* (México, D.F.: Editores Siglo XXI 1972).

16. *2 de octubre*, 60 mins, videocassette, 1969. I thank Dr. David Maciel for sharing this film with me. Footage from *2 de octubre* also appears in Oscar Menéndez, *México, 1968*, TV UNAM, 1996, Latin American Video Archive, New York, NY.

17. Ibid.

18. Rubén Jaramillo fought with Emiliano Zapata. He and his followers continued their struggle into the 1960s.

19. *2 de octubre.*

20. Carmen Landa, interview with author.

21. Juan de Onis, "Mexican Students Open Drive to Free 100 Political Prisoners," *New York Times*, July 9, 1970.

22. Juan de Onis, "Mexico is Urged to Free Students," *New York Times*, November 29, 1970.

23. "Lista de los 68 presos políticos por el movimiento estudiantil de 1968 sentencias a diversas penas de cárcel el 12 de noviembre de 1970," in "1968: El fuego de la esperanza," edited by Raúl Jardón, (unpublished manuscript in possession of author, 1996), 210–12.

24. Ibid., Mika Seeger was arrested in an early round-up in the movement on July 30, 1968. She was arrested with William Rosado Laporte. Seeger's arrest

was reported in the United States and Mexico. In the Mexican press, however, the connection to her father Pete Seeger was not made because her name was misspelled in the initial notifications. See *Excélsior* (July 31, 1968). Her arrest served to bolster the statements of the Mexican government that foreign agitators were inciting Mexican students. See *New York Times*, July 31, 1968. Pete Seeger visited and performed in Mexico frequently.

25.　"Lista de los 68 presos políticos por el movimiento estudiantil de 1968," 211.

26.　White House, Secret Memorandum, "Mexican Riots—Extent of Communist Involvement," October 5, 1968, Lyndon B. Johnson Library, National Security Files CO-Mexico, vol. IV, box 60, "Mexico, memos & misc., 1/68–10/68" National Security Archive, Tlatelolco Massacre: Declassified U.S. Documents on Mexico and Events of 1968, document 102, http://www.gwu.edu/~nsarchiv/.

27.　Raúl Alvarez Garín, "La dispersión," in *Pensar de 68*, ed. by Raúl Alvarez Garín, et al. (México, D.F.: Cal y Arena, 1988), 157.

28.　Ibid., 157–58.

29.　See Luis González de Alba, *Los días y los años*; and "Los que pudo ser," interview with Salvador Martínez della Roca, in *Pensar de 68*, 224.

30.　Echeverría also made other overtures to the students and to the left. Article 145 and Article 145 bis were repealed; however, both continued to exist through other statutes. José López Portillo (1976–1982) gave a general amnesty in late 1978. Then, many of the last of the 1968 activists could finally return to Mexico or they were finally released from prison. Of course, the release of political prisoners and the amnesty that they were given questioned the whole assertion made by Mexican politicians that they did not imprison people from the opposition. Echeverría, as well as López Portillo, succumbed to international and national pressure to release the prisoners, hoping that by doing so, they could further promote their careers.

31.　U.S. Consul in Monterrey, confidential telegram, "Student Violence in Monterrey," May 26, 1971, National Archives RG 59, 1970–73, POL 23–8 Mex, Box 2476. National Security Archives, The Corpus Christi Massacre, document 12, http://www.gwu.edu/~narchive/.

32.　Mabry, *The Mexican University and the State*; Krauze, *La presidencia imperial*; For an overview of the movement, see Manlio Tirardo, José Luis Sierra, and Gerardo Dávila, *El 10 de junio y la izquierda radical* (México, D.F.: Editorial Heterodoxia, 1971).

33.　Yroam, Shapira, "Mexico: The Impact of the 1968 Mexican Student Movement on Echeverría Reformism," *Journal of Interamerican Studies and World Affairs* 19, no. 4 (November 1977): 569; Schmidt, *The Deterioration of the Mexican Presidency*, 93–95; Mabry, *The Mexican University and the State*, 268–69.

34. While the National Autonomous University of Mexico is autonomous from the federal government, states also fund universities that are autonomous from them as well.

35. U.S. Consul in Monterrey, confidential telegram, "Change in Government and the University Problem," June 7, 1971, National Archives RG 59, 1970–73, POL 23–8 Mex, Box 2476, National Security Archives, The Corpus Christi Massacre, Document 13, http://www.gwu.edu/~narchive/NSAEBB/NSAEBB91.

36. Ibid.

37. Mario Huacuja and José Woldenberg, *Estado y lucha política en el México actual* (México, D.F.: El Caballito, 1978), 99; also quoted in Schmidt, *The Deterioration of the Mexican Presidency*, 94.

38. Mabry, *The Mexican University and the State*, 269.

39. Tarjeta enviada al secretario de Gobernación sobre las actividades del grupo Halcones, September 25, 1969, Archivo de Bucareli, Informes de la Dirección Federal de Seguridad, 1964–1972, reprinted in *Nexos* (June 1998).

40. Declaración a la DFS de Leopoldo Muñiz Rojas, alias "El Guilligan," exmiembro del grupo del Halcones, January 14, 1972, report compiled by Luis de la Barreda Moreno, Director of Federal Security, Archivo Bucareli, Informes de la Dirreción Federal de Seguridad, 1964–1972, reprinted in *Nexos* (June 1998).

41. *Excélsior*, June 11, 1971.

42. Ibid. The term "gorilla" refers to paid thugs.

43. Ibid. The role of journalists in the opposition was captured by Gabriel Retes, *El bulto*, 120 minutes, 1991. videocassette.

44. Tarjeta enviada al secretario de Gobernación sobre las actividades del grupo Halcones.

45. *Excélsior*, June 11, 1971.

46. Heberto Castillo, "Alfonso Martínez Domínguez: 'La matanza fue preparado por Luis Echeverría,'" *Proceso*, (June 4, 1979), 6–13. Castillo was surprised that Martínez Domínguez agreed to meet with him. In the article, Castillo described his sentiments about meeting with Martínez.

47. Ibid., 11.

48. U.S. Embassy in Mexico, confidential telegram, Student Demonstration, National Archives RG 59, 1970–73, POL 23–8 Mex, Box 2476, National Security Archives, The Corpus Christi Massacre, document 15, http://www.gwu.edu/~narchive/.

49. Ibid.

50. Department of State, Bureau of Intelligence and Research, Mexico: Government Repression of Students Causes Crisis, National Archives RG 59, 1970–73, POL 23-8 Mex, National Security Archives, The Corpus Christi Massacre, document 20,

http://www.gwu.edu/~narchive/NSAEBB/NSAEBB91.

51. U.S. Embassy in Mexico, secret telegram, Group Alleged to be Plotting Ouster of Echeverría, National Archives RG 59, 1970–73, POL 23-8 Mex, Box 2476, National Security Archives, The Corpus Christi Massacre, document 28, http://www.gwu.edu/~narchive/NSAEBB/NSAEBB91. Conservative politicians and elites were greatly concerned with Echeverría's policies that did appear to embrace leftists by offering them positions in the government.

52. Schmidt, *The Deterioration of the Mexican Presidency*, 92–102. Schmidt views June 10 as one of Echeverría's mobilizations of the masses to do his political bidding.

53. Department of State, Bureau of Intelligence and Research, Mexico: Government Repression of Students Causes Crisis.

54. See Declaración a la DFS de Víctor Manuel Flores Reyes, alias "El Coreano," ex-miembro del grupo "Halcones," January 17, 1972, and Declaración a la DFS de Leopoldo Muñiz Rojas, January 14, 1972, both compiled by Barreda Moreno, Archivo Bucareli, reprinted in *Nexos* (June 1998).

55. For a discussion of the life of a political prisoner, see Luis González de Alba, *Los días y los años* (México, D.F.: Biblioteca Era, 1971); Heberto Castillo, 1968: *El principio del poder* (México, D.F.: Proceso, 1980) and Castillo, *Si te agarran, te van a matar* (México, D.F.: Ediciones Oceano, 1983); and Oscar Menéndez, *Los años difíciles*, videocassette, 28 mins., 1997. Menéndez's film is a documentary about Heberto Castillo and his incarceration as a political prisoner.

56. Arturo Warman, "Secreto de familia," *Pensar el* 68, 132.

57. Mercedes Perelló, interview with author, June 10, 1997, Mexico, D.F. The Mexican guerrilla movement of the 1970s has still not been studied in great detail.

58. Throughout the 1950s, IPN students were very active. They demanded curricular changes and greater institutional control. They also protested the presidential elections. In 1956, they demanded more dorms, scholarships, and changes to the Medical School curricula.

59. Jesus Ramirez Cuevas, "La guerrilla en las regiones de México: La academia recupera la memoria," *Masiosare: La Jornada*, August 18, 2002.

60. "Ciudad Madera, un legado con raíz viva," *La Jornada*, September 25, 2000.

61. Informe sobre actividades guerrillas Atoyac de Alvarez estado de Guerrero (unsigned documents dated April 24, 1968), Archivos de Bucareli, Informes de la Dirección Federal de Seguridad, reprinted in *Nexos* (June 1998).

62. Issued in Siempre! January 26, 1972, reprinted in Juan Miguel de Mora *Las guerrillas en México y Jenaro Vázquez Rojas (Su personalidad, su vida, y su muerte)* (Mexico: Editora Latino Americana, 1972), 29.

63. For a discussion on contemporary guerrilla groups that sprang from *Partido*

de los Pobres, see Gustavo Hirales Morán, "Radical Groups in Mexico Today," Center for Strategic and International Studies (CSIS) *Policy Papers on the Americas* vol. XIV, September 2003.

64. Gustavo Hirales, "La Guerra secreta, 1970–78," Nexos 34 (June 1982): 36. Hirales was a militant with the *Liga Comunista de 23 de septiembre* (Communist League of September 23, LC-23).

65. Schmidt, *The Deterioration of the Mexican Presidency*, 86; Tamayo, "The 20 Mexican Octobers," 229; See also Generado Lissardy, "Las huellas criminales de Echeverría," *Proceso* (2002), "Una Supesta Conspiración para derrocar a Echeverría," *Proceso* (2002);, and "Documentado, el Entreamiento de los 'halcones' en Washington," *Proceso* (2002).

66. Hirales, "La guerra secreta," and Barry Carr, *Marxism and Communism in Twentieth Century Mexico* (Lincoln: University of Nebraska Press, 1992), 267.

67. Arnoldo Martínez Verdugo, ed, *Historia del Comunismo en México* (Mexico,D.F.: Grijalbo, 1985). Also see de Mora *Las guerrillas en México y Jenaro Vázquez Rojas*.

68. Tamayo, "The 20 Mexican Octobers," 221.

69. Informe de la Dirreción Federal de Seguridad sobre la detención de los miembros de un movimiento guerrillero orginado en Chihuahua en los años sesentas, Archivos de Bucareli, Informes de la Dirección Federal de Seguridad, reprinted in Nexos (June 1998).

70. Gilberto Guevara Niebla, "Escuelas en la izquierda," in *Pensar* el 68, 152–53.

71. Carr, *Marxism and Communism*, 270; Hirales, "La guerra secreta."

72. Tim Weiner, "Mexico Indicts Former Chief of Secret Police," *New York Times*, March 30, 2003.

73. Comisión Nacional de los Derechos Humanos, Comisión Nacional de los Derechos Humanos Mexico: *Informe Especial Sobre las Quejas en Materia de Desapariciones Forzadas Ocurridas en la Decada de los 70 y Principios de los 80*, http://www.cndh.org.mx/Principal/document/informe/index.html.

74. "No permitirá la policía la marcha de estudiantes," *Novedades*, December 13, 1968; "Para proteger a la sociedad, no se permitirá la marcha de estudiantes," *El Sol de México*, December 13, 1968.

75. Although the Dirty War or *guerra sucia* usually refers to Brazil, Chile, and Argentina, Mexico now discusses the period of 1972 to 1977 as a Dirty War. See for instance, Rosa Rojas, "Lamentas ONG la muerte del senador, 'hombre del sistema,'" *La Jornada*, October 31, 2000; Gretchen Peters, "Mexico Begins to Face Legacy of 'Dirty War,'" *Christian Science Monitor* vol. 9: 5, November 29, 2001. In Rojas' interviews with human rights activists, they referred to that period of time as the guerra sucia.

76. Recently, more documents have been released on Mexico's Dirty War, see

Human Rights and the Dirty War in Mexico, The National Security Archive, http://www.gwu.edu/~nsarchive.

77. "Irate Leftists Attack Echeverría at Mexico's National University," *New York Times*, March 15, 1975. In the days following the visit, Echeverría blamed the CIA for the attacks. "Mexico Blames CIA for Stoning," *New York Times*, March 18, 1975.

Chapter Six

1. See Shirlene Soto, *Emergence of the Modern Mexican Woman: Her Participation in Revolution and Struggle for Equality, 1910–1940* (Denver, Colorado: Arden Press, 1990); Elizabeth Salas, *Soldaderas in the Mexican Military: Myth and History* (Austin: University of Texas Press, 1990); Instituto Nacional de Estudios Históricos de la Revolución Mexicana, *Las mujeres de la Revolución Mexicana* (México, D.F.: Instituto Nacional de Estudios Históricos de la Revolución Mexicana, 1992).

2. Anna Macías, *Against All Odds: The Feminist Movement in Mexico to 1940* (Westport: Colorado: Greenwood Press, 1992); Alaide Foppa, "The First Feminist Congress in Mexico, 1916," trans. Helene F. de Aguilar, Signs 5 (Autumn 1979); and Gabriela Cano, "The Porfiriato and the Mexican Revolution: Constructions of Feminism and Nationalism" in *Nation, Empire, and Colony: Historicizing Gender and Race*, edited by Ruth Roach Pierson and Nupur Chaudhuri (Bloomington: University of Indiana Press), 106–20.

3. Rosario Castellanos, "La liberación de la mujer, aquí," *Excelsior* September 5, 1970, reprinted in *Debate Feminista* 12 (October 1995), 351–54.

4. Ibid. Castellano is referring to Samuel Ramos' discussion of Mexican character. See Ramos, *Profile of Man and Culture in Mexico*, trans. Peter G. Earle (Austin: University of Texas Press, 1962).

5. Ibid., 354.

6. Ibid., 354–55.

7. Marta Acevedo, "Nuestro sueño está en escarpado lugar," *Siempre*, supplement La Cultura de México, September 30, 1970, num. 901, reprinted in *Debate Feminista* 12 (October 1995), 355–70.

8. As quoted in Marta Acevedo, Angelina del Valle, Marta Lamas, María Elena Sánchez, and Guadalupe Zamarrón, "Piezas de un rompecabezas," *fem* 2 (October–December 1977), 12.

9. Acevedo, "Nuestro sueño está en escarpado lugar," 356.

10. Ibid., 357. Acevedo called the National Organization for Women the National Organization *of* Women.

11. Ibid., 364.

12. Ibid., 366–68.

13. Ibid., 368.

14. Marta Lamas, "Mis diez primeros años: el MAS y el MLM," *fem* 20 (October 1996), 8.

15. Mother's Day is a national holiday in Mexico on May 10.

16. Acevedo, et al., "Piezas de un rompecabezas," 12–13.

17. Ibid.

18. Lamas, "Mis primer diez años;" In interviews conducted by the author, three women Aída González, Carmen Landa, and Lilian Liebermann recalled this statement. González, interview; Landa, interview; and Lilian Liebermann, interview with author, April 4, 1997, Mexico City.

19. González, interview; Landa, interview; Liebermann, interview.

20. See Luisa Passerini, *Fascism in Popular Memory* (New York: Cambridge University Press, 1987); Elizabeth Tonkin, *Narrating Our Pasts: The Social Construction of Oral History* (New York: Cambridge University Press, 1991); and James Fentress and Chris Wickham, *Social Memory: New Perspectives on the Past* (London: Blackwell Press, 1992).

21. Liebermann, interview.

22. Liebermann, interview; González, interview. See also María Cristina Gonzalez Gicolini, "El movimiento feminista en México: Aportes su análisis" (MA thesis, Universidad Nacional Autónoma de México, 1987).

23. As mentioned in chapter two, macho may also be termed "pelado." The term macho or machismo is not used, but is described by Ramos. Ramos, *Profile of Man and Culture in Mexico*; Octavio Paz, *The Labyrinth of Solitude and the Other Mexico, Return to the Labyrinth of Solitude, Mexico and the United States, The Philanthropic Ogre*, trans. by Lysander Kemp, el. al (New York: Grove Press, 1985); and Oscar Lewis, *Five Families* (New York: Mentor Book 1959).

24. Interview with Sontag, published in *Excelsior* supplement *Diorama de la Cultura*, November 1971.

25. Landa, interview.

26. Lamas, "Mis diez primeros años;" 8, Landa, interview; Liebermann, interview; and María Cristina Gonzalez Gicolini, "El movimiento feminista en México."

27. Lamas, "Mis diez primeros años," 8; Landa, interview; and Liebermann, interview.

28. Anonymous, reprinted in Acevedo et al., "Piezas de un rompecabezas," 13.

29. Landa, interview; Gonzalez, interview; Liebermann, interview; and Marta Lamas, interview with author, June 5, 1997, Mexico, D.F.

30. Lamas, "Mis diez años primeros." The group in the south was also comprised of many students and young faculty due to its closer proximity to UNAM.

31. Ibid.; Landa, interview; Acevedo et al., "Piezas de un rompecabezas," and Gonzalez Gicolini, "El movimiento feminista en México."

32. "La situación de la mujer en México," *Punto Crítico*, 8 (August 1972).

33. Ibid.

34. "La mujer y el trabajo," *Punto Crítico* 13 (January 1973); "Puebla 10 de Mayo, Mujeres en Lucha," *Punto Crítico* 17 (May 1973).

35. By 1974, Fidel Castro began to address these issues. See Fidel Castro, *Speeches: Women and the Cuban Revolution*, edited by Linda Jennes (New York: Pathfinder Press, 1970), Ministerio de Justicia, *La mujer en Cuba socialista* (La Habana: Federación de Mujeres Cubanas, 1977). The declaration of formal equality, however, did not come to fruition in actual practice. For a discussion of the inability of revolutions to bring equality see Margaret Randall, *Gathering Rage: The Failure of Twentieth Century Revolutions to Develop a Feminist Agenda* (New York: Monthly Review Press, 1992).

36. Lamas, "Mis diez primeros años," 9; "Piezas de un rompecabezas," 19; Liebermann, interview.

37. Lamas, interview.

38. Reprinted in "Piezas de un rompecabezas," 20.

39. This image is found in the United Nations reports. See United Nations, *Meeting in Mexico: The Story of the World Conference of the International Women's Year, Mexico City, 19 June–2 July 1975* (New York: United Nations, 1975).

40. World Conference of the International Women's Year. *Report of the World Conference of the International Women's Year, Mexico City, 19 June–2 July 1975*, no. E/Conf.66/34 (New York: United Nations, 1976), 120–22.

41. Quoted in Adalijiza Sosa Riddell, "The Status of Women in Mexico: The Impact of the International Year of the Woman," in *Women in the World: 1975–1985: The Women's Decade*, edited by Lynne B. Iglitzin and Ruth Ross (Santa Barbara, California: ABC-CLIO Press, 1986), 305.

42. United Nations, *Action Survey of IWY, Part 1* (New York: UNESCO Publishers, 1976), and Sosa Riddell, "The Status of Women in Mexico: The Impact of the International Year of the Woman," 305–24.

43. Quoted in Sosa Riddell, "The Status of Women in Mexico," 305.

44. Landa, interview.

45. This idea is not new to Latin America. See Margaret Randall, *Sandino's Daughters: Testimonies of Nicaraguan Women in Struggle* (Vancouver, British Columbia: New Star Books, 1981); Francesca Miller, *Latin American Women and the Search for Social Justice* (Hanover: University of New England Press, 1991); Rigoberta Menchú, *I Rigoberta Menchú: An Indian Woman in Guatemala*, ed. by Elisabeth Burgos Debray, trans. by Ann Wright (Norfolk,

England: The Thetford Press, 1984); and see Graciela García, *Páginas de lucha* (Tegucigalpa, Honduras: Guymuras, 1981). In Randall's work, the women interviewed discuss their roles as revolutionaries, not feminists. Rigoberta Menchú explicitly states that her struggle is for all people, not solely women.

46. Liebermann, interview.

47. Mercedes Perelló, interview.

48. This is not an uncommon perception. Women of color and lesbians in the United States criticized feminist entities such as the National Organization for Women for similar reasons.

49. Mercedes Perelló, interview.

50. Vida Valero Borrás, interview with author, April 10, 1997.

51. Valero Borrás and Alejandra Herrera, interview with author, April 10, 1997.

52. Herrera, interview; See also Fuentes Molinar, "Las épocas de la universidad mexicana," for his discussion on university reform

53. Herrera, interview.

Conclusion

1. Herbert Braun, "Protests of Engagement: Dignity, False Love, and Self-Love in Mexico during 1968," *Comparative Studies in Society and History* 39, no. 3 (July 1997): 511–49; and "Irate Leftists Attack Echeverría at Mexico's National University," *New York Times*, March 15, 1975.

2. "Files Point to Official Use of Snipers in '68 Mexico Massacre," *New York Times*, October 2, 2003.

3. Theoretically, Mexico's Dirty War does not qualify as a genocide by the United Nations Convention on the Prevention and Punishment of the Crime of Genocide. For a discussion on the definition of genocide and the application of the convention, see Samatha Powers, *A Problem from Hell: America in the Age of Genocide.* (New York: Perennial, 2002), 31–85.

4. Enrique Krauze, "Past Wrongs, Future Rights." *New York Times* (August 10, 2004). Vicente Fox of the *Partido Acción Nacional* (National Action Party, PAN) won the presidential election in 2000 ending seventy-one years of PRI rule.

5. *La Jornada*, July 29, 2004 and July 30, 2004.

6. Editorial: "Justice for Mexico's Dirty War," *New York Times* (July 29, 2004)

7. Krauze, "Past Wrongs, Future Right;" Ignacio Carrillo Prieto, letter to the editor, *New York Times* (August 6, 2004).

8. Roger Bartra, "Culture and Political Power in Mexico," *Latin American Perspectives* 16, 2 (Spring 1989), 69.

Selected Bibliography

Archives and Libraries

Archivo General Nación, Mexico City

Archivo Histórico de Universidad Nacional Autónoma de México-Centro de
Estudios Sobre la Universidad (AHUNAM-CESU), Mexico City

Biblioteca Daniel Cosío Villegas, El Colegio de México, Mexico City

Biblioteca Nacional, Mexico City

Centro de Estudios del Movimiento Obrero y Socialista (CEMOS), Mexico City.

Fototeca Nacional, Pachuca, Hidalgo

Hermeoteca Nacional, Mexico City

Hispanic Reading Room, Library of Congress, Washington, D.C.

Latin American Video Archive, New York City

National Security Archive

New York Public Library, New York City

Primary Sources

Published Material

Alvarez Garín, Raúl, Gilberto Guevara Niebla, Hermann Bellinghausen, Hugo Hiria,
editors. *Pensar el 68.* México, D.F.: Cal y Arena, 1988.

Arriola, Carlos, editor. *El movimiento estudiantil mexicano en la prensa francesa.*
México, D.F.: El Colegio de México, 1979.

Ayala, Leopoldo, editor. *Nuestro Verdad: Memorial popular del movimiento estudiantil popular y el dos de octubre de 1968.* México, D.F.: Joaquín Porrda, 1989.

Barta, Eli, María Brumm, et al., editors. *La revuelta: Reflexiones, testimonios, y
reportajes de mujeres en México, 1975–1983.* México, D.F.: Martín Casillas
Editores, 1983.

Campa, Valetín. *Mi testimonio: Experiencias de un comunista mexicano.* México,
D.F.: Ediciones de Cultura Popular, 1978.

Cano Andaluz, Aurora, editor. *1968 Antología periodística.* México, D.F.: Instituto
de Investigaciones Bibliográficas: Universidad Nacional Autónoma de
México, 1993.

Castillo, Heberto. *1968: El principio del poder.* México. D.F.: 1980.

———. *Si te agarran, te van a matar*. México, D.F.: Ediciones Oceano, 1983.

Cazés, Daniel, editor. *Memorial de 68: Relato muchas voces*. México, D.F.: La Jornada Ediciones, 1993.

Celis, Lourdes et al., editors. *Historia de la acción pública: Adolfo López Mateos, 1958–1964*. Volume I: *Sus Ideas*. México, D.F.: Fondo para la Historia de las Ideas Revolucionarias en México, Partido Revolucionario Institucional, 1978.

Díaz Ordaz, Gustavo. *A Political Handbook*. Translated by Luis Quintanilla. México, n.p., 1964.

Fisera, Vladimir. *Writing on the Wall, May 1968: A Documentary Anthology*. London: Allison and Bushby Press, 1978.

Fuentes, Carlos. *Tiempo mexicano*. México, D.F.: Joaquín Mortiz, 1973.

García Canú, Gastón. *Javier Barros Sierra: 1968*. México, D.F.: Siglo Veintuno Editores, 1993.

Gil, Carlos, editor. *Hope and Frustration: Interviews with Leaders of Mexico's Political Opposition*. Wilmington, Delaware: Scholarly Resources Press, 1992.

González de Alba, Luis. *Los días y los años*. México, D.F.: Biblioteca Era, 1971.

Gordillo, Elba Esther. *La construcción de un proyecto sindical: Mi testimonio*. México, D.F.: Aguilar, Altea, Taurus, 1995.

Guevara, Ernesto Che. *The Motorcycle Diaries: A Journey Around South America*. Translated by Ann Wright. London: Verso Books, 2003.

Instituto Nacional de Estádistica, Geográfica e Informática. *La Mujer en México: Una visión traves de estadisticas nacionales: Encuentro Nacional de Mujeres Legisladores*. México, D.F.: El Colegio de México, Programa Interdisciplinario de Estudios de la Mujer, 1992.

Instituto Nacional de Estudios Históricos de la Revolución Mexicana. *Las Mujeres de la Revolución Mexicana*. México, D.F.: Instituto Nacional de Estudios Históricos de la Revolución Mexicana, 1992.

Jaramillo, Rubén, and Froylán López Manjares. *Rubén Jaramillo, Autobiografía y Asesinato*. México, D.F.: Editorial Nuestro Tiempo, 1967.

Jardón Arzate, Edmundo. *De la Ciudadela a Tlatelolco*. México, D.F.: Fondo de Cultura Popular, 1969.

Jardón, Raúl. *1968, El fuego de la esperanza*. México, D.F.: Siglo Veintiuno Editores, 1998.

———. *El espionaje contra el movimiento estudiantil : Los documentos de la Dirección Federal de Seguridad y las agencias de inteligencia estadounidenses en 1968*. México, D.F.: Ithaca, 2003.

Meany, Guillermina. *Canoa: El crimen impune*. México, D.F.: Editorial Posada, 1977.

Monsiváis, Carlos. *Días de guardar*. México, D.F.: Biblioteca Era, 1970.

Mora, Juan Miguel de. *Las guerrillas en México y Jenaro Vázquez Rojas (Su personalidad, su vida, y su muerte)*. México, D.F.: Editora Latino Americana, 1972.

Morelet de Varela, Claudia. *Yo dirigí la porra universitaria*. México, D.F.: Imprenta

Carma, 1976.

North American Congress on Latin America. *Latin American Women: The Gendering of Politics and Culture*, July–August 1993.

———. *Mexico 1968: A Study of Domination and Repression*. 1968.

Olivera, Luis. *Impresos sueltos del movimiento estudantil mexicano, 1968*. México, D.F.: Universidad Nacional Autónoma de México, 1992.

Paz, Octavio. *The Other Mexico: The Critique of the Pyramid*. Translated by Lysander Kemp. New York: Grove Press, 1972.

Poniatowska, Elena. *Fuerte es el silencio*. México, D.F.: Ediciones Era, 1980.

———. *Massacre in Mexico*. Translated by Helen Lane. Columbia: University of Missouri Press, 1991.

_____. *Nothing, Nobody: The Voices of the Earthquake*. Translated by Aurora Camacho de Schmidt and Arthur Schmidt. Philadelphia: Temple University Press, 1995.

Ramirez, Alfredo. *Yo, porro: retrato hablado*. México, D.F.: Editorial Posada, 1984.

Ramirez, Ramon. *El movimiento estudiantil de México: Julio/diciembre de 1968, Análisis/Cronología*. México, D.F.: Ediciones Era, 1969.

———. *El movimiento estudiantil de México: Julio/diciembre, Documentos*. México, D.F.: Ediciones Era, 1969.

Revelo, Renato. *Los jaramillistas*. México, D.F.: Editorial Nuestro Tiempo, 1978.

Revueltas, José. *México: una democrácia bárbara*. México, D.F.: Editorial Posada, 1958.

———. *Ensayo sobre un proletariado sin cabeza*. México, D.F.: Ediciones Leninista Espartaco, 1962.

———. *México 68: Juventud y revolución*. México, D.F.: Ediciones Era, 1978.

Romero Valenzuela, María. *Hoy Maestro: Ayer joven del '68*. México, D.F.: Casa de la Cultura del Maestro Mexicano: Claves Latinoamericanas: Centro de Estudios del Movimiento Obrero y Socialista, 1990.

Scherer García, Julio, and Carlos Monsiváis. *Parte de guerra, Tlatelolco 1968: Documentos del general Marcelino García Barragán: los hechos y la historia* México, D.F.: Nuevo Siglo, 1999.

Sevilla, Renata, ed. *Tlatelolco: Ocho años después*. México, D.F.: Editorial Posada, S.A., 1976.

Taibo, Paco Ignacio. *68*. México, D.F.: Editorial Joaquín Mortiz, 1991.

United Nations. *Demographic Yearbook, 1968, 1969*. New York: Department of Economic and Social Affairs, Statistical Office, 1969.

———. *Meeting in Mexico: The Story Behind the World Conference of the International Women's Year, Mexico City, 19 June–2 July 1975*. New York: United Nations, 1975.

———. Report of the World Conference of the International Women's Year. Document Number E.76.IV.1. New York: United Nations, 1975.

Selected Bibliography

United Nations Association, Al-Ber Costa Chapter, *Women in Action*. The Al-Ber Costa Chapter of the United Nations Association, USA, 1976.

Valle, Eduardo. *Escritos sobre el movimiento del 68*. México: Universidad Autónoma de Sinaloa, 1984.

Vallejo, Demetrio. *Yo acuso*. México, D.F.: Editorial Hombre Nuevo, 1973.

Newspapers, Journals, and Bulletins

Boletin Mensual de Union Nacional Mujeres Mexicano

Compañeras

Excélsior

El Día

El Heraldo de México

El Sol

El Universal

Debate Feminista

fem

La Jornada

Look

Milenio

Mujeres

The Nation

New York Times

Nexos

Nosotras

Novedades

Por que

Proceso

Punto Crítico

Ramparts

Revista y Revista

Siempre

Time

La Voz de México

Films and Photography

2 de octubre. 60 minutes. 1969. Videocassette.

Casasola, Ismael, José Revueltas, Victoria Novelo. *La caravana del hambre: reportaje fotográfico*. Puebla, Mexico: Universidad de Puebla, Fototeca de INAH, 1986.

Cáceres, Olga. *Luis Echeverría: El Presidente Predicador*. 46 minutes. 1998. Videocassette.

———. *Luis Echeverría. La empeñosa ambición.* 45 minutes. 1998. Videocassette.

Canal 22. *La battalion Olympica: Acoumento abierto.* 35 minutes. 1998. Videocassette.

Cazals, Felipe. *Canoa.* 120 minutes. 1975. Videocassette.

Fons, Jorge. *Rojo manecer.* 95 minutes. 1988. Videocassette.

Fuentes, Reuben and Jesús Salmerón. *Historia 1960: Grafica de un movimiento social.* Chilpancingo, México: Universidad Autónoma de Guerrero, 1991.

Grupo Mira, *La gráfica del '68: Homenaje al movimiento estudiantil* México, D.F.: Ediciones Zurda, 1993.

López, Leobardo Arteche and CUEC. *El Grito.* 120 minutes. 1969. Videocassette.

Mendoza, Carlos. *Operación Galeana: La historia inédita del 2 de octubre de 1968,* 70 minutes. 2000. Videocassette.

Menéndez, Oscar. *México 68.* 85 minutes. 1992. Videocassette.

———. *Los años difíciles.* 28 minutes. 1997. Videocasete.

Nexos. *El movimiento estudiantil.* 6 vols. 1993. Videocassette collection.

Pineda, Elid. *Gustavo Díaz Ordaz: El rompecabezas.* 45 minutes. 1998. Videocasete.

———. *Díaz Ordaz y 1968.* 44 minutes. 1998. Videocassette.

Pliego, Julio. *México Antes 1968.* 6 vols. 1996. Videocassette collection.

Ramirez, Enrique R. *Historia Gráfica del movimiento estudiantil, México 1968.* Guadalajara: Editorial Godina, 1993.

Retes, Gabriel. *El bulto.* 120 minutes. 1991. Videocassette.

Sarquiz, Oscar. *Historia del Rock Mexicano I. Yo no era un rebelde: Rock mexicano 1957–1970.* 45 minutes. 2000.

———. *Historia del Rock Mexicano II. La célula que se explota: Rock mexicano 1970–1999.* 45 minutes. 2000. Videocassette.

Novels, Plays, Poetry, and Music

1968: Música, Imágenes, e historia. Mexico, D.F: Universal Music México, 1998, Compact Disc.

Agustin, José. *Cerca del Fuego.* Mexico, D.F.: Plaza y Janes, 1986.

Azuela, Mariano. *The Underdogs.* Translated by Frederick H. Fornoff. Pittsburgh, Pennsylvania: University of Pittsburgh Press, 1992.

Burroughs, William. *The Yage Papers.* San Francisco, California: City Lights Books, 1975.

———. *The Naked Lunch.* New York: Grove Press, 1992.

Castellanos, Rosario. *Another Way to Be: Selected Works by Rosario Castellanos.* Translated by Myralyn Frizzelle Allgood. Athens: University of Georgia Press, 1990.

Fuente, Carmen de la. *La expatriada.* Curico, Chile: Editorial la Noria, 1995.

Fuentes, Carlos. *Where the Air is Clear.* Translated by Sam Hileman. New York: Ivan Oboliensky, 1960.

———. *The Death of Artemio Cruz.* Translated by Alfred MacAdam. New York: The

Noon Day Press, 1991.

Garro, Elena. *First Love; Look for my Obituary: Two Novellas*. Translated by David Unger. Williamantic, Connecticut: Curbstone Press, 1997.

———. *Recollections of Things to Come*. Translated by Ruth L. C. Simms. Austin: University of Texas Press, 1969.

Martinez Zúñiga, Alonso. *Los 68: Drama político-social en catorce cuadros*. México: Editorial Manuscrito 68, 1994.

Paz, Octavio, *The Labyrinth of Solitude and The Other Mexico; Return to the Labyrinth of Solitude; Mexico and the United States; The Philanthropic Ogre.* Translated by Lysander Kemp, Yara Milos, and Rachel Phillips Besh. New York: Grove Press, 1985.

Reyes, Judith. *Tlatelolco*. Lyrics in Leopoldo Ayala, *Nuestro verdad: Memorial popular del movimiento estudiantil popular y el dos de octubre 1968*. México, D.F.: Joaquín Porrúa, 1989.

———. *Marcha de los caidos*. Lyrics in Ayala, *Nuestro Verdad*.

Paso, Fernando del. *Palinuro en Mexico*. México: Diana, 1987.

Paz Paredes, Margarita. *Memorias de hospital; Presagio: dos poemas*. México, D.F.: Miguel Angel Porrua, 1983.

———. *Litoral del tiempo: antologia poética*. Guanajuato, México: Ediciones del Gobierno del Estado de Guanajuata, 1978.

Velasco Piña, Antonio. *Regina*. México, D.F.: Editorial Era, 1987.

Secondary

Aguayo Quezada, Sergio. *1968: Los archivos de la violencia*. México, D.F.: Grijaldo, 1998.

Aguila, Anita, and Rosalind Rosoff. *Emiliano Zapata: Hombre de Tierra*. México, D.F.: Editorial Alhambra Mexicana, 1986.

Aguilar Camín, Héctor, and Lorenzo Meyer. *In the Shadow of the Mexican Revolution: Contemporary Mexican History, 1910–1989*. Translated by Luis Alberto Fierro. Austin: University of Texas Press, 1993.

Aguilar García, Javier. *Historia de la CTM, 1936–1990: El movimiento obrero y el estado mexicano*. México, D.F.: Universidad Nacional Autónoma de México, 1990.

Agustín, José. *La contracultura en México: La historia y el significado de los rebeldes sin causa, los hipitecas, los punks, y las bandas*. México, D.F.: Grijalbo, 1996.

Alatorre Angeles, Mendietta. *Juana Belén Gutiérrez de Mendoza, precursora de la Revolución Mexicana*. México, D.F.: Talles Impresores de Morelos, 1983.

Alonso, Ana María. *Thread of Blood: Colonialism, Revolution, and Gender on Mexico's Northern Frontier*. Tucson: University of Arizona Press, 1995.

Anguiano, Arturo. *Entre el pasado y el futuro: La izquierda en México, 1969–1995*. México, D.F.: Universidad Autónoma Metropolitana, 1997.

Aranda, Clara Eugenia. *La mujer: explotación, lucha, liberación*. México, D.F.:

Editorial Nuestro Tiempo, 1976.

Azala Blanco, Jorge. *La condición del cine mexicano (1973–1985)*. México, D.F.: Editorial Posada, 1986.

Aziz Nassif, Alberto. *El estado mexicano y la CTM*. México, D.F.: Centro Investigaciones y Estudios Superiorers en Antropología Social, 1989.

Balderston, Daniel and Donna J. Guy, editors. *Sex and Sexuality in Latin America*. New York: New York University Press, 1997.

Bantijes, Adrian A. *As If Jesus Walked on Earth: Cardenismo, Sonora, and the Mexican Revolution*. Wilmington, Delaware: Scholarly Resources Press, 1998.

de Barbieri, Teresita. *Mujeres y vida cotidiana*. México, D.F.: Fondo de Cultura Económica, 1984.

Bartra, Roger. *La jaula de la melancolía: Identidad y metamorfosis del mexicano*. México, D.F.: Grijalbo, 1987.

———. "Culture and Political Power in Mexico." *Latin American Perspectivas* 16, no. 2 (Spring 1989): 61–69.

Basurto, Jorge. *Vivencias femeninas de la Revolución*. México, D.F.: Instituto Nacional de Estudios Historicos, 1993.

Bederman, Gail. *Manliness and Civilization: A Cultural History of Gender and Race in the United States*. Chicago: University of Chicago Press, 1995.

Bedolla Miranda, Patricia. *Estudios de género y feminismo*. México, D.F.: Universidad Nacional Autonoma de Mexico, 1989.

Beattie, Meter M. "The House, the Street, and the Barrack: Reform and Honorable Masculine Spacce in Brazil 1864 to 1945." *Hispanic American Historical Review* 73, no. 3 (August 1996): 439–73.

Benítez, Fernando. *Lázaro Cárdenas y la revolución mexicana*. Volume 3, *El Cardenismo*. México, D.F.: El Colegio de México, 1978.

Bergman, Emilie, et al., editors. *Women, Culture, and Politics in Latin America: Seminar on Feminism and Culture in Latin America*. Berkeley: University of California Press, 1990.

Berman, Paul. *A Tale of Two Utopias: The Political Journeys of the Generation of 1968*. New York: W.W. Norton & Company, 1996.

Bethell, Leslie, editor. *Mexico Since Independence*. New York: Cambridge University Press, 1991.

Brading, David, editor. *Caudillo and Peasant in the Mexican Revolution*. Cambridge: University of Cambridge Press, 1980.

Brandenburg, Frank Ralph. *The Making of Modern Mexico*. New York: Prentice Hall, 1944.

Braun, Herbert. "Protests of Engagement: Dignity, False Love, and Self-Love in Mexico During 1968." *Comparative Studies in Society and History* 39 (July 1997): 511–49.

Selected Bibliography

Brunk, Samuel. "Zapata and the City Boys: In Search of a Piece of the Revolution." *Hispanic American Historical Review* 73, no. 1 (February 1993): 33–65.

———. *Emiliano Zapata: Revolution and Betrayal in Mexico*. Albuquerque: University of New Mexico Press, 1995.

Butler, Judith. *Gender Trouble: Feminism and Subversion of Identity*. New York: Routledge, 1990.

Camacho, Daniel, and Rafael Menjívar. *Los movimientos populares en América Latina*. Mexico, D.F.: Siglo Veintiuno Editores, 1989.

Camp, Roderic Ai. *Politics in Mexico*. New York: Oxford University Press, 1993.

Carr, Barry. *Marxism and Communism in Twentieth Century Mexico*. Lincoln: University of Nebraska Press, 1992.

Castañeda, Jorge. *Compañero: The Life and Death of Che Guevara*. New York: Alfred A. Knopf, 1997.

Castañeda, Marina. *No somos minoria: una movilización estudiantil, 1986–1987*. México, D.F.: Editorial Extremporaneos, 1987.

Caute, David. *The Year of the Barricades: A Journey Through 1968*. New York: Harper and Row, 1988.

Cazés, Daniel. *Crónica 1968*. México, D.F.: Plaza y Valdés, 1993.

Colmenares, David, Luis Angeles, and Carlos Ramírez. *La devaluación de 1982*. México, D.F.: Tierra Nova, 1982.

Daniels, Robert Vincent. *Year of the Heroic Guerrilla: World Revolution and Counterrevolution in 1968*. New York: Basic Books, 1989.

Davis, Diane. *Urban Leviathan: Mexico City in the Twentieth Century*. Philadelphia, Pennsylvania: Temple University Press, 1994.

Dore, Elizabeth, editor. *Gender Politics in Latin America: Debates in Theory and Practice*. New York: Monthly Review Press, 1997.

Espejel, Laura, Alicia Olivera, and Salvador Rueda, editors. *Emilano Zapata: Antología*. México, D.F.: Instituto Nacional de Estudios Históricos de la Revolución Mexicana, 1988.

Espinosa Altamirano, Horacio. *Toda la furia*. México, D.F.: Ediciones Universo, 1973.

Faris, Wendy B. *Carlos Fuentes*. New York: Frederick Ungar Publisinging Company, 1983.

Fernández Christlieb, Paulina. *El espartaquismo en México*. México, D.F.: Ediciones El Caballito, 1978.

Fisher, Josephine. *Mothers of the Disappeared*. London: Zed Books, 1989.

———. *Out of the Shadows: Women, Resistance, and Politics in South America*. London: Latin American Bureau, 1993.

Foppa, Alaide. "The First Feminist Congress in Mexico, 1916." Translated by Helen F. de Aguilar. *Signs* (Autumn, 1979): 192–99.

Foweraker, Joe. *Popular Mobilization in Mexico: The Teachers' Movement, 1977–87*.

New York: Cambridge University Press, 1993.

Franco, Jean. *Plotting Women: Gender and Representation in Mexico*. New York: Columbia University Press, 1989.

Fuentes Molinar, Olac. "Universidad y democracia: La mirada hacia la izquierda." *Cuadernos Políticos* 53 (January–April 1988): 4–18.

Galeana de Valdes, Patricia, editor. *La condición de la mujer mexicana: Memoria del II Seminario Nacional de la Federación Mexicana de Universitarias*. México, D.F.: Universidad Autonóma de México, 1992–1993.

García, Carola. *Revistas femeninas: la mujer como objeto de consumo*. México, D.F.: Ediciones El Caballito, 1980.

García Tsao, Leonardo. *Felipe Cazals habla de su cine*. Guadalajara: Universidad de Guadalajara, 1994.

Gilbert, César. *El habito de la utopía: Análsis del imaginario sociopolítico en el movimiento estudiantil de Mexico*. México, D.F.: Instituto Moro: Miguel Angel Porrua, 1993.

Gilly, Adolfo. *México, la larga travesía*. México, D.F.: Nueva Imagen, 1985.

Goodsell, John N. "Mexico: Why the Students Rioted." *Current History* 56 (1969): 31–35.

González Gicolini, Cristina. "El movimiento feminista en México: Aportes su análisis." MA Thesis. Universidad Autónoma de México, 1987.

González Casanova, Pablo. *Democracy in Mexico*. New York: Oxford University Press, 1970.

González Casanova, Pablo, and Hector Aguilar Camín, editors. *México ante la crisis: El contexto internacional y la crisis económica*, 2 vols. México, D.F.: Siglo Veinteuno Editores, 1985.

González Casanova, Pablo and Jorge Cadena Rosas, editors. *Primer informe sobre la democrácia: México, 1988*. México, D.F.: Siglo Veinteuno Editores, 1988.

González y González, Luis. *Los artífes del Cardenismo* México, D.F.: El Colegio de México, 1979.

———. *Los días del Presidente Cárdenas* México, D.F.: El Colegio de México, 1979.

González Navarro, Moisés. *La Confederación Nacional Campesina: Un grupo de presión en la reforma agraria mexicana*. México, D.F.: B. Costa-Amic 1968.

Guerrero Tapia, José. *Y después de mi, quien?* México, D.F.: Editorial Scorpio, 1987.

Guevara Niebla, Gilberto. "Antecedentes y desarrollo del movimiento de 1968." *Cuadernos Políticos* (July–September 1978).

———. *La crisis de la educación superior en México*. México, D.F.: Nueva Imagen, 1981.

———. *La luchas estudiantiles en México*. 2 vols. México, D.F.: Linea, 1983.

———. *La democrácia en la calle: Crónica del movimiento estudiantil mexicano UNAM*. México, D.F.: Instituto de investigaciones sociales, 1988.

———. *La rosa de los cambios: Breve historia de la UNAM*. México, D.F.: Cal y Arena, 1990.

Selected Bibliography

Gutmann, Matthew C. *The Meanings of Macho: Being a Man in Mexico City*. Berkeley: University of California Press, 1996.

Guy, Donna. *White Slavery and Mothers Alive and Dead: The Troubled Meetings of Sex, Gender, Public Health, and Progress in Latin America*. Lincoln: University of Nebraska Press, 2000.

Hart, John. *Revolutionary Mexico: The Coming and Process of the Mexican Revolution*. Berkeley: University of California Press, 1987.

Hernández García, Nieves. *Los errores de Díaz Ordaz: El conflicto medico, la tragedia de Tlatelolco*. Mexico, D.F.: Costa-Ammic Editores, S.A., 1984.

Hellman, Judith Adler. *Mexico in Crisis*. New York: Holmes & Meier Publishers, Inc., 1979.

Hurtado Márquez, Eugenio. *La Universidad Autónoma, 1929–1944*. México, D.F.: Universidad Autónoma de México, 1976.

Iglitzin, Lynne B., and Ruth Ross, editors. *Women in the World, 1975–1985: The Women's Decade*. Santa Barbara, California: ABC-Clio, 1986.

Jelin, Elizabeth, editor. *Ciudadania y participación: Las mujeres en los movimientos sociales latino americano*. Geneva, Switzerland: Instituto de Investigaciones de las Naciones Unidad para el Desarrollo Social, 1987.

Josephs, Gilbert, Anne Rubenstein, and Eric Zolov, editors. *Fragments of a Golden Age: The Politics of Culture in Mexico Since 1940*. Durham, North Carolina: Duke University Press, 2001.

Josephs, Gilbert and Timothy Henderson, editors. *The Mexico Reader: History, Culture, and Politics*. Durham, North Carolina: Duke University Press, 2002.

Josephs, Gilbert M and Daniel Nugent, editors. *Everyday Forms of State Formation: Revolution and Negotiation of Rule in Modern Mexico*. Durham, North Carolina: Duke University Press, 1994.

Katsiaficas, George. "1968 Revisited: Student Activism Coupled with International Cultural Revolt." *The Chronicle for Higher Education* 34 (March 1988).

Kimmel, Michael. *Masculinity in America: A Cultural History*. New York: The Free Press, 1996.

Koppen, Elke. *Movimiento sociales en México*. México, D.F.: Universidad Autónoma de México, 1989.

Knight, Alan. *The Mexican Revolution*. 2 Vols. New York: Cambridge University Press, 1986.

———. "Cardensimo: Juggernaut or Jalopy." *Journal of Latin American Studies* 26, no. 1 (Feburary 1994) 73–107.

Krauze, Enrique, and Aurelio de los Reyes. *General misionero: Lázaro Cárdenas*. México, D.F.: Fondo de Cultura Económico, 1987.

———. *Mexico Biography of Power: A History of Modern Mexico, 1810–1996*. Translated by Hank Heifetz. New York: HarperPerennial, 1998.

Küppers, Gaby, editor. *Compañeros: Voices from the Latin American Women's Movement*. London: Latin American Bureau, 1992.

Kuznesof, Elizabeth and Robert Oppenheimer. "The Family and Society in Nineteenth Century Latin America: An Historiographical Introduction." *Journal of Family History* 10, no. 3 (1985): 215–34.

Lagarde, Marcela. *Género y feminismo: Desarrollo humano y democrácia*. Madrid: Horas, 1997.

Lamas, Marta, editor. *El género: La construcción cultural de la diferencia sexual*. México, D.F.: Grupo Editorial Miguel Angel Porrda, 1996.

Lavrin, Asunción. *Women, Feminism, and Social Change in Argentina, Chile, and Uruguay, 1890–1940*. Lincoln: University of Nebraska Press, 1995.

Lewis, Oscar. *Five Families*. New York: Mentor Books, 1959.

Lomnitz-Adler, Claudio. *Exits from the Labyrinth: Culture and Ideology in the Mexican National Space*. Berkeley: University of California Press, 1992.

López Villegas-Manjarrezas, Virginia. *La CTM vs. Las organizaciones obreros*. México, D.F.: Ediciones Caballito, 1983.

Loyp Brambila, Aurora. *El movimiento magisterial de 1958 en México*. México, D.F.: Ediciones Era, 1979.

Mabry, Donald. *The Mexican University and the State: Student Conflicts, 1910–1971*. College Station: Texas A&M Press, 1982.

Macías, Anna. *Against all Odds: The Feminist Movement in Mexico to 1940*. Westport, Colorado: Greenwood Press, 1982.

Maciel, David and Joanne Hershfield. *Mexico's Cinema: A Century of Film and Filmmakers*. Wilmington, Delaware: Scholarly Resources Press, 1999.

Martínez Della Roca, Salvador. *Estado y universidad en México, 1920–1968: Historia de los movimientos estudiantiles en la UNAM*. México, D.F.: J. Boldi i Climent, 1986.

Martínez Verdugo, Arnoldo, editor. *Historia del Comunismo en México*. México, D.F.: Grijalbo, 1985.

Martré, Gonzalo. *El movimiento popular estudiantil de 1968 en la novela mexicana*. México, D.F.: Universidad Nacional Autonoma de Mexico, 1986.

Massolo, Alejandra and Martha Schteingart, editors. *Participación social, reconstrucción y mujer: El sismo de 1985*. México, D.F.: El Colegio de México, 1987.

Massolo, Alejandra, compiler. *Mujeres y ciudades: Participación social, vivienda, y vida cotidiana*. México, D.F.: Colegio de Mexico, 1992.

———. *Por amor y coraje: Mujeres en movimientos urbanos de la ciudad de México*. México, D.F.: Colegio de México, 1992.

McGee-Deutsch, Sandra. "Gender and Sociopolitical Change in Twentieth Century Latin America." *Hispanic American Historical Review* 71 (1991): 259–306.

Medina Valdez, Gerardo. *El 68, Tlatelolco, y el PAN*. México, D.F.: Partido Acción

Nacional, 1990.

Méjia Prieto, Jorge. *Fidel Velazquez: Cuarenta-siete años y poder*. México, D.F.: Editorial Diana, 1991.

Melhuus, Marit, and Kristi Ann Stølen. *Machos, Mistresses, and Madonnas: Contesting Power of Latin American Gender Imagery*. New York: Verso Press, 1996.

Meyer, Michael, and William Sherman. *The Course of Mexican History*. New York: Oxford University Press, 1995.

Middlebrook, Kevin J, editor. *Unions, Workers, and the State in Mexico*. San Diego: Center for U.S.-Mexican Studies, University of California-San Diego, 1991.

Miller, Francesca. *Latin American Women and the Search for Social Justice*. Hanover, New Hampshire: University of New England Press, 1991.

Million, Robert Paul. *Mexican Marxist—Vicente Lombardo Toledano*. Chapel Hill: University of North Carolina Press, 1966.

Mitchell, Kenneth. *State-Society Relations in Mexico: Clientalism, Neoliberal State Reform, and the Case of CONASUPO* London: Ashgate Publishing, 2001.

Mohanty, Chandra Talpade, Ann Russo, and Lourdes Torres, editors. *Third World Women and the Politics of Feminism*. Bloomington: University of Indiana Press, 1991.

Monsiváis, Carlos. "The Movements Finds a Cause in Mexico." *Minerva* 7 (1969): 563–69.

Mosse, George L. *The Image of Man: The Creation of Modern Masculinity*. New York: Oxford University Press, 1995.

Navarro, Armando. *Mexican American Youth Organization: Avant-Garde of the Chicano Movement in Texas*. Austin: University of Texas Press, 1995.

Niblo, Stephen. *Mexico in the 1940s: Modernity, Politics, and Corruption* Wilmington, Delaware: Scholarly Resources Press, 1999.

Ochoa, Cuauhtémoc. "La reforma educativa en la UNAM (1970–74)." *Cuadernos Politicos* 9 (July–September 1976): 67–82.

O'Malley, Irene V. *The Myth of the Revolution: Hero Cults and the Institutionalization of the Mexican State, 1920–1940*. New York: Greenwood Press, 1986.

Pelaez, Gerardo. *Historia del Sindicato Nacional de Trabajadores de la Educación*. México, D.F.: Ediciones de Cultura Popular, 1984.

Pescatello, Ann, editor. *Female and Male in Latin America: Essays*. Pittsburgh, Pennsylvania: University of Pittsburgh Press, 1973.

Quiñónez, Sam. *True Tales from Another Mexico: The Lynch Mod, the Popsicle Kings, Chalina, and the Bronx*. Albuquerque: University of New Mexico Press, 2001.

Ramos Escandon, Carmen. *Presencia y transparencia: La mujer en la historia de México*. México, D.F.: Colegio de México, Programa Interdisciplinario de Estudios de la Mujer, 1987.

Ramos, Samuel. *Profile of Man and Culture in Mexico.* Translated by Peter G. Earle. Austin: University of Texas Press, 1962.

Randall, Margaret. *Gathering Rage: The Failure of Twentieth-Century Revolutions to Develop a Feminist Agenda.* New York: Monthly Review Press, 1992.

Rascon, Maria Antonieta. *Mujer y la lucha social.* New York: Women's International Resource Exchange, 1987.

Rosas, Javier, et al. *50 años de oposición en México.* México, D.F.: Universidad Nacional Autónoma de México, 1979.

Rubenstein, Anne. *Bad Language, Naked Ladies & Other Threats to the Nation: A Political History of Comic Books in Mexico.* Durham, North Carolina: Duke University Press, 1998.

Salas, Elizabeth. *Soldaderas in the Mexican Military: Myth and History.* Austin: University of Texas Press, 1990.

Schmitt, Karl M. *Communism in Mexico: A Study of Political Frustration.* Austin: University of Texas Press, 1965.

Schmidt, Samuel. *The Deterioration of the Mexican Presidency: The Years of Luis Echeverría.* Translated by Dan A. Cothran. Tucson: University of Arizona Press, 1991.

Scott, Joan W. "Gender: A Useful Category of Historical Analysis." *American Historical Review* 91, no. 5 (Dec. 1986): 1053–75.

Semo, Enrique. *Viaje alrededor de la izquierda.* México, D.F.: Editorial Nueva Imagen, 1988.

Semo, Ilan. editor. *La transición interrumpida, México, 1968–1988.* México, D.F.: Editorial Patria, 1993.

Shapira, Yroam. "Mexico: The Impact of the 1968 Mexican Student Movement on Echeverría Reformism." *Journal of International Studies and World Affairs* 19, no. 4 (November 1977): 557–80.

Sherman, John. "The Mexican Miracle and Its Collapse." in *The Oxford History of Mexico.* Edited by Michael Meyer and William Beezley. New York: Oxford University Press, 2000.

Slick, Sam. *José Revueltas.* Boston, Massachusetts: Twayne Publishers, 1983.

Soto, Shirlene. *Emergence of the Modern Mexican Woman: Her Participation in Revolution and Struggle for Equality, 1910–1940.* Denver, Colorado: Arden Press, 1990.

Stavans, Ilan. *The Riddle of Cantinflas: Essays on Hispanic Popular Culture.* Albuquerque: University of New Mexico Press, 1998.

Steele, Cynthia. *Politics, Gender, and the Mexican Novel, 1968–1988: Beyond the Pyramid.* Austin: University of Texas Press, 1992.

Sternback, Nancy Saporta, Marysa Navarro-Arranguren, Patricia Chuchryk, and Sonia Alvarez. "Feminism in Latin America: From Bogatá to San Bernardo."

Signs 17 (Winter 1992): 393–433.

Stevens, Evelyn. *Protest and Response in Mexico.* Cambridge: Massachusetts Institute of Technology Press, 1974.

Story, Dale. "Policy Cycles in Mexican Presidential Politics." *Latin American Research Review* 20, no. 3 (1985): 139–61.

Taibo, Paco Ignacio. *Guevara: Also Known as Che.* New York: St. Martin's Press, 1997.

Tamayo, Sergio. "The 20 Mexican Octobers: A Study of Citizenship and Social Movements." PhD diss., University of Texas at Austin, 1994.

Tirardo, Manlio, José Luis Sierra, and Gerardo Dávila. *El 10 de junio y la izquierda radical.* México, D.F.: Editorial Heterodoxia, 1971.

Trejo Delarde, Raúl. "The Mexican Labor Movement: 1917–1975." Translated by Aníbal Yáñez. *Latin American Perspectives* 3, no. 1 (Winter 1976): 144–47.

Tuñón Pablos, Esperanza. *Mujeres que se organizan: El Frente Unico Pro Derechos de la Mujer, 1935–1938.* México, D.F.: Porrúa, 1992.

Tuñón Pablos, Julia. *Mujeres en México: Una historia olvidada.* México, D.F.: Planeta, 1987.

Tutino, John. *From Insurrection to Revolution in Mexico: Social Bases of Agrarian Violence, 1750–1940.* Princeton, New Jersey: Princeton University Press, 1986.

Twinam, Ann. *Public Lives, Private Secrets: Gender, Honor, Sexuality and Illegitimacy in Colonial Spanish America.* Stanford, California: Stanford University Press, 1999.

Vaughn, Mary Kay. *Cultural Politics in Revolution: Teachers, Peasants, and Schools in Mexico, 1930–1940.* Tucson: University of Arizona Press, 1997.

Wallace, Michelle. "Reading 1968 and the Great American Whitewash" In *Remaking History: Discussions in Contemporary Culture,* edited by Barbara Kruger and Phil Mariani. Seattle, Washington: Bay Press and the Dia Art Foundation, 1989.

Wences Reza, Rosalio, *El movimiento estudiantil y los problemas nacionales.* México, D.F.: Editorial Nuestra Tiempo, 1971.

Womack, John. *Emiliano Zapata and the Mexican Revolution.* New York: Vintage Books, 1970.

Yeager, Gertrude M. *Confronting Change, Challenging Gender: Women in Latin American History.* Wilmington, Delaware: Scholarly Resources Press, 1994.

Zermeño, Sergio. *México, una democrácia utópica: El movimiento del 68.* México, D.F.: Siglo Veinturno Editores, 1978.

Zolov, Eric. *Refried Elvis: The Rise of the Mexican Counterculture.* Berkeley: University of California Press, 1999.

Index

Numbers in bold type indicate photos or illustrations.

Index

Huerta, Isabel, 88, 89

Iberoamericano, 63; demands removal
    of troops from UNAM, 129
Institute of Insurance and Social
    Service of State Workers
    (ISSSTE), 22
Institute of Mexican Youth, 103
International Year of the Woman:
    MLM excluded from Mexico
    City meeting of, 184
Isaac Ochoterena Preparatory
    School, 39
Isabel, Margarita, 86–87

jaramillistas, 26
Jaramillo, Rubén, 26–27, 159
Jaramillo family: assassination of, 27
Jardón, Raúl, 30, 64, 88
Jardón Arzate, Edmundo, 31
Johnson, Lyndon B., 145
La Journada, 137, 138
Juárez, Benito, 100
July 26 Movement, 7, 14

Khrushchev, Nikita, 32
kidnapping, 172, 173, 174
kitchen brigades, 88
Krauze, Enrique, 193

labor struggles, 11
The Labyrinth of Solitude (Paz), 17
Lamas, Marta, 88, 184, 212n. 18
Landa, Carmen, 51–52, 54, 87, 88, 160,
    181; changes in life of, 186
law of social dissolution. *See* Article 145
León, Jesús de, 24
Leonhardy, Terrance George, 172–73
Lewis, Oscar, 182
Liebermann, Lilian, 181
lightning brigades, 82–89, 187, 192; cir-
    culation of Six Point Petition,
    97; invites public to join Great
    Silent March, 111; reliance upon
    young women, 95
Líneas Nacionales (railroad), 26
López, Ñico, 14
López Mateos, Adolfo, 21–22, 25, 26, 28,
    143, 201n. 42; and emasculation
    of workers' leadership, 32
López Osuna, Florencio, 135, 137–38, 143
López Portillo, José, 225n. 30
López Rodríguez, José, 65, 114
Lozano Bernal, Alfonso, 24
lynching incident, 120–22

Mabry, Donald, 63
machismo, 182

machos, 181; women's contribution to
    creation of, 182
Madera military compound, 171
Madera Paz, Candelario, 165
Madrazo, Carlos A., 143, 144, 145, 147
Maldonado, Braulio, 143, 144, 145
Mandel, Ernst, 180
March for the Path of Liberty, 48
Marcuse, Herbert, 13
Marino (newspaper caricaturist), 45
Martínez della Roca, Salvador, 163
Martínez de Ovando, Angel, 91–92
Martínez Domínguez, Alfonso, 166–67
Martínez Manatou, Emilio, 108
Martínez Verdugo, Arnoldo, 32–33
Marx, Karl, 13
Massacre in Mexico (Poniatowska), 86
Massieu, Guillermo, 62, 66, 68, 69
Mendiolea Cerecero, Raúl, 38, 39, 41,
    77, 95
Mendivil, Leopoldo, 123
Mendoza, María Luisa, 57
Meste, María Eugenia, 65
Metropolitan Autonomous University
    (UAM), 158, 187
Mexican Communist Party (PCM), 32,
    48, 81, 123; police raid offices of,
    42–44; and prison sentences,
    161; targeted by Mexican gov-
    ernment, 47; ties to National
    Union of Mexican Women, 59
Mexican Economic Miracle, 6, 18, 23,
    48, 134; labor movements chal-
    lenge, 12
Mexican Electricians Union (SME), 23
Mexican Institute for Infant Protection
    (IMPI), 158
Mexican Institute of Social Security
    (IMSS), 20–21
Mexican Railroad Workers' Union, 24
Mexican Republic Railroad Workers'
    Union (STFRM), 25–26
Mexican Revolution, 3, 7, 106; criticism
    of, 11; massacre was requiem
    for, 150; novels inspired by, 18;
    students accused of opposing,
    84; women and, 178
Mexican Senate, 139
Mexican University Student Front
    (FUM), 70
Mexico: and failure to maintain ideals
    of revolution, 17; and social
    issues, 37
Meza, Enrique, 121
Military Camp 1, 142, 147
Le Monde, 76
Monsiváis, Carlos, 68, 128
Morelos, José María, 100

250

Index

Index